Once will be better

or

My life story

By

Ronnie Downtoo

Copyright © 2024 Ronnie Downtoo

ISBN: 978-1-917293-63-1

All rights reserved, including the right to reproduce this book, or portions thereof in any form. No part of this text may be reproduced, transmitted, downloaded, decompiled, reverse engineered, or stored, in any form or introduced into any information storage and retrieval system, in any form or by any means, whether electronic or mechanical without the express written permission of the author.

Preface

I have read many books in my life but none of them have perturbed me as much as the last one I read. I am a relatively sensitive type of person and I've cried at a sad movie or romance book more than once, but who hasn't? However, I always knew they were just fictional stories, that someone had written or filmed well. This one was different.

A dear colleague of mine, Jacklyn, wrote a book about her life and I was probably touched by her story because I knew the main character personally. But why did it upset me so much? Why did the memories I had managed to suppress for so many years burst to the surface? It was like when you keep a bottle of champagne in the cellar for thirty years and then someone suddenly brings it up from the dark and shakes it. The cork pops and the champagne sprays out.

Well, that's what this book did to me. It shook up memories lying dormant in the depths of my soul and there was no going back, though I still don't understand why because Jacklyn's life was so different from mine. We had two separate destinies, lived in two different worlds. What did we have in common?

I was born in Ukraine, in the former Soviet Union, in a poor family with many children, while Jacklyn was born in England, in a small and loving family. She was still a child when she got pregnant by a teenage boy almost her own age. Overcoming her fear and shame of becoming a mother, she finally gave birth to her beautiful daughter.

Her parents stood by her side, supported her in every way and helped her to raise the child. After a year, however, her family moved to Jamaica leaving Jacklyn with the baby and teenage dad. Another baby came along, and trouble followed. She had to grow up fast because she had no one to rely on but herself. For years she nursed her partner, who became seriously ill, and at the same time she had to raise her children alone.

In the book, we learn how a little girl becomes a loving mother and wife, how she finds her place in life. Her story is truly heart breaking, but it is very different from mine – so why did it have such an impact on me and why did it upset me so much? I wasn't even halfway through when I decided not to read any further. Memories were coming at me with such force that I felt an almost physical pain in my chest and it terrified me.

In my mind I was reliving the past: more and more of it was coming back to me, and I wasn't happy about it. I had already closed the door to the past and opened a new door to the future; I had started a new life in a foreign country, so why was this happening?

I told Jacklyn what her book had done to me and that I'd stopped reading it because I just couldn't continue. She encouraged me to keep reading and see if it would get better.

So I did and she was right; by the time I finished the book, I was completely liberated. I no longer had a crushing sensation in my chest; I no longer had the pain of the past. I was relieved – no more searching for answers to the whys, it just happened and that was that.

That particular bottle of champagne was emptied to the last drop. Certain memories from the past that I couldn't talk about before now don't hurt so much. I not only feel that I can talk about them but I can also write them down and tell you all about them. Like everyone, I've made good and bad choices and done things I'm not proud of, but now I have the courage to share them with you.

I think I've had an interesting, eventful life so far. There will be parts of my story that are painful and you may feel you can't read any further, but please don't stop. Keep reading and you'll see: it will get better.

So let's get started!

Chapter 1

As I have already mentioned, I was born in Ukraine – in Transcarpathia to be precise – in the mid-sixties. I have an older and a younger brother, two older and two younger sisters: I'm in the middle. We could say there are seven of us, like evil – well fortunately, there are still seven of us to this day.

A person's life is very much influenced by his or her childhood. If you were to ask my brothers and sisters, they would say that ours was relatively good, though it all depends on what you compare it with.

True, we were poor but we never starved. I paid a price for that because I spent half my childhood queuing. Back then, grocery shopping was strictly regulated and we got one of everything per person, so my mother always took two children with her to the shop so that we could buy enough bread, meat, milk, etc.

Can you imagine being seven or eight years old and queuing for three hours on Saturdays in a crowded shop just to have broth on the table the next day? When we were older we tried to rebel, saying we'd rather not eat meat so we wouldn't have to queue so much. It didn't work and I ate chicken broth every Sunday until I was eighteen.

My mum brought us up strictly. She was a really bossy type; with her five-foot-six height and her strong voice, she always got what she wanted. From when we were very young, she tried to raise us to be hard workers. We each had our own duties and did our share of the household chores – not willingly because which nine- or ten-year-old child wants to do the washing up or cleaning when they could be outside playing with the neighbours' children? But my mum always said 'must is superior', and we stuck to it.

When I was about six or seven years old, I had to sweep the kitchen. I remember the broom was twice my size and kept falling out of my hands, but I did it because I had to. I was a relatively good child and I was not much trouble, though later I became the black sheep of the family. But we will come to that.

There were a lot of us children, so there were never enough fruit or sweets. We learnt early on how to share what little we had. My mother always bought the second-class damaged fruit and the cheapest sweets. If she brought a kilo of cherries, we'd put seven cups on the table and count them one by one so that everyone got the same amount.

I was in third grade when my classmates, twin girls from the neighbourhood, invited me to their house to play. Their mum brought out a big bowl of cherries and I'll never forget sitting on the swing and just eating and eating the delicious, juicy cherries. It was incredible to me that we didn't have to share and we could eat as much as we wanted.

Later, when we were older, we went up into the mountains to pick fruit. Yes, that's right: up into the mountains. What you should know about Transcarpathia is that everywhere you look you see mountains, hills, forests and fields. The scenery is stunningly beautiful; it's impossible to get enough of it and the air is so fresh you can almost bite it. Naturally we didn't notice it back then; what surrounded us was all so normal.

As soon as school was over and the good weather came, we would take the train up into the mountains to pick raspberries or blackberries. A lot of people made a living out of it: what they picked one day, they sold at the market the following day. We used to make jam and syrup, which we consumed during the winter.

In August, we picked blueberries and bilberries on high hills, so high up that we had to walk two or three hours on serpentines.

Then came the walnut and chestnut season. I don't know if you've ever seen a chestnut on a tree when it's in the shell, but it's very spiky. It has millions of thorns sticking out of it and stings so badly that a hedgehog is nothing compared to it! Even when we wore gloves we could feel the thorns in our fingers days later, but it was worth it. Chestnuts were expensive at the market and we might have never eaten them if we hadn't picked them ourselves.

The thing I liked most in the summer was picking mushrooms. The peace and quiet that surrounded us in the forest were indescribable: all you could hear were the birds chirping and the leaves rustling under your feet. When the weather was rainy enough, plus we had enough luck, we would take home a bunch of mushrooms. The next day we would string them up and take them up to the attic to dry. We weren't bored; we were like busy ants gathering them all summer and eating them in the winter.

What I haven't talked about yet is fishing. I grew up about ten minutes away from the Latorca river where we often went fishing even if only for a couple of hours. Many people think fishing is a pastime for boys or men but that's not true; if anybody asks me what my hobbies are, my answer is always reading and fishing. It wasn't just a pastime like for my other sisters, for me it was a real pleasure that has remained to this day.

I remember one time my two brothers and I caught a hundred fish in a couple of hours (yes, a hundred, we counted!). It was great fun, though it was less fun when we had to clean them. Then my mum fried them so crispy that we licked our fingers afterwards. I've never eaten anything so delicious since, that's for sure.

In the winter, at minus twenty degrees, the Latorca (or at least the surface) froze over and it became an ice-skating rink. We didn't have skates, but we still had a lot of fun sliding on the ice. If it wasn't snowing, the ice was so transparent that we could see fish swimming under our feet. That was the underwater world for us and we really enjoyed it.

One day there was an accident. My two brothers and I were about to go sledging across the river when the ice cracked underneath me. Luckily the water was only up to my knees, but it was terribly cold. I didn't have time to get scared because my brothers quickly pulled me out of the freezing water, put me on the sled and ran all the way home with me. That little adventure, plus the telling off we got that day, made us realize how quickly trouble can happen.

I don't want you to think that we or my parents were irresponsible because they weren't. Going on the ice in the winter was as natural for us as swimming in the river in the summer. At least we learned to swim!

I loved that part of my life but that doesn't mean I had a good childhood. What I've written about so far is only half of it, the better half. You may think I'm over-reacting because it could have been worse but that doesn't change how I felt at the time. I was a miserable nobody whose self-confidence was down the drain.

One of the things that made my life miserable was poverty. I was probably the only one in my class who was happy that school uniforms were compulsory. The few clothes I had were the ones I'd inherited from my sisters; when I outgrew them, and if they were not completely ruined, I passed them on to my younger sister.

This went on for years. Then one day, luck smiled on me because my mother bought me a light-blue coat, which I was delighted with. I was ten years old and it was the first piece of brand-new clothing I'd ever had. A few days later I was crossing the road on my way home from school when a cyclist hit me. I fell on the muddy road and my nice new coat was covered in dirt. So much for my luck – although now that I think about it, I was lucky that I was hit by a cyclist and not a car.

The other thing I was very ashamed of was our house. If I wanted to sugar coat things, I could say that I grew up in a detached house with a big garden and courtyard, but in reality it was a mud house with a kitchen and a bedroom, which was gradually falling down.

Seven kids and their parents in one room – can you imagine that? I never invited anyone over to play, not that there was anyone to play with. Most of my classmates looked down on me or ignored me; if they did talk to me, they only wanted to copy my homework.

The twin girls from the next street (where I ate the cherries) invited me over a couple of times but then that stopped, too. My only company was a few street kids who were similarly poor. My childhood didn't include birthday parties, hanging out with friends nor, later, having fun and going to discos.

I haven't really talked about my dad so far but I will now. He was a good man but strict, kind of a hard head. Although he never hurt us, we were afraid of him. He was only home a few months a year, so we didn't know him that well. In those days it was very common for men to leave their families and travel thousands of kilometres in search of a better job and a better salary. Unfortunately, my dad had to do that.

He boarded a train at the beginning of March and the next time we saw him was in late October or November. He usually travelled to Yalta, Riga or Odessa and worked as a labourer on construction sites. While he was away trying to earn money, my mum was trying to make ends meet, which didn't always work out. By the time my parents paid off their debts in the autumn, bought firewood and the few things we needed, there was hardly any money left.

This went on for about fifteen years until the time came when my dad stopped taking the train. He was fed up with it all. Unfortunately, even though he was away from his family for eight months a year, we didn't get from A to B, we were not much better off. So, he decided to stay home and worked as a guard in a factory.

If you have children, you know what it takes to raise them. In my family, a child was born every year or every two years, which was not easy. Because my dad was home so little, my mum had to do all the work around the house. Most of my childhood memories are of her queuing at the shops, cooking lunch or dinner in the kitchen and doing the laundry by hand because we didn't have a washing machine.

It's not easy to raise seven kids, and she would have probably gone crazy if she'd had to do it all by herself, but luckily we had Nana. She was the most wonderful grandmother in the world and the best person I've ever known. Unlike my mom, she never yelled at us because she didn't need to. We would do anything for her, it only took one word. I don't know why it was so, but she was certainly a second mum to us.

She often took us to the cemetery to clean Grandpa's grave and then we'd go to the forest nearby to pick mushrooms. She taught us to distinguish the edible ones from the poisonous. There was a big cherry tree between the cemetery and the forest that Nana could climb the tree to pick cherries for us. If we'd had a camera, that would have been a moment worth capturing: a sixty-five-year-old woman in a black shawl picking cherries in a tall tree for her grandchildren. She would have done anything for us.

Other times she took us to pick herbs in the fields. It was so nice to listen to her as she explained which plants were good for which diseases. Many years have passed since then and I can't remember everything, but there are some herbs that I still use to this day thanks to her.

In the autumn when the fruit was ripe, we picked sloes or rosehips to make tea. The bushes scratched our hands like we were playing with ten kittens but we didn't mind; we'd go anywhere she wished.

She taught us to pray, to believe in God. She was a special person and when she died she left a huge empty space. But I believed – and it felt good to believe – that she had gone to heaven and would take care of us from there.

You may laugh at what I'm about to tell you, but I don't mind. Many, many years later I had a serious car accident in which the car was totalled, but I escaped with a few scratches. You may say that I was lucky because I was wearing my seatbelt, but I'm sure it wasn't just that. Nana was there with me; I felt her presence and I know she saved me. I couldn't die there and I was given another chance.

Now let's get back to my childhood because I have more to tell you. It's true that my Nana made life beautiful, but it was ruined by my brother. Before you get the wrong idea, there was no abuse – at least not sexual abuse. There were a few slaps for sure, but that's natural between siblings. My brother terrorised me psychologically and made my childhood miserable.

In the spring, as soon as my dad left the house, he appointed himself head of the family. There might have been a conversation between father and son like, 'Son, you're the eldest, look after your siblings,' like in the movies, but my dad certainly didn't say 'Son, from now on you're the man of the house and everyone does what you say.' But he treated us as if he were a boss and we were his servants.

My problem was not that he told us what to do, because things *had* to be done; what really made me angry was that he never did any work. bosses don't work, they just give orders.

My brother was a real tyrant who enjoyed humiliating us. He gave us each an ugly nickname; I was called Fatty because he thought I ate too much and was fat. I didn't think that name suited me at all because I was a skinny, scrawny, anaemic little girl. After I became Fatty, I ate less and lost even more weight.

I was about seven when my parents bought our first television. In those days there was only a ten-minute story on TV for kids in the evenings, and no broadcasting at all on Mondays, but even that programme was only on if the bully allowed it and we kissed his hand. I thought this was humiliating and I was the only one who refused to do it. As punishment, I was taken to the kitchen and had to stay there until the end of the programme.

No matter how much I cried or complained to my mum, nothing changed – in fact, it got worse. Since I rarely gave into him, he picked on me more than the others. My brother enjoyed torturing me.

I gave him a nickname, though I never dared to say it out loud. I called him a sadistic animal, although at the time I didn't know what that really meant.

Once I was sitting at my desk doing my homework while he was kicking my chair with his foot behind my back. I repeatedly told him to stop but he kept kicking. Something inside me screamed, 'ENOUGH! *ENOUGH!*' and I grabbed the first thing I could lay my hands on and threw it at him.

It was a glass cutter and to this day I don't understand how it got there. The next thing I saw that my brother had his hands over his face and there was blood running down.

I was terrified. I ran out of the house, slept at Nana's and didn't go home until the next morning. It turned out that the glass cutter had only slashed his face and his eyes were unharmed. When I finally dared to go home, he slapped me so hard that my nose started bleeding.

The bullying and teasing continued. I hated my brother and when he was finally drafted into the army, I wished he would never come home again. A few days later we found out that he had been taken to Afghanistan where there was a war between the Russians and the Afghans. At that time, hundreds of dead soldiers were being brought home in zinc coffins, supposedly cruelly mutilated. It was then that I became aware of what I really wished.

'I wish he'd never come home!' How could I think that about my own brother? But I was only thirteen at the time, still a child. When I saw my mother's worried face, I felt even more guilty and afterwards I prayed that he would come home safely.

Three years passed before I saw him again and it was as if he'd had been reborn. A serious, grown-up man returned from the war and our relationship changed. Although we rarely see each other, we are always happy when we do so.

My brother was taken off to the army and the mental terror was gone, yet I wasn't much happier. I always felt that we didn't have a proper loving family. I don't know how my brothers and sisters perceived it because we never talked about it, but as a child I suffered a lot from feeling that my parents didn't love me.

It's not that my siblings were treated differently to me because they weren't. In our family we didn't kiss or hug, and we never said 'I love you' to each other.

I didn't expect that from my dad because he was hardly ever home, and the few months he spent with us were not enough for us to really get to know him. But I do have one good memory of him that I will never forget. On New Year's Eve, after the clock struck midnight, we made a toast (even the little ones got a sip of sparkling wine) and then my dad kissed everyone in turn and wished us all a happy new year. We had to wait exactly one year for the next kiss.

But what about my mum? Why don't I have such clear memories of her? I know she did everything she could for us and much more. She took care of us, there was always food on the table, we wore clean clothes and we were never cold in the winter. But that wasn't enough for me, I wanted to feel her love.

I know now that she loved us, but why didn't she make us feel that love? Why didn't she show us her feelings? I grew up knowing that no one loved me.

I deserved to be loved because I was a good child, quiet and obedient. I was a good student and my teachers never complained about me, they only praised me. Even as a skinny, weak little girl, I got sick very rarely – although I loved being sick. When I was lying in bed with a fever, my mother would put a wet cloth on my forehead and caress my face and I was so happy. I could see the worry in her eyes and the hope that she loved me would flash through me. But why did I never hear her saying 'I love you, my little girl'?

Maybe it would have been easier to ask her but I never did. Instead I continued with self-torture and suffering. I'm making my mother look bad, but even so I know I couldn't have asked for a better mother. She was strict and maybe shouted at us more than she should have, but she cared for us and loved us, even if she didn't let us feel it.

I think we had a good upbringing because, thanks to her, we all made our way in life as we grew up. I've always admired her strength, her perseverance and the fact that she never gave up, no matter how hard things were.

My dad worked hard, too, but to no avail because we remained poor. As a teenager I found that hard to accept because I had dreams and aspirations. I wanted to wear nice clothes, eat good chocolate, or at least have an umbrella so I wouldn't get wet in the rain so often.

I didn't want to live like that, but what was there to do? When I complained to my Nana, all she said was, 'Once will be better.'

'But when?' I asked. There was no answer.

I assumed that if there weren't so many of us brothers and sisters, we'd be better off so I bombarded my mother with questions. Why did she have so many children? Why wasn't three or four enough for her, like other families? When she told me that her pregnancy with her seventh child had been dangerous and she could have died in childbirth, I was completely freaked out. She'd risked her life for my sister, not even thinking that the six of us could have been left motherless. She'd been brought up to believe that all children are given by God and can only be taken by God, and abortion is a sin. But how could she be more attached to her baby than to her own life or to us?

All she responded was, 'If it wasn't for her, you wouldn't be here now either!'

It turned out that my little sister saved our lives. She was born in mid-November and was about a month old when one night she started crying. My mum woke up and sensed that there was something wrong.

She was feeling dizzy, nauseous, her stomach was upset and her legs were collapsing. We were sleeping deeply, perhaps too deeply. She realised that there was carbon monoxide in the room, which must have been coming out of the tiled stove. Somehow she managed to open the door and windows to ventilate the house, then she woke us up one by one. Fortunately no tragedy occurred.

My mother believed that everything happened for a reason. Had she not given birth to her youngest child, the whole family would probably have died.

There was a middle-aged Jewish couple who lived in our street and they couldn't have children. They had everything – a nice house and even a car, which not many people had in the early seventies. They ran a small shop and made a very good living; all they needed was a child to make them happy.

One day they approached my mother with a strange request: they wanted her to give them a child because my mum had so many. They were interested in my middle sister, Potyi. Of course, my mum didn't want to hear about it and she immediately shooed them away. They asked her to think it over because they could give my sister everything, but my mother was adamant.

As a teenager I once threw this in her face (and I'm ashamed of it now but teenagers are like that). I asked why she didn't give Potyi to those people so at least one of us could have had a better life.

'You'll know when you have children of your own,' she said.

She explained that the thought of her little girl living down the street with another family where she would rarely see her was completely unimaginable. A few months later the couple moved to America, which proved that my mother had made the right decision as it would have broken her heart not to see her child again. I am now a mother myself and I know I would have done the same.

I was in the middle of the story about when my brother was still a soldier and we were living in the mud house with a room and kitchen. As time went on and we grew bigger, the room seemed smaller and smaller. We literally outgrew the house and ruined it.

We only had as much furniture as we needed – three beds, a table and chairs, a chest of drawers and a wardrobe – and we could barely fit in the room. There was a ceiling-high tiled stove to heat the room and the kitchen at the same time. Three of us slept in one bed, which was no problem when we were four or five, but at thirteen or fourteen?

Then one day my older sister fell in love, got married and moved away from home. My brother was moved into the kitchen where we had bought a bed, so that the four girls could fit more comfortably in the room.

I have no idea how old our house must have been, but it was getting worse. The plaster was falling off the outside walls and the inside walls were mouldy, but those were the least of our problems. A crack appeared in the kitchen wall which got bigger and scarier until you could see through it into the courtyard. It was obvious that sooner or later that side of the house would give way.

One night we woke up to find a large chunk of plaster had fallen from the ceiling of the room. We were in big trouble; it was only a matter of time before the house collapsed on us. Now you understand why I felt so miserable and ashamed to invite anyone to our house.

We had been waiting for years for a council flat but without success. A lot of people wanted free housing, so the waiting list was long. Now we couldn't wait any longer because our house could collapse at any moment.

On the advice of a neighbour, we wrote to the municipality asking them to put us at the top of the waiting list as our house was in a life-threatening condition. My uncle took some photos and we sent them and the letter and waited for a miracle. And the miracle happened!

The happiest day of my life was when we went to see our new home. We were given a beautiful three-bedroom flat on the fifth floor with a living room and three balconies. Yes, three balconies! I had never seen anything like that before.

The rooms were spacious and bright, and the balconies overlooked the whole city. The kitchen was quite small but that didn't matter because we could have lunch or dinner in the living room. Finally, the bathroom and separate toilet were a big advantage for a family with so many children.

I entered the rooms again and again, and kept going onto the balcony because I couldn't get enough of the view. I couldn't believe we were going to live there! It was like a dream I didn't want to wake up from – but it was true. We'd been lucky.

The flat needed a good paint job, but as we couldn't afford a painter we did everything ourselves; then we packed up and moved into our new home. Since there were more rooms than furniture, we had to buy a few things but we settled in.

Unfortunately the dream home had several flaws that we didn't realise until later. The windows didn't close properly and the balcony doors were deformed, so when it rained water came in under them. In the winter the cold came in, so it was never warm enough.

It was also a problem that in those days there were no lifts in these buildings. Climbing up and down the stairs to and from the fifth floor several times a day was not easy, especially when we were carrying heavy shopping bags.

But our biggest problem was the lack of water. We had water three times a day for an hour at a time and it barely came up to the fifth floor. We had to fill buckets, pots and the bathtub to flush the toilet. For washing up and bathing we heated water on the stove because even though we had a boiler, there was no chance of hot water coming out of it.

We repaired and beautified the flat as much as we could, but we couldn't do anything about the water problem so we adapted and after a while we got used to it. We still loved living there, though, because we never forgot where we'd come from.

A few months later my other sister got married and moved out, leaving just the four of us. My brother was in the same room with my younger sister, and I was with my middle sister, Potyi. She was my dearest sister and also my friend. We got along very well, we never fought, or at least I don't remember us fighting. I was glad at the time that my mother hadn't give her to that childless couple because I would have missed her.

Potyi was only a year younger than me so we became teenagers at almost the same time. As happens at that age, we were unhappy with everything but especially with ourselves. We looked alike: we were the same height and build with the same cropped brown hair. The only difference between us was that she had brown eyes and a nice little nose, while I had blue eyes and a long nose. Apparently, I looked like my grandfather, though that didn't comfort me.

From the moment I saw my nose sticking out of my face in the mirror, I was devastated. My mother was so beautiful so how could I be so ugly? Why hadn't I inherited her features? At the age of fifteen that was my biggest problem, not poverty. Maybe I read too many romantic books but I wanted to fall in love, get married and have children. I felt that no one would want me looking like I did and I had no chance of happiness.

I couldn't accept myself as I was, so I complained a lot to my mother. Then one day she got fed up and said, 'You have two legs, two hands, you are healthy – what more do you need? A woman who spends her whole life in a wheelchair would gladly trade places with you. She wouldn't care how long her nose is or how tall and skinny she is. The only thing that would make her happy is to be able to walk. There is nothing wrong with you – accept yourself as you are.'

It was effective; I thought about it and agreed with her. I still couldn't accept myself but I stopped complaining, at least not out loud.

Not long ago I had a conversation with my mum. Somehow, old things came up about my teenage years and how ugly I thought I was.

I was shocked by what she said. 'But you were beautiful! You were the most beautiful child of all.'

'Me?' I couldn't believe my ears! If she really thought I was beautiful, why didn't she ever tell me? Maybe if I'd had more confidence, my life would have been different. Or maybe not; who knows since no one can avoid their fate.

My aunt had a small grocery store not far from our new flat. She needed help and asked if I could work for her a few hours a day during the summer holidays.

'Of course, I can. At least I'll have something to do and the little money will come in handy.'

I'd always wondered what it would be like to stand on the other side of the counter and serve people. The year before, I'd had a student job sorting fruit in a cannery; it wasn't bad, but I particularly enjoyed working in the shop.

For someone who was shy and reserved, it was a pretty good experience. I loved working there and I learned more and more from my aunt; you could say that she had the trade in her blood.

She was friendly to everyone and that's why the customers loved her. I looked up to her and I wanted to be as smart and confident as she was, but I didn't see much chance of that.

By the time the summer was over, I knew what I was going to be when I grew up: I would finish secondary school and, with my certificate in hand, I would go to trade college. These were bold dreams and I knew it wouldn't be easy because it cost money to go to college, lots of money.

When I was at school, I found out that one of my classmates was going to the same school as I was. So, while we were planning our future, we became very good friends.

Months went by and we lived our lives. It had been three years since my brother had joined the army. The war in Afghanistan was still raging and many soldiers lost their lives. Sometimes we didn't hear from him for months, so we could only hope that he was okay.

Then one day the doorbell rang and I answered the door. A tall, thin soldier with a moustache was standing on the doorstep. I didn't recognise him; only when he called my name did I realise it was my brother. When I'd last seen him, he'd been shorter and much fatter, or at least that was how I remembered him.

It was a great joy that he'd returned home safe and sound. I would be lying if I said that I did not fear that the psychological terror and bullying would continue, but fortunately it did not. My brother had matured and become a completely different person. All the horrors he'd experienced in the war had changed him. The stories he told us were similar to the ones we'd heard up to then. I remember two of them clearly and would like to share them with you.

The first story is about two Russian soldiers sneaking into a nearby village one night to steal grapes. They were caught, killed, and their bodies mutilated. Hopefully, that's what happened and not the other way round and they were mutilated first and then killed. Finally, they had their bellies cut open and loaded with grapes. In the morning when their comrades found them, they were barely recognisable: their eyes had been gouged out and their noses and ears cut off. This explains why the dead soldiers were brought home in closed zinc coffins.

According to my brother, the food they were given was often inedible and fruit was scarce. No wonder his comrades had a craving for grapes but the price they paid was too high.

The other story began when there was a ceasefire and the soldiers were standing and talking to each other. My brother was one of them. Suddenly an old Afghan man came up to them and said that he would like to exchange his watch for a hat – mind you, the Russians had very warm hats with ear flaps. The watch looked good, so it seemed like a good barter. One of the soldiers indicated that he would give his hat for the watch, so they moved a few feet away to make the deal.

No one expected what happened next. The Afghan man took out a knife and slit the soldier's throat, then killed himself. By the time the others rushed over, they were both dead. Everyone was shocked by the sight, as they had been talking to each other a moment earlier. My brother could only imagine that it could have been him lying there with his throat cut. It had also crossed his mind to exchange his hat but his comrade had acted first – and it had cost him his life.

The Soviet-Afghan war lasted ten years and hundreds of thousands of soldiers were killed or injured. My brother was one of the lucky ones who survived. After he came home, he didn't stay with us for long because he met a girl, got married and moved in with his wife's family.

In the meantime, my sister had a baby boy and I became his godmother. I visited them often to babysit, especially on weekends.

When my godson was ten months old, my sister wanted to go back to work part-time. That was the start of my summer holidays, so she asked if I wanted to babysit. I was happy to do it as I loved the baby and I could spend more time with him. I was only sixteen at the time but I felt grown up because my sister trusted me with her baby. During the week I looked after my godson for four hours a day and we spent weekends outdoors when the weather was nice.

As I mentioned earlier, we used to go hiking in the mountains or to pick fruit and mushrooms, and having a small child in the family didn't change anything. It is true that we didn't go very far or high with him, but there was always somewhere to go.

Sometimes we organised a two-day trip and slept in tents. During the day, we fished or picked mushrooms and made goulash soup in the cauldron over an open fire. In the evenings we fried bacon and potatoes over the campfire, or the mushrooms we had picked in the forest. Those were good times and it's nice to think back to them.

Once, my brother-in-law invited his friend for a weekend trip, which I was not happy about. I'd met him a few times at my sister's house but we'd never spoken. He was about three years older than me, tall and very handsome and, of course, quite vain.

I always felt awkward when I saw him but he didn't even notice me; he looked right through me like all boys did at that time. I was angry with my brother-in-law for inviting him because I knew how uncomfortable it would make me.

However, he behaved quite differently out there in the open. He played with my godson, made my sisters laugh and talked to me. By the end of the day, I was completely relaxed and didn't mind having him there. We made a fire in the evening and sat around it like scouts in a camp. The atmosphere was good and we talked and laughed a lot.

We put a strip of bacon on a skewer made of tree branches, held it over the fire and dripped the fat onto slices of bread; this was our supper with a little tomato and red onion. How delicious it was out there in the fresh air!

My brother-in-law and sisters went to sleep, so it was just the two of us at the campfire. The boy talked about himself, about his childhood, that he had never known his parents and had grown up in an orphanage. He said he didn't want the day to end because he felt like he was part of our family.

I was happy to hear what he said but at the same I felt guilty for being angry that he'd been invited. We talked for a long time; I would have liked to stay longer, but it was getting late. When I got up to leave, he was standing next to me and he kissed me with a passion as if his life depended on it.

I didn't really realize what was happening to me because I hadn't even dreamt of something like this would ever happen. Then he stopped, mumbled something and left me in the dark. Needless to say, I barely slept that night, because my thoughts were swirling around in my head.

'What was that kiss? A confession or a moment of madness? Could it be that he likes me, since he wouldn't have kissed me if he didn't have feelings? Or would he?'

I couldn't have known because I had no experience. Not only had boys never asked me out, they had never even flirted with me. This guy could have had anyone he wanted, so why would he want me? No, I couldn't believe it.

I tried to remember what he'd said before he left, but I couldn't. I was so confused, I couldn't understand what he was saying. I had mixed feelings: on the one hand, I was happy to have had my first kiss and hoped it wouldn't be my last, but on the other hand I knew it was too good to be true. I realised that it was a waste of time thinking about it because sooner or later I'd find out what it was all about.

The next day it became clear. He acted as if nothing had happened, was pompous and arrogant again, and looked right through me like before. I was very disappointed: where was the nice guy I'd spent hours talking to the night before and who I thought I had come to know? The guy who had kissed me with such passion and made me feel special had disappeared – or had never existed.

Maybe he hadn't wanted that day to be over because he knew the next day everything would be the same. I ran into him on another two occasions at my sister's house, but we were like strangers.

Summer was over and school started. It was my last year of secondary school and after graduation I was looking forward to going to college. I was planning to work in the meantime as I would have to pay my college fees, travel expenses and other costs. I knew my parents wouldn't support me financially and I didn't expect them to.

They didn't really like the idea of college because they thought I should have studied some kind of trade after eight years of primary school and then found a job somewhere. However, my class teacher had said my grades were too good to end up in a vocational school and I could do better. And I wanted to go further.

I studied hard; all I could see was that I would be the first college student in my family, maybe the only one. The only problem was that I went to a Hungarian school and studied all my subjects in Hungarian but the colleges were in Russian or Ukrainian.

We had Russian language and literature classes, but they were only good for learning to read, write and to be able to communicate. Back in primary school, I'd taken part in an inter-school competition and really struggled because everything was in Russian. The only test I did well with was the maths one because numbers are numbers in any language, so my fear of the entrance exams was understandable.

It turned out that if I continued to be a straight B or A student, I would get a so-called 'referral' to college, which meant that I would not have to take the entrance exams. I didn't understand this referral system but that's how it worked at the time. Even those who wanted a job in a factory or a sewing shop were given a referral at the end of school. Since our class teacher promised us this, it was up to me and my friend to make our dreams come true.

Before I continue with my story, I need to explain my nationality. Although I was born in the Soviet Union, in Ukraine, I had nothing to do with Russians or Ukrainians. My maternal grandfather was born in Transcarpathia, which at that time was still part of Hungary. Unfortunately, after the First World War Hungary was split up and all the neighbouring countries 'got' a piece of it; one day my grandfather was a Hungarian citizen, the next day he was Ukrainian.

My father, on the other hand, was German. About 150 or 200 years ago, hundreds of families were resettled from Germany to Hungary in empty, abandoned villages and that was how my father's ancestors had ended up in Transcarpathia. Despite Russian being the official language at that time, we spoke Hungarian among ourselves as it was our mother tongue, so naturally my parents sent us to Hungarian schools.

Finally, the day came when we were waiting for our referrals in the school principal's office. It had been a hard year but I'd studied a lot, and I got my reward: I passed my school-leaving exams and I did well. My grades were good and I even improved in some subjects.

Everything went according to my plan and I finally was feeling fortunate. The headmaster started to list the names and handed each of us our referrals. My friend's name came up, then the name of the trade college. Next was a guy in my class and also a trade college. I was a little surprised by that, as I didn't know he was also applying for college.

'That means three of us are going there,' I thought. I waited impatiently to hear my own name and finally it came: factory referral.

WHAT? FACTORY REFERRAL?

Then everything went black and I fainted. When I came around, I was lying on the floor with my classmates looking at me. I was confused; I didn't understand what had happened to me. Someone held out a glass of water to me and I sat up. While I was sipping the water, I looked around and suddenly I remembered everything. I started sobbing bitterly, no longer caring that everyone was looking at me.

The world collapsed around me; my dream of going to college was just a dream and it was time to wake up. But how could it happen – why was life so unfair? The boy who received my referral had worse marks than me and he'd copied my homework several times, yet he was going to be sitting in my seat at college and it hurt.

I was not naïve and it was obvious what had happened: he was an only child from a wealthy family who was destined for a better future because of his parents. I was smarter than him but I was just a nobody. What had been the point of all that studying, all those sleepless nights before the exams? Learning wasn't easy for me and I'd suffered and made lots of sacrifices, but it was all in vain. I should have listened to my parents and not have dreamed about doing better. I had my school leaving certificate in my hand, but what was the point of it if I was going to end up in a factory?

Now you might wonder why I didn't try to reapply if I was so keen on college, but it's because I gave up. I knew that even if I spent the whole summer studying, my Russian would still not be good enough to pass the exams. Instead I saved myself from another disappointment and tried to accept my fate.

The interesting thing is that a few years later I ran into this classmate in an electronics shop. He was standing behind the counter (where I should have been standing). He didn't even say hello and served me with a smug look on his face as if he owned the whole store.

I never went in there again. I used to see my friend often in one of the grocery stores, but we were no longer friends and had drifted apart.

Chapter 2

A new chapter in my life began when I was hired at the metal factory. I was seventeen years old, no longer a child and a schoolgirl but an adult working woman.

I was assigned to Department 26 where I had a job doing distribution work. I wasn't part of the office staff or the workers but somewhere in between. Forty-five of us worked there; only three of us were women.

For someone who was initially afraid of working in a factory, I settled in quite well. Everyone was friendly, so I got more and more relaxed every day. My colleagues often teased me or made me feel embarrassed in a silly way, which we laughed about together. After a couple of weeks, I was enjoying going to work and I felt good there.

My first pay day arrived. It wasn't hard to work out how much I was going to get as I'd been hired on minimum wage. I was planning to give some money to my mum for bills and food and keep the rest for myself. I needed new shoes because the ones I was wearing were completely ruined, and some new clothes wouldn't have hurt either. The last time I'd bought something for myself was when I was helping my aunt in the shop and that was a long time ago.

I went home in a good mood with my wage in my pocket, but as soon as I got home that changed. My mother told me that I had to put all the money in the kitty; there were many of us and every rouble counted.

'Now that you're earning money, it's time for you to help the family so we can live a little better,' she said.

I felt bad because that meant that even though I worked all month, just like before I wouldn't have any money for myself; on the other hand, I knew my mum was right. I had my three school-age brothers and sisters, and my Nana was living with us and she was sick a lot and needed medication. My mum cleaned offices part-time, and my dad was a security guard on minimum wage, so it was understandable that the two of them could not support seven people. I knew I couldn't be selfish and spend the money on myself because the family needed it more.

With a heavy heart, I put it all on the table then my mother gave me some of it back, which I spent on my first umbrella.

Though I was still no better off financially, my life had changed. At work, I was finally someone who wasn't looked down on or ostracised. I didn't have to worry about being made fun of for my shabby shoes, as I had done at school. My colleagues didn't ignore me but paid attention to me. I was an equal and that was a very good feeling. I'm sure that this period shaped my personality a lot because I gained a bit of self-confidence and started to feel more comfortable in my own skin.

As I said, there were only two other women working in the department: one in the office and one in the warehouse. The woman in the office took me under her wing from the very first moment and helped me in any way she could. After a while we became almost friends, although we never met outside the factory. She told me a lot about her life and her family; she said that she was content because she had a good marriage, a loving husband and two young daughters.

'They deserve to be happy,' I thought to myself. I hoped that one day I would find the right man and have a nice family like hers.

She loved gardening but she didn't have the opportunity because they lived in a concrete block of flats. They had bought a plot of land in a nearby village where they often went. Half of it was planted with fruit trees but there was also a small vegetable garden and lots of flowers. In time, her husband built a small wooden house there. As my colleagues used to say, it was her little garden of paradise. She spent almost every weekend there, sometimes with the whole family, sometimes on her own.

One Saturday morning her husband had things to do, so he stayed at home with the children. My friend got on her bike and went to the plot alone. When she didn't come home that night, the family was not concerned because she'd spent the night in the wooden house before, but when she didn't come home the next day either, they knew something had happened to her.

They went to the police. The following day, people went searching for her only to find her body at the bottom of a dried-up well. She had been brutally raped, murdered and thrown into the well. A few days later, the culprits were caught while trying to sell the woman's bicycle in the village. Three local men, who no one would have thought capable of such a thing, were arrested.

Needless to say, we were shocked by this incident. These killers had taken the life of a person who had never harmed anyone. They had destroyed a beautiful family – and for what? A second-hand bicycle. A hobby farm, which used to be a little paradise, turned into hell for them on that Saturday.

I couldn't decide whether to share this memory with you or not because everything I have written about so far has happened directly to me or to my family members, but thinking back to the years I spent in the factory I realised that I couldn't leave out this tragic story. Sadly, I lost a dear person whom I still remember more than thirty years later.

But now let's go back to my first months in the factory, when this colleague was still alive and sitting in the office. Not only did I get a lot of help from her, but also from my immediate colleagues. When they finished a piece of work, they always brought it to me and talked to me while they waited for their next job. I didn't mind as I learned a lot about the factory and about them.

Slowly I got to know everyone. One of them was a man called Robi, who was always teasing our colleagues, always joking with them. He was the kind of man who liked to be the centre of attention. He was full of fun and self-confidence, but he didn't seem pretentious.

I noticed he was at my desk more and more often whether he needed a job or not. He was always kind and considerate to me, which I liked. Once we left the factory together at the same time and we got talking. He asked me if I wanted to have a coffee with him and I said yes.

We sat at a nearby café. While we were drinking our coffee – my first-ever espresso – he kept talking and talking, what about I don't know, but I remember that it was very enjoyable to listen to him.

We'd been sitting there for about two hours and I didn't want to go home because I was having so much fun with him. I barely slept that night; I blamed the coffee because it was too strong – but all I could really think about was Robi. It was like I was mesmerised by him and I just couldn't get him out of my mind.

I was nervous about the next day, wondering how he would behave with me. I shouldn't have worried because he greeted me by saying that he thought yesterday afternoon had been good and we should do it again.

When I finished work, he was waiting for me at the exit. This time we went to a different café where I only had a soft drink because I wanted to sleep better that night. The afternoon passed in the same way as the previous one: Robi talked and talked, and I listened curiously to his words.

It was as if the world around us had stopped, and it was just him and me. I didn't even care if it was late, or what I was going to tell my parents when I got home. There was something about him that was magnetic, that was both exciting and scary, especially when he said that he liked me and wanted to see me at the weekend.

I almost jumped out of my skin because this would be a date, a real date! I said yes and couldn't wait for Sunday afternoon to come but first there was something I had to do: talk to my parents. Somehow I had a feeling they wouldn't be as excited about it as I was; after all, Robi was more than ten years older than me and had been married. His four-year-old son was living with his ex-wife somewhere in Russia.

Unfortunately my fears were confirmed because my parents were not happy about what they heard. My dad yelled at me like never before. 'Have you lost your mind that you want this old, divorced man? Who knows why he got divorced, what he did to his family? You could do better for yourself. There are plenty guys in the factory.'

'I didn't choose him, he chose me,' I thought, but of course I didn't tell him that.

'Just because he's divorced doesn't mean he can't be a good man! And the fact that he's older than me doesn't bother me, so why does it bother you? I'd like to go out with him, get to know him better, and then I'll decide whether he's right for me or not.'

No matter what my parents told me, I was stubborn.

'Do what you want, just don't regret it,' my father said finally.

This was our first serious confrontation because I usually obeyed them, but I felt I had to stand up for Robi because it was my future, my happiness.

Finally the long-awaited Sunday came, and then another and another. The more time we spent together, the more I liked what I saw, or at least what he showed me of himself. They say opposites attract, which in our case proved true; he had everything I lacked and that impressed me. Whereas I was quiet and reserved, he was a loud and confident, always the centre of attention. He made me laugh all the time and I was never bored around him. Wherever we were, he would perform until everyone's attention was on him. He had an opinion about everything.

I looked up to him and was proud to be his girlfriend. I was totally in love with him and the happiest I'd ever been: he was the one for me. After two months I felt I couldn't live without him. Although he never said it, I hoped he felt the same way about me because he spent all his free time with me.

It is true that our natures were different but there were similarities. We both liked fishing, picking mushrooms and hiking in the mountains. Since our family had moved into our new flat we went down to the river less frequently, usually just to swim or sunbathe. That changed when I got together with Robi. He had a motorbike and we used to go fishing on the lakes and rivers in the area.

Sadly we didn't enjoy the benefits of motorcycling for long because on one occasion, after dropping me off at the staircase, Robi had an accident on his way home. Luckily, he had only minor bruises but his bike was wrecked. We went hiking in the mountains by train instead, no longer with my family but with him and his friends.

My life was completely different after I started working in the factory. I stopped thinking about college because I felt like I was travelling in the right direction. I was in love and happy. Did I need more?

One day Robi told me he wanted to introduce me to his parents. 'Before you meet them, you need to know something about them,' he said.

He went on to say that when he was a little boy, his parents were well off. They had everything: a big house, a car in the garage, an expensive television in the room. When his mother became pregnant with their second child, she had a miscarriage and lost a lot of blood. Her family doctor advised her to have half a glass of red wine with her lunch every day to improve her condition. Half a glass became a whole glass, and then she didn't even need lunch, just the wine.

This went on for years. His father tried to make her see sense but it didn't work. One day he gave up and started drinking too, so by the time Robi was a teenager his parents had become complete alcoholics. They sold their house, cashed in everything they could and spent it all. There were daily arguments in the family, and even fights on more than one occasion.

It was awful to imagine what he must have experienced as a young boy. I used to think I'd had a difficult childhood, and sometimes my dad had a glass of wine or two, but I never saw him drunk or aggressive. I was lucky that my life hadn't included that.

When we arrived at Robi's parents' house I knew roughly what to expect, but it was worse than that. They lived in a small house with one room and a kitchen that didn't look too bad from the outside, but inside it was awful as if there were no woman in the house. It was a mess: it was dirty and everywhere I looked there were empty beer and wine bottles lying around.

His parents were kind to me, but even though they knew when I was coming they couldn't stay sober. A bottle of wine was found somewhere and they poured me a glass. We drank to our meeting then to our health, and then just carried on drinking. I wasn't used to alcohol and I didn't want to get used to it so I sipped my wine, but it went to my head after a while. I knew that if I didn't stop, I was going to get drunk so didn't touch my glass again. They didn't bother and soon opened another bottle of wine.

Since they made me feel welcome, I went to see them more often from. There was always wine on the table but fortunately they didn't pour any more for me, for which I was grateful as I could easily have got into the habit of drinking.

It was time for me to introduce Robi to my parents, who were still not happy about our relationship. I hoped that meeting him would change their opinion. We didn't greet my boyfriend with wine but with lunch and a delicious cake. I thought the meeting went well because my mum and my Nana liked Robi straight away. He did his best to make a good impression but my dad barely spoke to him; you could tell he was angry.

When Robi had left, the bomb exploded. 'Do you know who this man is?' my father shouted angrily in my face.

'Of course I do!' I shouted back. 'I know him!'

'You know his family, too? They're alcoholics, a bunch of useless people! Open your eyes! Is that what you want?'

'Yes, it is!' I answered back. 'And I know who his parents are. It's bad enough for him to have to live in a family like that. You can't judge him for that, it's not his fault.'

'You could do better than that,' my father said finally and that was the end of the argument.

'But I want him! Why can't you understand that?' I said to myself. How could he be so unfair to someone he didn't even know – or maybe he did know Robi, since he knew his parents were alcoholics.

The next day I questioned my mother about what she knew. My dad had told her that a friend of his lived in the same courtyard as Robi, so he knew the family by sight and had seen them drunk more than once. That explained why dad was so angry when he recognized Robi, but even so he had no right to judge him; one cannot choose one's relatives.

Months went by and Robi and I were still a couple. We got along well, hung out almost constantly and talked about everything – except his marriage. When that came up, Robi went quiet and you could tell he didn't like to talk about it. I wondered where it had gone wrong.

He did tell me that his wife had a bad relationship with his parents; she looked down on them and it caused tension in the family. The bigger problem was her jealousy, which, needless to say, was unfounded. They fought more and more and it ruined their marriage. When his son was one year old, his wife packed up and moved to live with relatives in Odessa. Robi had not heard from them since and had no contact with his child apart from paying alimony. He said he missed his son very much and had no idea when he would see him again.

'A few years ago, I had a family and plans for our future,' he said sadly. 'Now there's nothing left. Luckily I have you, and with you it will be different.'

I was happy with what I heard and sure it would happen. I didn't think I was a jealous person, so that shouldn't be a problem between us. Robi and I had been dating for more than ten months and our relationship was working well. We trusted each other and we never fought, although sometimes we disagreed about something. In the end, he always convinced me that he was right.

One time I used my pocket money to buy mascara and a light pink lipstick. I wanted to look a bit more attractive because next to Robi I was just a grey mouse. He had black wavy hair, a black moustache and a handsome face; he was good looking, so no wonder his wife was jealous. There was nothing beautiful about me except perhaps my blue eyes. With my pale face, long nose and ugly brown hair, I was not a noticeable figure.

In the morning, when I went to work wearing a little make-up, I didn't hear what I expected. Robi told me, almost angrily, that I didn't need it, that he liked me as I was.

Other times I curled my hair to make it a wavier and not so boringly straight. Then he would question me, 'Why are you doing this to yourself?'

'I want to look a little better, why else?'

'I like you the way you are and that's the main thing, isn't it?'

'Yes.' What else could I say because he was right.

I didn't even think about arguing with him, because he said what I wanted to hear; he liked me and that was the important thing.

I was increasingly preoccupied with the idea that I had to do something with myself because I was over eighteen and I wanted to live my own life. As long as I was living with my parents and bringing my salary home, I had no independence. They still treated me like a child even though I was an adult.

When this came up with Robi, he suddenly said, 'You know what? Let's change it! Let's get married.' It wasn't exactly a proposal, but it served its purpose. I said yes and we started planning our future together.

Every few years, the factory built a block of flats and sold them to the workers. This seemed like a good opportunity for us, as we would only have to pay a third of the total price; the rest would be deducted from our monthly salary.

'We could stay with my parents while waiting for our turn and save up money for the first instalment,' I said.

The plan was good; it just needed to be implemented. First, we told Robi's parents that we were getting married and they were very happy. I knew they liked me; they were always nice to me and had called me daughter for some time. They were good people at heart although alcohol had ruined them.

I wasn't sure that my parents would be so happy to hear the news. My dad continued to be very cold to Robi but at least he wasn't yelling at me or trying to talk me out of it. Maybe he realised he was losing this battle, because the more he forbade it, the more I clung to Robi.

I was a little afraid to tell them at home that I was getting married but strangely, my father didn't raise his voice. All he said was, 'I thought by now your eyes would be open and you would realise who this man is – a nobody.'

My mother came to my defence. 'No matter who he is or what he has, as long as he's a good person.'

'Of course he's a good person,' I said. 'I've known him for a year. I would have noticed if he wasn't.'

'It's your life, you can ruin it any way you want. If you love him so much, marry him – but you can't bring him here! Live wherever you want,' my dad said, ending the discussion.

I certainly hadn't expected him to say that; I would rather he'd yelled at me or argued with me but let us live with them. I was very angry with him; I just didn't understand how a father could do that to his daughter. Did he really think I'd change my mind and give up Robi? Well, no! We were getting married whether he liked it or not! But then what were we going to do? Where were we going to live? Renting was not a good idea because we wouldn't be able to save up any money. Should we live with Robi's parents until we got our own place?

We had no choice. I'd been visiting them a lot lately, so I had the chance to have a better look around. If we threw out all that junk and cleaned it up, the little house wouldn't look so bad. Of course, the walls could do with a good paint job and sooner or later the old furniture would have to be replaced...

Robi agreed with everything I suggested and we agreed to start renovating once I was living there after the wedding.

A month later we got married. It wasn't a big ceremony as we barely had any money and we couldn't rely on our parents for financial support. We bought my wedding ring but Robi's was borrowed from his cousin. I rented the simplest, cheapest wedding dress. Since I was marrying a divorced man, we couldn't have a church wedding only a civil one. After the ceremony, we went home and had a small family meal. That was it: no wedding ceremony, no honeymoon. But it didn't matter; we were married and that was the point.

For a few days it felt strange to leave the factory and not go home to my fifth-floor apartment. My mother-in-law kept telling me to make myself at home but I just couldn't. I thought that if we painted and cleaned the place up, it would feel more like home and I would feel better.

A week after our wedding, we were walking home in high spirits when I brought up the issue. 'I want to get on with the renovation and finish it as soon as possible.'

'We'll start next week,' Robi said. 'There's a match tomorrow afternoon and I want to watch it.'

'Then I'll go to my sister's. It's been so long since I've been to their house.'

'No, you can't!' he said angrily.

'Why not?' I asked.

'Because I forbid it!' Then he slapped me so hard in the middle of the street that I almost fell. At first I didn't understand what had happened. The last time my brother had hit me was years earlier for throwing a glass cutter at him. That hadn't hurt so badly because I was expecting it – but what was this? Why had Robi hit me?

I started crying and my face was burning with pain and shame because anyone on the street could see us. Then Robi grabbed my arm roughly and dragged me into their courtyard. He started shouting, 'You think I don't know why you want to go there? To meet your lover!'

'Who?' I couldn't understand what he was talking about. Did he mean my brother-in-law?

'You know who! Your brother-in-law's friend, the one you kissed.'

'But he's not my lover. I only want to see my godson.'

'I don't care, you can't go there anymore! You'll see them at your parents'.'

So he was jealous and that's why he'd hit me. Back then, when I'd told him about that guy and the kiss, all he'd said was that the boy must have liked me. Now he was banning me from my sister's house so I didn't run into him. I still felt guilty about neglecting my godson, because two years before I'd been with him all summer, and for the last year I'd spent all my time with Robi.

I'd never seen Robi so angry as when he slapped me. I thought that when he calmed down, he would regret what he'd done and stop hurting me because we loved each other. But no apology was made; everything seemed fine to him, as if nothing had happened.

We did nothing in the house for the next week or the weeks that followed. Robi either didn't feel like it or he was tired because he thought he had worked hard enough at the factory. I wasn't happy about it, but what could I do? I couldn't start painting on my own.

The next time I asked him about the renovations, he shouted angrily in my face, 'Enough! Shut up! There will be no renovation!'

'But we agreed,' I said quietly.

'I don't care what we discussed! It's fine as it is! I don't want to hear any more about it!'

'I don't care what we discussed,' I repeated to myself as I was laying the table for lunch. I was fighting back tears, my hands shaking with nervousness. Did that mean the house would remain like that? I felt betrayed because Robi had agreed to everything before the wedding.

When we sat down to lunch, he suddenly slammed his fist on the table. 'Where's my spoon? What am I eating with? My hands?'

He hit me with such force that if I had not been sitting down,, I would have ended up on the other side of the room. His mother quickly jumped up and got a spoon for her son to calm him down. I felt dizzy, sick and I couldn't hold back the tears. I started sobbing. This slap had opened my eyes and I could see clearly; the pink mist that had been lingering around me until that moment was gone.

I was so blinded by love that I hadn't seen what was going on around me. Who was this man who would beat me like this over a spoon? Who had I married? I could forgive him the first slap by convincing myself that he was jealous and he'd lost his temper, but there was no excuse for that now, especially when he knew I was pregnant.

I wanted to run out of the house and never look back, but where could I go? Home? I remembered my father's words: 'Open your eyes! Is that what you want?'

My God, how could I have been so blind? My dad only wanted the best for me; I should have listened to him and then I wouldn't have been in this mess. I'd wanted so much to be loved that I'd ignored everything else. I was caught in a trap and I had to get out of it by myself.

I was disappointed in Robi but I was ashamed to admit it to my parents so I kept quiet. I tried to make the best of the situation as I had to think of my child.

I knew I could not live in such filth and mess but unfortunately, whenever I started to do anything, my mother-in-law waved me away, telling me to relax, she would do it tomorrow. But she didn't do anything, she didn't even try.

Since everything was fine for them but not for me, I had to do something. I waited until they were all asleep and then I started cleaning. After a while, the place started to look a little better, although sometimes I felt like I was fighting a windmill.

There was something I liked about that house, though, and that was the five paintings on the wall. They had been painted by Robi's uncle, who was not a famous painter but who obviously had talent. After I'd dusted them off and cleared all the spider webs, they brightened up the room quite a bit and looked good on the dirty walls.

Not that any of my family could have seen them as no one came to see us, which I didn't mind at all. I did, however, often go home where I sometimes ran into my sisters. Since I was forbidden to visit them, it was the only way I could see my godson. I told everyone I was busy, so I didn't have time to visit.

I naively thought that if I avoided conflict and tried to accommodate my husband in every way, maybe he'd be less aggressive but I was wrong about that, too. Robi was unpredictable: one minute he'd be cheerfully telling me something, the next minute he was screaming and slapping me.

It was the same when he saw me plucking my eyebrows with tweezers. My mum had seven children and was in her fifties, but she still plucked her eyebrows because it was natural for women do these things. Robi didn't think it was and got terribly angry. 'What are you doing?' he yelled. 'Who do you want to please?'

He didn't even wait for an answer – the slap was already coming. Somehow this one didn't hurt as much as the last two; either he didn't hit me as hard or I was getting used to them.

But I couldn't let it go, I screamed back. 'What are you doing? You should have hit me when I was putting on my make-up for you! I certainly wouldn't have married you.'

'Shut up!' shouted Robi.

But I couldn't stop. 'What happened to you? What has changed since then?'

'Shut up if you don't want another one!' he threatened.

I didn't need another slap so I kept my mouth shut. There was no point in asking him, because I already knew the answers. Robi wasn't a good man, as I had believed and had tried to prove to my parents, he just played his part well. I was easy prey because I was starved for the love he seemingly gave me. But after the wedding, the real him came out and he didn't have to pretend anymore.

I remembered how many times we'd sat here in the evenings with his parents. There was always wine or beer on the table but Robi was never drunk. Now he was drunk almost every day. I'd thought that only his parents were alcoholics but then I realised that all three of them were. When my dad said they were alcoholics I hadn't wanted to hear it, but he'd been right about everything. The proof was right in front of my eyes.

One day Robi and I came home from work and found his parents already drunk. He joined them and the three of them continued drinking. When the last bottle of wine had been poured into the glasses, Robi went into the kitchen for some reason. Meanwhile, my mother-in-law drank her own glass quickly then reached for his glass and drank it too. All Robi saw was his mother putting the empty glass on the table.

I will never forget what happened next: Robi punched his mother in the face so hard that she collapsed. I was so scared that I thought he had killed her.

My father-in-law's only reaction was, 'Hey, son!' He brought a glass of water and splashed it in her face and thankfully she came to. She was completely confused, but when she looked at me for a moment I thought I saw shame in her eyes. Then she climbed onto the bed and fell asleep.

Perhaps the best word for what I felt for Robi at that moment was contempt. How could he hit his mother like that? What kind of person did that? Was he even human? I didn't close my eyes all night because I just couldn't digest what I had seen. I was sure it wasn't the first time, as my father-in-law had so routinely brought round his unconscious wife. He wasn't as frightened as I was. The poor woman needed help, not a beating.

The previous year at this time I'd been the happiest person in the world and now I was the most miserable. If Robi treated his mother like this, what could *I* expect?

Unfortunately, the brutal behaviour wasn't the only thing that worried me. Before the wedding we had agreed to start saving money for our own apartment, as it would be our turn in the factory in a few years' time. Robi hardly gave me anything from his salary, saying that he had expenses: two packs of cigarettes a day, five or six cups of coffee and the wine or a beer certainly cost money. His parents spent most of their pension on drinks, not food. What was left was my salary, which was barely enough for the four of us for a month.

It was then that I really understood my mother's situation. She'd had to look after seven people; of course she couldn't wait for me to start working and contribute a little to the family budget.

But what should I do now? If this went on, we'd be stuck in the house forever because we'd never have money for a new flat. It looked like we wouldn't even be able to buy a pram or a cot when the time came.

I was absolutely devastated. I remembered Nana's words: 'Once will be better.' But when? Not the next day, that was for sure.

My mother-in-law went to the shop twice, so there was enough beer and wine to drink late into the night. They were in a good mood, talking loudly but not quarrelling.

At one point, Robi turned to me and said almost boastfully, 'Guess what, I knocked out all my father's teeth!' That must have been true because his father had hardly any teeth, but I couldn't laugh. It made my stomach turn.

'Congratulations. You should be proud of yourself,' I thought, though I didn't say it out loud.

My father-in-law got very angry with Robi and started shouting at him. Word followed word, and they had a big argument and ended up fighting. My mother-in-law tried to separate them but to no avail. One of them pushed her so hard that she fell under the table and stayed there.

The two men continued to fight. My father-in-law had blood coming out of his nose but he wouldn't stop. Bottles and glasses were smashed and there was blood everywhere. I sat curled up on the edge of the bed watching them. It was so scary, it was like being in a horror movie. I wouldn't have minded if they'd killed each other, as long as it was over.

When they finally stopped, my father-in-law shouted, 'Get out of here! This is my house and you can't behave like this! Both of you get out!'

I didn't need to be told twice. I grabbed my coat and boots and ran. Robi followed me and my father-in-law quickly locked the door. It was mid-December, eleven o'clock at night and we were standing outside, clueless.

Where to go, what to do? Robi seemed to have sobered up, perhaps because of the cold air or the seriousness of the situation. He thought we should wait until his father fell asleep then try to find a way into the house.

'I'm not going back there,' I said. 'Let's go to my mum's. They won't let us sleep on the street.'

I was right: they let us stay. The next day Robi told a slightly different story about the night, but that was to be expected: he said it was his father's fault, not his. Since I couldn't tell the truth,

I kept quiet and let him deceive my parents. He succeeded because my dad finally let us move back home.

Finally something had changed in my life and I hoped that things would get better. My parents moved into the living room and we got one of the big rooms; Potyi and my youngest sister lived in the other, and my brother and Nana lived in the third.

Nana was very ill by then and had only a few days left. Months before, the doctors had diagnosed stomach cancer and given her only a few weeks, but she was very resilient and fought to the end. I can't imagine the pain she felt but she never complained.

Once I entered her room without her noticing and I heard her crying. When she looked up at me, her terrible pain was written on her face. My heart broke for her but I couldn't help her.

A few months earlier when I'd announced I was getting married, she was the only one who'd really supported me. All she'd said was, 'If you love him, marry him.'

Nana had said that the age difference didn't matter because there were twelve years between her and my grandfather yet they were fine together. The interesting thing is that they weren't in love; they hadn't even known each other before they were brought together.

My grandfather had never planned to get married and had wanted to be a Catholic priest. He had already started at the seminary when his father died suddenly. His mother and younger siblings were left without a head of the household, and as the eldest son he had to look after them. He gave up his studies and went to work to support his family. He was forty years old when his youngest sister married, and he was left alone without a wife and children.

Like my grandfather, my Nana also had no luck in life. She was the youngest child in the family and her parents were very old. Shortly after she was born, her father died and her eldest brother dispossessed them – she was still a baby when she and her mother were dumped on the streets. Relatives took them in and let them live with them in exchange for work.

Nana had no house and no dowry, so she had no chance to marry. At the age of twenty-eight, acquaintances introduced her to my grandfather. It is true that they did not marry for love, but they did fall in love and lived happily together for thirty-two years. According to her, she was very fortunate to have my grandfather because she could not have had a better man.

She believed that Robi and I would make a good couple and have a happy marriage. Oh, if only she'd known how wrong she was because our marriage was anything but happy. I didn't regret keeping the truth from her so she didn't have to worry about me. She lived her last weeks believing that Robi and I were doing well and that the baby was coming in the summer. The poor thing knew she wouldn't see her great-grandchild, but she was happy to hear the news.

At the beginning of February she gave up the fight and died, leaving a big hole in our hearts. I knew it was better for her because she had suffered so much, but it was still hard to let her go. She was the best grandmother in the world and my second mom, whom I will never forget. We named the cherry tree she climbed for us when she was sixty-five years old 'Nana's cherry tree'. It stood between the cemetery and the forest for many years to remind us of her.

Life went on and time slowly but surely healed our wounds. We patched things up with my father-in-law, but something had changed between us. I couldn't like him as much as I had done because I had seen the other side of him, the worst side of him.

I wasn't angry with him for throwing us out of his house because he was drunk and only the booze was talking. According to him, he regretted what he had done and he called us back several times, but I didn't want to live with them again so we stayed with my family.

Robi visited his parents often and continued to drink with them, but at least he didn't get drunk every night like before. He did his best to ingratiate himself with my family and he succeeded; my dad started to like him. Ironically, by the time I was completely disillusioned with my husband the two of them had become friends.

Unfortunately, living in my parents' house did not make our marriage better. Nothing I did was good enough for Robi; he picked on me and criticised me for everything. He didn't think I was a good housewife or wife – but what did he expect? I married too young to have had any experience. When I was younger I used to help my mum to bake or cook, so I tried to learn as much as I could from her. I felt I was doing my best, but to be a good housewife you need time and patience, which Robi didn't have.

We fought a lot and sometimes his hand would come and go, but only in private in our room so that my parents wouldn't know how he treated me. His behaviour made me feel like a miserable nobody again and destroyed what little self-confidence I'd been starting to build up. I improved my cookery skills because I wanted to learn to cook well, but I couldn't deal with his jealousy. He had made me believe that his ex-wife was the jealous one, but that was just one of his many lies.

One day while shopping, I ran into one of my former classmates; I knew him from primary school but I hadn't seen him since. I was surprised that he said hello to me, since we hadn't been that close.

We started talking and I introduced him to my husband. He had a bag of sweets in his hand, which he politely offered to both of us. Robi didn't want any but I couldn't refuse so I took one. Maybe it was my pregnancy that made me crave that chocolate so much, or maybe it was because I'd been craving such a treat since childhood.

When I caught Robi's piercing look, I knew I had made a mistake but it was too late. On the way home he nearly exploded, but at least he didn't hit me in the middle of the street like he had done a few months before.

He hissed angrily in my ear, 'Now you've accepted the chocolate, next time he'll buy you a coffee and then you'll end up in his bed!'

No matter what I said, he didn't hear me. I got three slaps in the face at home to make sure I wouldn't forget his words.

Robi's sick jealousy continued to grow. As I worked mainly with men in the factory, he was jealous of anyone who smiled at me or joked with me. Since I'd got married, my relationship with my colleagues hadn't changed and they behaved the same as before. We were like one big family but Robi didn't see it that way and I was the one who paid the price.

After the fights and slaps in the face that night, it wasn't easy to pretend the next day that nothing had happened but I did. I played my part and did it well, because no one suspected anything. We made people believe that everything was fine between us, that we were in a good marriage.

Robi seemed happy that he would soon be a father again and hoped for a son, but I was terrified that if I had a son he might be like his father or grandfather. But girls in that family could become as much a victim as me or my mother-in-law.

These worries were dwarfed by what I was really worried about. My child's health was the most important thing, not whether it was a boy or a girl. Since I'd married, I had been very stressed and I hoped it wouldn't affect the baby. At that time, we didn't have ultrasound scans so I couldn't know anything for sure. There were only three weeks left until the baby was due, so we would find out then.

One day Robi and I were walking in the city centre when we felt hungry and went into a diner to get something to eat. While we were waiting for our food, a group of people came through the door and sat at the table behind my husband. They were in a good mood, talking loudly and laughing a lot. I'm sure you know what it's like when someone next to you laughs out loud and you unknowingly look over. Apparently, I did that – I didn't even realise.

Robi got very angry and demanded, 'Why are you staring at those men? Do you know them?'

The truth is that until then I hadn't even realised that the merry company was all men. 'I don't know them,' I replied but he called me a liar.

'Then why are you eyeing them? Maybe you've got your eye on someone?'

'You're talking nonsense,' I said, but I immediately regretted it.

Word followed word and Robi got more and more upset. Suddenly he jumped up and ran out, leaving me alone at the table. I had no idea whether those around us had heard our quarrel, but I felt very ashamed. I could hardly hold back my tears and I was shaking with nerves.

I tried to eat the last bites on my plate but I couldn't; all I could think was that this was not over yet. That's when I realised I had no money on me and I couldn't pay for what we'd ordered.

I sat there with no idea what to do. Should I beg them to let me go without paying, or promise to come back with the money? They wouldn't believe me anyway. Should I get up and run out of the door like my husband had done? But I couldn't run with my big belly, and I wouldn't survive the shame if I was caught at the door like a thief.

I was feeling sick and could hardly breathe. I don't know how long I sat like that, but suddenly I looked up and Robi was standing in front of me. He'd come back for me. He paid the bill and said we had to stop at his uncle's on the way home.

'I don't care where we go, just get me out of here,' I thought.

Robi didn't say a word to me, but he seemed calmer although you could never tell with him. I hoped that the scene in the diner would have no consequences, but I was wrong. When we arrived at his uncle's house, we greeted him in the kitchen and then Robi motioned for us to go to the bathroom. He hadn't even closed the door before he started shouting at me.

'I'll teach you not to stare at other men!' He raised his hand and started hitting me. To protect my baby, I automatically put my hands in front of my belly, leaving my face free. I received one slap after another.

When he stopped for a moment, I quickly turned away from him. 'Don't turn your back on me, look me in the eye!' he shouted, but I didn't listen and that made him even angrier.

He hit me repeatedly on the head and back with his fist. I was crying loudly but he was unaffected. Finally he stopped and left the bathroom. I sat on the edge of the tub, my hands still covering my belly, afraid because he could come back at any moment. But he didn't come back; he'd finished taking out his aggression on me for now. He chatted with his uncle outside as if nothing had happened.

That day my hopes for a better life were completely dashed. The love I so longed for would never come from my husband. A man who could beat his eight-months' pregnant wife like that had no heart, and without a heart love is impossible.

I sat on the edge of the tub and cried; I couldn't stop. I was crying for myself, for my ruined life. I'd made a bad decision and this was the result. But it wasn't just about me anymore, it was about my unborn child, too. What kind of life was waiting for a child with such a father?

The next morning at dawn I woke up with a terrible cramp in my belly. I was really scared because surely these couldn't be the labour pains yet, could they? Then my waters broke and there was no doubt – today my baby would be born.

In the ambulance on the way to the hospital I prayed that everything would be okay and that I would deliver a healthy baby. But my baby didn't want to be born; it was as if he felt safer in my tummy.

After I had been in labour for eight hours, my strength was gone. A nurse took my hand, leaned over and whispered in my ear, 'Pull yourself together. Your baby needs you. Help him to be born.'

'Yes, you're right, my baby needs me.' That thought gave me strength and finally I did it: my baby boy was born. I heard him cry out loud and then he was quickly taken out of the room. I was a little disappointed because I wanted to see him, but I couldn't.

'Never mind, they'll bring him to breastfeed tomorrow,' I thought. But they did not bring him the next day or the third day. Mothers who'd had their babies a day later than me already had them in the room.

I didn't understand what was happening. Was there something wrong? The obstetrician had said everything was fine and I could hear my son crying, so why couldn't I see him? When I asked the paediatrician, he didn't look me in the eye; he talked but didn't say anything specific.

I was very scared – I felt that something was wrong. My baby was almost three days old and I hadn't held him. I couldn't sleep at night, so I sneaked out of the ward to look for my baby. I knew that the room where they keep newborns was down the corridor, because that's where the crying came from. Luckily, the nurse had gone somewhere so I could look around undisturbed.

There were a lot of babies so I had to hurry to find mine. Each cot had the baby's name on the front and I looked at them in turn,. Finally, I saw a familiar name – but what I saw made me freeze. My child's face was covered with a piece of white gauze the size of a handkerchief. I looked around to see if there was one on any other babies, but there was only one on mine.

I leaned closer to see if he was breathing but the gauze wasn't moving around his mouth. I can't describe the feeling I had at that moment. My scalp began to go numb and my heart, which had been beating so hard, seemed to stop. I couldn't breathe and I was shaking like a leaf.

I reached for his face to take off the gauze but then I didn't; I was afraid of what I would see, afraid to face reality. Instead I ran out sobbing and didn't stop until I reached my room. There I buried my face in the pillow and cried all my sorrow into it. I didn't want to believe that I had lost my little boy. This couldn't happen, not to me! I needed him, he was the best thing in my life.

I cried and cried until my pillow was soaked with tears. I tried to calm myself by thinking that maybe I'd misread his name or maybe there was another child with the same surname. Maybe he was just sound asleep, so you couldn't tell if he was breathing. But why was his little face covered? I didn't manage to calm down but I was exhausted from all the crying and I fell asleep sometime around dawn.

When they woke me in the morning, I was almost out of my mind. I had a splitting headache and my chest felt like it was being crushed by a stone. My first thought was that I'd had a bad dream, but when I went to the bathroom and saw myself in the mirror I knew it had really happened. My eyes were swollen from crying and my face was white as a sheet.

The nurses started bringing the babies into the room. I cried again, knowing that they would never bring mine.

'Don't cry, Mommy,' one of the nurses said. 'I brought your baby.'

WHAT? I didn't understand what she said as she handed me a baby. *My* baby! He was lying on my lap, looking at me with his big, beautiful eyes. He had a round face, a tiny nose and a mouth that looked like mine.

I couldn't take my eyes off him, I was completely enchanted. My little boy, my darling little boy! There was nothing wrong with him, he was breathing nice and steadily, and he even gave a big yawn. I was over the moon; I had been waiting for this for days.

'Now it's time to feed him,' the nurse said kindly.

Of course he was hungry, this little boy. I started to cry again while I was feeding him, but they were tears of joy because I was happy, very happy. If I hadn't been so impatient the night before and sneaked into the newborns' room, I could have saved myself from the worst night of my life.

I never found out why they covered his little face with that gauze or why I couldn't see him for three days. But that was in the past and I had to concentrate on the future.

Before I continue with my story, I need to go back a bit in time to my pregnancy. There is something I forgot to mention and I would like to make up for it now. A few weeks before the baby was due, we bought a pram where the baby could sleep for a while because we didn't have the money for a cot. I didn't spend much on baby clothes because luckily I got several things from my sister. We had to sew the nappies ourselves as there were no disposable ones at that time; I did that a few days before the birth, so the baby had pretty much everything he needed for the first few weeks. The only thing we hadn't thought of was a name. We really didn't: we didn't name the baby.

From what I have told you so far about my marriage, you can see that we were not a normal couple. Robi was not the kind of man who would put his ear to his wife's belly and listen to the baby's heartbeat, feel it move or kick. Somehow we had never talked about what we would name our baby, so when I was asked after the birth what I would call my boy I had no idea what to say. The only thing I knew for sure was that I would not be allowed to name him; I knew Robi well enough to know that I had no right to decide. If I dared to utter a boy's name, that would mean trouble.

The next morning the nurse handed me a small piece of paper with a note saying it was from my husband. On the paper there was only one word: ZOLTÁN. So the father had named his son and, as I'd thought, I'd had no word in the decision. But I was happy that he hadn't give him his own or my father-in-law's name. My little boy became Zoltán, or rather Zoli.

It was only when I was discharged from hospital that I really experienced what life was like with a baby. During the day we could manage, but the nights were tough. The baby would often wake up crying and then struggle to fall back asleep.

We had been home for about a week when Zoli cried for the second time one night. I changed his nappy and tried to calm him down but it didn't work. Robi woke up, came to me and yelled at me, 'Shut that child up. I want to sleep!'

He slapped me so hard that the room spun around; I probably would have fallen had I not been holding on to the pram. I picked up the baby and ran out to the kitchen with him, closing the door behind us. There we were, both crying, but at least we didn't disturb my husband.

I don't know what I had thought, what I had expected from him. Why did this slap hurt more than the previous ones, why did it hurt so badly? I'd naively thought that if I gave Robi a son he might appreciate me more, but of course I was wrong about that like everything else.

That slap in the face made me realise that I couldn't expect any help or understanding from Robi, I could only rely on myself. I swore I would do my best to be a good mother to my son because he meant the world to me.

Days went by and I got more into the routine of being a mother. It was not easy as there were hardly any nights that the baby slept through. The midwife said he must have a tummy ache, that's why he was so restless, but I thought that all the bad things I had experienced during my pregnancy might have affected him, though I couldn't be sure.

Anyway, Zoli was growing nicely and he gained half a kilo by the time he was one month old. I could not say the same for myself: the few kilos I had gained during my pregnancy had long since disappeared, and more. I was tired all the time, and the circles under my eyes were getting deeper from lack of sleep.

One day, Robi decided to take a break and go hiking in the mountains. It was a tempting offer as the last time we'd been chestnut picking was the previous autumn before our wedding. But much as I wanted to go, I couldn't leave the baby at home for a whole day.

'No need,' said Robi. 'We'll take him with us.'

Climbing up the mountain with a one-month-old baby seemed crazy, but I didn't dare argue so I agreed. After all, feeding shouldn't be a problem; I still had plenty of breast milk and I could take enough nappies.

The inside of the pram was removable and portable; it looked like a bassinet. The next morning we put Zoli in it and went to the Carpathians, which were twenty minutes away by train.

It was the middle of summer, and the weather couldn't have been more beautiful. Robi carried the bassinet with the baby from one mountain to another without any complaint as we picked mushrooms in the forest.

We came to a meadow full of the most beautiful flowers and sat down to rest by a stream. Robi was in a very good mood, and after a while so was I. He told me interesting stories about his years in the army, some of which made us laugh. We had a great time, an incredible time! It was so familiar, as if we had just gone back a year in time and I saw again the man I had fallen in love with, the man who had completely enchanted me, who had made the world around me disappear until it was just him and me. How beautiful our relationship had been then, how different.

I don't know what happened to me that day but I felt I was in love with Robi again and I forgot all the bad things he had done to me in the last months. Maybe it was the beautiful landscape that had such an effect or the nostalgia, but I was hopeful again. Maybe our relationship could change and we could be happy again.

Since our trip had gone so well, we agreed to leave the house more often. The baby didn't complain either; he ate and slept almost the whole time.

Needless to say, things did not turn out as planned. Soon my milk dried up and feeding became a problem, so we couldn't take the baby anywhere for long.

It's true that we didn't talk about it, but that day changed something in Robi too. He was less fussy with me and didn't hit me for weeks – though he still didn't help with the housework or child-rearing.

When we had moved in with my parents, from the very first moment we lived on separate money in separate households. My mother offered to cook for us but Robi refused; he thought it was the wife's job to cook and I agreed. But how hard it is to do everything on your own with a baby; only someone who has been there knows. I appreciated my mum even more for what she'd done for us; I couldn't imagine how hard it had been for her with seven children, especially when a new baby was born every other year, but she never complained, she just did her job.

Because of her many children, my mother retired early but she still had no more time than before. The previous year my aunt had bought a hobby farm plot with a wooden weekend house on a hill on the other side of the river. At first my mother only went there to help but later she spent almost all her free time there.

Since my aunt worked and didn't have time to take care of the land, she left tending it to my mother in exchange for fruit and vegetables. My mother was happy to do it and her dedication paid off.

The ground on the hill was as hard as concrete and watering was only possible with rainwater collected in barrels, but she still managed to grow vegetables that amazed the neighbours.

I remember that once she told me that when she and my dad went down to the bus stop with two buckets of tomatoes, people surrounded them. They couldn't stop praising the huge tomatoes and asking for advice on how to grow them. We weighed them at home and some of them weighed up to eight hundred grams. I'd never seen anything like it before, and the important thing was that they grew so big without chemicals.

My dad used to go on his days off to help, and sometimes he took my brothers and sisters, but my mum really deserved the credit. She took pride in what she did because her hard work made my aunt's plot the most beautiful on the mountain. She had incredible strength and perseverance, never backing down from adversity.

When she wasn't working on the land she was at home boiling tomato juice or storing pickles for the winter, so I couldn't expect her to help me with the baby. It was a great help that she kept us supplied with fruit and vegetables all summer.

Then autumn came and Zoli was almost three months old. Unfortunately, his sleeping at night got worse. So as not to wake Robi, every night I went to the kitchen with the crying baby and soothed him, walked around with him until he finally fell asleep, but after two hours it would start again. If you were to ask me now if you could ever get used to this, the answer is no: you can't but you must.

Motherly love and the hope that it would get better got me through those nights, but it didn't. My dad finally had enough and said he was too old to listen to Zoli every night; he'd heard enough children's cries in his life. Old? He was only fifty-three, and the one who had heard enough children's cries in their life was my mother, not him.

What was I supposed to do with my little one to stop him waking up and disturbing everyone with his crying? My parents' room was only separated from the kitchen by a thin wall so Dad could hear everything that went on. He was tired because he was working during the day or was on the plot with my mum, and at night he couldn't sleep. Even so, I was angry with him because he practically threw us out of the apartment.

Finally, Robi said what I didn't ever want to hear. 'We are moving back to my parents. They won't mind their grandchild crying.'

We had no choice but to move back in with my in-laws. They didn't mind their grandson crying because by the end of the night all three of them were so drunk that they slept like babies.

Had anything changed there since we'd left? Not a thing: it was just as dirty and messy as when I'd first moved in. I had to start from scratch, and I could only do the cleaning and tidying up when the parents were asleep. They were real hoarders, not eager to part with anything, and our room was cluttered with unnecessary things. When we finally managed to buy a cot for Zoli at least my father-in-law agreed, albeit grumpily, to get rid of some of the old stuff. That made the room feel a bit better, although I never really felt at home there.

One thing that helped me a lot was that I didn't have to cook; Robi no longer insisted that it was the wife's job to cook. I didn't mind because it gave me time for other things. Obviously I helped my mother-in-law with the cooking, often finishing what she couldn't because she got too drunk before the meal was ready.

Unfortunately, alcohol continued to be an important part of their lives and not in small amounts. With Robi back in his own environment, it started again; he no longer had to play the role of the good boy because my parents could not see his behaviour.

He hasn't raised his hand to me for the last two months, but he quickly made up for it. It was foolish of me to think that something in his soul had stirred on that outing and that our relationship would improve. At his parents' house he was back to being the rude, pushy, aggressive man he'd always been. The man I had once fallen in love with and expected to see again was lost to me forever. With that went hope: hope of happiness, hope of a better life.

We had been married for just over a year but I was completely disillusioned with my husband. The terrible thing was that I couldn't see a way out.

A month passed and nothing good happened. Zoli was awake more and more at night, although he did not cry as much. By the age of five months, he had completely switched from day to night; supposedly this is not uncommon for babies, but of course Robi blamed me for that too.

The truth is that I loved the sleepless nights, even if they were tiring. While Zoli slept most of the day, I could also sleep for four or five hours, but the night was mine and my little boy's. When everyone went to sleep, he woke up and it was just the two of us. I would talk to him, read him stories, and he would listen attentively as if he understood every word I said.

I enjoyed the silence and the peace, even though I knew it wasn't normal and couldn't last forever. It was tiring but at the same time it recharged me and gave me the strength to endure the days.

Usually Zoli was asleep by six in the morning, at which time I would wake my husband for work and go to bed. Unfortunately, more than once I woke up to fighting and shouting. If they had money, my in-laws were drunk by ten in the morning and they couldn't keep quiet.

Once, after a few hours' sleep, I was woken up by my mother-in-law wailing. I had barely opened my eyes when I saw my father-in-law hitting her on the head with his heavy winter boots. I was frightened he was going to beat that poor woman to death in front of me.

He was a big man, but at that moment I didn't even think about it; I only knew that I had to protect my mother-in-law from that beast. I jumped out of bed and charged at him, shouting, 'What are you doing? Stop it! Aren't you ashamed?'

My father-in-law was so shocked that he let me take the boot out of his hand without a word. Zoli woke up because of the noise and started crying bitterly. I put on my coat, grabbed the baby and his blanket and ran out into the cold. Only then did I really realize what I had done. Without thinking, I had rushed at my father-in-law without anticipating the consequences; he could have beaten me to death with that boot, even though he had never laid a hand on me before.

I managed to calm my little boy but I was still shivering from the nerves and the cold. When I finally went into the house, my in-laws were both fast asleep.

After a few hours they woke up and only my mother-in-law's black eye revealed what had happened that morning. My father-in-law either didn't remember or didn't want to remember what he had done.

I decided not to tell Robi because I didn't know how he would react; he might praise me for defending his mother, or I might get punished for interfering in someone else's business. One fight a day was enough so I kept quiet.

The next day I took Zoli to the doctor for his monthly check-up. If it hadn't been compulsory, I would have preferred not to go because it was always busy and we had to wait our turn. I was the poorest of the mothers and they made me feel it: they barely acknowledged my greetings, looked at me with contempt and then turned away. I felt just as excluded as I had felt in school among my classmates.

Although the women didn't speak to me, I could hear their conversations. They complained constantly about their husbands: one who wouldn't get up at night to look after their child, another who wouldn't help with bath time, and a third who refused to change nappies.

I listened to them and thought, 'You don't know how lucky you are if that's all you have to worry about. I'm lucky if I don't get a slap in the face because the baby is crying. But that's my problem.'

I always thought of my dad's words: 'Is that what you want?'
'Yes, it is!' Well, I got it! I had wanted it, hadn't I?

Finally it was our turn to see the doctor. Zoli's weight and height were fine for his age and apart from his poor sleeping habits he was a perfect baby.

The doctor advised me to keep him awake as long as possible after his feeds. 'The less he sleeps during the day, the more he'll sleep at night,' she said. 'But it's going to be a long process that won't happen overnight.'

I didn't realise how long it would take. We had been struggling for months to make the days be daytime and the nights be nighttime. You can't imagine how hard it is to keep a child awake when the poor thing's eyes are stuck shut, and I felt bad that I had to do this to him, but I had no choice. I had to go through with it.

Back at my mum's house, I used to walk round the kitchen to put him to sleep and now I had to keep the poor thing awake, but I finally did it! Zoli was a year old when he finally slept through the night.

It was late June, and the weather was beautiful. Robi wanted to celebrate his son's birthday outdoors so we went to the Carpathians again.

It seemed easier this time as Zoli was no longer a baby. He ate more or less the same food as we did, though I took some of his usual baby food in a tub. In the previous weeks we'd been fishing to the Latorca several times, which the little one had really enjoyed. He'd slowly started to walk, although not on his own yet; I had to hold his little hands.

As it was going to be a full day trip, we took the tent in which I could put Zoli to sleep at noon. We ended up in the same meadow where we'd been almost a year ago. Nothing had changed – the same stream meandered, the meadow was full of flowers – but something was different. The magic, the nostalgic feeling I had felt in this place was gone. Any hope that our relationship could change had been completely dashed.

We had a good time cooking soup in the pot and enjoying the sunshine, then father and son huddled in the tent while I went down to the stream to wash the dishes. On my way back, I saw Zoli standing outside the tent looking for me. When he saw me, his face lit up and he started walking towards me. Yes, he walked towards me without any help! It was his gift to me that he started to walk on his first birthday.

The following Saturday we celebrated again with dinner and a cake with candles. I invited my parents; it was only right that they should be there for their grandchild's first birthday. My relationship with my dad was still quite tense, but it had been like that ever since I'd first confronted him about Robi. Interestingly, the two of them had become very good friends.

Thankfully I still had a good relationship with my mum, even though I no longer lived with my parents. I tried to visit them and my brothers and sisters often, but it was not easy. My mother continued to work on the farm and spent all her free time there from spring to autumn. My brothers and sisters were getting older: Potyi had been working in a sewing shop for a year, and my brother had finished his vocational training and was enjoying his summer holidays. Only my youngest sister was still at school, but at fifteen she was no longer a child.

Our family had grown nicely. My older sister, who'd moved thousands of kilometres away to be with her husband's family, had three children. My other sister had a daughter after my godson, and my brother who'd survived the Afghan war was the proud father of two little boys.

But now back to my little boy's birthday. I tried very hard to make the day memorable. I cooked a lovely dinner and bought a nice big cake from the shop. I cleaned the house thoroughly, not listening to my mother-in-law's usual rant, 'Leave it, daughter, I'll do it.'

I knew she wouldn't, so I did it myself. I wanted to make a good impression on my parents because that was the first time I'd invited them.

The evening went quite well, although my dad didn't seem to be enjoying himself. My father-in-law was too pushy and kept filling their glasses, which my parents didn't appreciate. Even Robi noticed; he knew that this was not their world.

When my parents finally went home, the two men had a big quarrel. As usual, it was followed by a fight. My mother-in-law was so drunk that she just curled up in the corner of the bed and watched them with intoxicated eyes.

In an instant everything turned upside down. The table was knocked over in the jostling, and plates, glasses and empty bottles fell to the floor. This made Zoli very frightened and he was almost screaming in terror.

As I had done before, I grabbed him out of his cot and ran into the courtyard. If you can imagine the scene, you will probably understand my thoughts: I wished they would kill each other in that house and finally it would all end. I know I shouldn't have wished that but I couldn't help it. I believed in God and prayed to Him every night; what had I done to deserve this fate? Why did I have to suffer so much when I had harmed no one? Why was life so unfair?

Since I had no answers to my questions and it was very late, Zoli and I had to go back to the house. I managed to calm him and he fell asleep in my arms.

I hoped that my wish had not come true and that the two men had not killed each other, but I was prepared for anything. The room looked like a battlefield: the table and the chairs had been overturned, Zoli's left-over birthday cake was trampled on the floor, and the three drunk people were lying on the bed, fully dressed, shoes on, sound asleep.

I wanted to spit on them but I didn't. I picked up the debris and went to bed.

The next day nobody talked about the incident as if nothing had happened. My father-in-law had a big black eye and I thought, 'He really deserved it.'

My little boy's first birthday was memorable – but not in the way I wanted.

Over the next few days, I became increasingly sick, dizzy and tired. I always found a reason – low blood pressure, iron deficiency or a problem with my blood sugar – but I had no excuse for the morning vomiting and nausea.

I was pregnant and desperate. I knew the baby would be a girl because I felt completely different from when I was pregnant with Zoli. That was why it was so hard to make the decision that I wouldn't have the baby. I really wanted a little girl, but not here in this family, from this father. I was sure that if I had her, I would be stuck with these alcoholic people forever.

At first Robi agreed that I should have an abortion then he changed his mind. He tried to convince me that we needed another child but I was adamant. 'Where am I going to put another one in this room? We barely have space as it is. We can't afford rent, and my dad won't take us in with a crying baby,' I argued.

Robi didn't know what to say; perhaps for the first time since we had been together he realised that I was right. In fact I was trying to convince myself with these arguments so that the decision would not be so difficult, but it was still one of the hardest decisions of my life.

If you've ever been in a situation like mine, you'll know how I felt. After the abortion, I felt so guilty that it almost hurt. My mind knew I'd done the right thing but my heart was almost broken. I shouldn't have thought about what my little girl would have been like if she'd been born, but I couldn't think about anything else. My mum was so brave and strong that she'd risked her life giving birth to her seventh child. Why couldn't I be that strong; why had I deprived my little girl of life?

I don't know how long I would have beaten myself up with these thoughts if it wasn't for Robi. Two big slaps to my face after an argument set my mind straight and my remorse was replaced by hatred. I no longer had any doubt that I'd done the right thing, made the right decision. I tried not to dwell on the matter; I had enough trouble as it was.

On 26 April, a major disaster occurred at the Chernobyl nuclear power plant. The Russians only made it public days later; they probably wanted to cover it up but they failed. An explosion released large amounts of radioactive waste into the air and contaminated hundreds of thousands of kilometres of land.

I remember that day well because it was the first Saturday that the three of us went fishing to Latorca. If the wind had been blowing contaminated air towards us, there was a chance that we had got a dose of it. Since the Russians were as secretive as usual and only told half-truths, we were not sure about anything, but there was always fear.

Soon they started calling in the men and sending them to the disaster site to clean up the contaminated rubble; they were called liquidators. I don't know what the selection was based on but at some point my brother's name was added to the list. It wasn't enough for him to have been involved in the Afghan war; now he had to go to Chernobyl as a liquidator. He was there for about a month before he was allowed to go home on the grounds that he had reached the permitted radiation dose limit.

In the meantime, Robi had quit his job at the factory and applied for a job as a plumber in the local municipality. He said he had worked there too long for too little money. That wasn't true: I had worked with him at the factory until my maternity leave and the workers were paid by the hour, not the piece, so no one worked too hard.

My husband was right that we needed more money as we were living on one salary. Once Zoli was one year old, I had no more child benefit. I could stay at home on unpaid leave for another six months but then I would either go back to work or lose my job. I thought Zoli was too young to go to kindergarten, and he had to be potty trained to be admitted. He was one year and four months old when I managed to teach him to use the potty.

I was glad that he only needed nappies at night because I had to wash so many of them every day. That reminded me of how my mum must have washed so many nappies over the years after seven kids and never complained.

Zoli didn't speak yet; the only word he knew was 'daddy'. Why? I have no idea because I was with him all day, not his father. He seemed to understand everything, although only in Hungarian. That would have been fine if he hadn't been sent to a Ukrainian kindergarten. At that time there was no Hungarian kindergarten in our town, so I had no choice but to enrol him in the Ukrainian one.

The kindergarten teachers were kind to him, and they spoke to him in Russian because they knew that a child with Hungarian as a mother tongue would learn it more easily than Ukrainian. It was the same with me: to this day I speak Russian well while I struggle with Ukrainian.

I'd like to tell you about my son's first day in kindergarten because it was another memorable day, at least for me. Zoli was always a sweet, friendly little child. Whenever we went to the playground, he always had fun and got on well with the other children so I didn't think there would be any problems in kindergarten.

The first day he only had to stay for four hours to get used to the environment. The morning started with the teacher having to take the crying baby out of my hands; Zoli clung to my neck so tightly, as if he sensed that something bad was going to happen to him there. He was too small to understand why I was giving him to strangers.

Four hours later, I rushed back to take him home. When I opened the door, I looked for my little boy among the children playing in the middle of the room but he wasn't there. That's when I saw him, sitting alone on the bench in the corner. His face was smeared and his eyes were barely visible because they were so puffy from crying.

He was no longer crying when I arrived, just looking with a blank expression on his face. He looked so forlorn that it almost broke my heart. I called his name several times and he looked at me, but it took him a few seconds to realize that I'd come back for him. Finally he ran into my arms. As I held him, I began to sob.

The teacher looked at me. 'Stop crying, you're scaring the child! You can see he's not crying anymore.'

'Of course he's not crying,' I retorted. 'He's cried enough.'

If it had been up to me I wouldn't have taken him there until he understood what was happening, but it wasn't up to me. I had to go back to work, so Zoli had to deal with the fact that he was a toddler. For understandable reasons, it never occurred to me that my mother- and father-in-law could look after their grandchild. I never left my son alone with them for a minute.

I hope you don't mind that I shared this story with you, but I want you to know that it is an important memory from my past. To this day, it still breaks my heart to think of my little boy's haggard face as he sat there alone on the bench.

Robi eventually managed to get a job in the municipality but his salary was no more than what he'd been paid in the factory. His friend who'd lured him there had said it was worth working there because the tips were good but, if that was true, I didn't see any of them.

It turned out to be the perfect job for Robi and he loved going there. Every day he was given a couple of addresses to fix something or clear a blockage. Once the job was done, no one cared what he did for the rest of the day. He had the office staff wrapped around his finger, so when they called about something he always explained himself.

There were times when he didn't do anything because he hadn't been given an address for the day. Then he'd be in the workshop playing cards and drinking beer with the others. He could not do that in the factory where there were strict rules and alcohol was forbidden.

Because his working hours were so irregular, he also drank eight to ten cups of coffee a day in the local cafes. He spent all his tips and even part of his salary on beer, cigarettes and coffee. It was impossible to put anything aside. We'd been queuing for a flat for more than two years, but it didn't look like we'd ever have the money.

It was time for me to start work because my unpaid leave was almost up. Zoli had been in kindergarten for a month and although I wouldn't say he was used to it, he was *getting* used to it. He started the morning crying but then he calmed down – at least, that's what the nannies said. Maybe he'd come to understand that there was nothing to be afraid of and I'd always come back for him.

My first day at the factory had finally come. Even though I had worked there for two years and knew exactly what to expect, I was as excited as the first day I was hired. It turned out that my colleagues were eager to have me back. Every single one of them came up to me, greeted me and said a few kind words. It was all so incredible and uplifting at the same time.

It was then that I realised how much I missed them; they were my second family and I'd always felt comfortable with them. Here I was not excluded, mocked or humiliated; here I was their equal. More than one of my colleagues called me 'sister', which made me feel very good.

It was this relationship between us that Robi was unable to understand. According to him, a man is only nice to a woman because he wants something from her. I thought that was silly but it was no use telling him.

I was not happy that he had quit the factory, I was angry with him about it, but now I realised it was the best thing that could have happened to me. If he had seen how happy the others were for me, I'm sure he would have had a jealous fit. I wouldn't have felt so good knowing that he was there watching every move I made with a wary eye. In the evening he questioned me thoroughly because he thought I was in such a good mood, but in the end he found nothing to quarrel about so there was no fight that day.

I became a working woman again. After work I rushed to the kindergarten to pick up Zoli as soon as possible. He grew out of his pram so we sold it and bought another one for a bigger child. Several times on the way home, Zoli did not sit in the buggy but pushed it in front of him so we were slower and got home later. On one of these occasions, Robi was waiting for us at home. He asked me angrily where I had been, why I had come home so late.

'Because we walked,' I said. 'Anyway, we're only twenty minutes late.'

'Twenty minutes was just enough time to go to the military base and hang out with the soldiers.'

I couldn't believe my ears. There was a military base down the street about fifteen minutes away from us, but what was he talking about? 'Are you serious? I was with our kid, and we came straight home from kindergarten.'

'You're lying!' he yelled and started hitting me. My poor little boy was so scared that he started crying loudly, but Robi ignored him and kept hitting me in the face.

Somehow I managed to pick up Zoli and calm him down. I hoped that the beating would stop but Robi had no intention of stopping. He came up behind me and continued to hit me on the head. Zoli cried even louder; he was almost screaming.

'Stop it, you're scaring the poor child!' I shouted.

As if he only then realised what he was doing, he immediately stopped and left the room. After I calmed myself and my son, I asked myself what had happened. What was all that about? How could he even think of accusing me of being with the soldiers? It was as if he wasn't conscious, but he wasn't so drunk that he didn't know what he was doing. The worst part was that he did it all in front of the child.

I knew that if this went on, history would repeat itself. Robi had probably seen his father beat his mother when he was a child, and when he was old enough he beat his parents because it was natural. If Zoli grew up in such an environment, sooner or later he would start hitting his father and me because it would be natural for him too. That thought was terrifying – I couldn't let that happen to us! I had to do something and as soon as possible.

I didn't speak to Robi all night, but that was normal; I wasn't in the mood to talk after such a circus. I kept thinking about what would be the right thing to do. I had to escape, but where to?

Suddenly my husband said, 'What is your problem? What are you thinking about? You're not going to leave me, are you?'

The question surprised me and I didn't answer. Was it so obvious what I was thinking or had he become a mind reader? Then he continued, 'You can go. I won't hold you back but the child stays!'

'What? Why would he stay? I'm his mother.'

'And I'm his father. The court will give my son to me.'

'Why would they do that? The child belongs with his mother,' I said.

'I'll tell them you're a bad mother, you drink and go to the pub.'

'They won't believe you because it's not true.' I said, a little discouraged.

'But it will be true. My mates will claim they saw you in the pub.'

I couldn't stand it anymore and I started to cry. I had gone to the pub a few times, but only to wait for Robi to finish his beer. He had proudly introduced me to his mates as his girlfriend, so now he could blackmail me? Maybe he already knew that he would use it when the time came, or maybe he was just making it up.

He scared me so much that I could hardly close my eyes that night. He was such a good talker that he could make a judge believe that I was the bad one, the alcoholic, and I'd be the loser. If they took my son away from me, I'd go mad. I'd rather be beaten than live without my son. Robi had found my weakness – my son – and he was trying to chain me to him.

I was desperate, but before I gave up I remembered something – or rather someone: my husband's ex-wife. She'd managed to escape and taken her son far away from his father. She could probably defend herself but if she could do it, so could I. I couldn't give up so easily – and I didn't; I just waited for the right moment.

A few days later something happened again to make our lives less 'monotonous'. We were coming home from kindergarten and a woman in her forties was coming towards us. I saw her looking, or rather staring, at Zoli. He was a very nice little boy so that did not surprise me because it had happened before. What surprised me was that Zoli started to cry loudly as she passed us. It was as if he was frightened by her, but there was no reason to be. The woman smiled at him kindly; she seemed to like him. So what's all the crying about?

I couldn't calm him down and he cried all the way home. The fact that he still hadn't stopped after three hours was very strange and I thought maybe he was sick or in pain, even though he'd been fine at nursery.

I took his temperature, pressed his tummy, looked in his mouth to see if he had a toothache, but he seemed healthy except that his face was very pale instead of being red from crying so much. After we got home, he didn't eat, drink or use the potty.

Failing to calm my little boy had never happened to me before. Something was wrong with him, I just didn't know what. I was thinking about taking him to the emergency room when my mother-in-law remembered something. Luckily, they hadn't drunk so much that day as they didn't have much money to spare because their pension wasn't due for a few more days.

She asked me if we'd met anyone before Zoli became so tearful. 'Yes, a woman was really staring at him on the street,' I replied.

'Then I know what's wrong with him – he's been cursed with eyes,' she said and hurried off to the kitchen.

'Cursed with eyes? You mean she bewitched him?'

My nana had told us this story, but somehow it had all seemed unbelievable. She said that there were people, especially women, who bring evil upon others with their eyes. They don't always know this about themselves, but when they admire an animal, or maybe a child, it immediately makes them sick. In villages such women were ostracised for bringing destruction to the animals. The child, on the other hand, could be cleansed of the curse with holy water if it was recognised in time. I didn't recall how to do this, or perhaps Nana didn't tell me.

Fortunately my mother-in-law knew what to do. Since we didn't have holy water, she came back from the kitchen with a glass of tap water. We were supposed to put charcoal in it, but we didn't have that either so she started lighting matches one after the other. When the match was almost burnt, she carefully took the charred end and let the other half burn, then she threw at least ten of them into the water.

What she did next really surprised me: she picked up the glass and began to pray. I would never have thought that my mother-in-law could pray or that she remembered her prayers from her childhood.

Which prayer she said I don't know because she was muttering it to herself. When she finished, she dipped her index finger in the water and drew a cross on Zoli's forehead. The second cross was placed on his chin and the third on his chest, again dipping her finger in the water. Finally, she wet the child's parched lips a little.

Zoli stopped crying and his face changed from snow white to a healthy pink in front of my eyes. He looked at me, then pointed to the corner and reached for the potty. When he finished, he ate his dinner with such a good appetite that it was a pleasure to watch. The child who had sat pale and weak in my lap half an hour ago was now playing merrily in the cot. It was a miracle!

I was grateful to my mother-in-law for what she had done because there was no telling what would have happened if she hadn't come up with the solution.

I know it all sounds unbelievable, even like a fairy tale, but believe me it really happened exactly as I told you. I don't dare to think what would have happened if I had taken Zoli to the emergency room and they had given us the wrong diagnosis, or if it had happened a few days later when my in-laws got their pension.

They were usually drunk before noon then they'd sleep for a couple of hours and then carry on drinking. One day they were drunk by the time we got home from kindergarten. Of course, Robi quickly joined them so as not to miss out on the good stuff. What was sad was that the grandparents didn't even think of using their pension to buy their grandchild clothing or a toy. For them, alcohol was the most important thing. The more they drank, the better their mood and the louder they became.

It was late and I couldn't get Zoli to sleep because there was too much noise. I knew them well enough to see that there would be trouble sooner or later. I don't remember exactly what they fought about, only what happened next.

It was almost the same as on Zoli's birthday: first father and son were shouting at each other, then they got into a fight. My mother-in-law also got involved as if she wanted to separate them – or perhaps she didn't know what she wanted. My father-in-law pushed her away so roughly that the poor thing went flying into the corner of the bed. She stayed there and perhaps passed out.

Zoli and I were sitting on the other bed and I couldn't move because of the cot in front of us. He was crying loudly again; he was very scared. The two men were hitting each other as if they were not father and son but two strangers full of hatred.

I never understood how drink could have such an effect on them. They got on quite well when they were sober, but unfortunately they were rarely sober. The fight went on and on, neither of them wanting to give up. They pushed each other against the cupboard and then the table, which promptly toppled over. Bottles and glasses crashed to the floor.

I don't need to tell you how frightened the poor child was, but I was angry, very angry that he had to see that. We had to get out of there somehow, and as soon as possible.

As the two men were wrestling in the middle of the room blocking the way to the kitchen, I couldn't escape. When they finally leaned the other way, I jumped up and ran out of the room with my child.

We quickly put on our coats and boots and went out into the garden. It was early December and I remember the night was very cold. I didn't know what to do because Zoli and I couldn't stay in the garden for long. I would have liked to go straight home to my mother, but I didn't dare to leave my parents-in-law in this state.

I didn't have to think about it for long because the problem solved itself. My father-in-law threw Robi out of the house like a bag of rubbish.

'Get out of here, get out of my house!' he shouted angrily, then slammed the door and locked it.

The evening ended the same way as it had two years ago, except that then the baby was still in my tummy. There was nothing more to be done and we left for my mum's without a word. As it was terribly cold and Robi had no coat, by the time we got home he was almost sober.

Luckily the next day was Saturday, so we didn't have to go to work. As I was still very upset, I hadn't slept for a long time but at least I'd had time to think about where to go next. I was absolutely sure that I would never go back there, at least not to live, but if it was up to my dad we were unlikely to stay with my parents. We couldn't afford rent and we needed somewhere to live, but where?

Suddenly, something dawned on me. Why did I need my dad's permission to live there? I had the same right to be there as my other brothers and sisters. Anyway, the flat was in my mum's name; she'd got it from the municipality because of the children.

Back then in the Soviet Union, mothers with many children were appreciated and even given commemorative medals. My mother had received one of these on which was engraved *Máty gerojinyá*, meaning 'Mother Heroine'.

Inspired by this thought, I decided to simply announce to them that we were moving in. I was prepared to argue with my dad and I would win.

I had no idea at the time that it wasn't my dad who would be the problem but Robi. He started the next morning by saying that we would go home when the child woke up.

'Home?' I asked. 'Don't you remember your father throwing us out last night?'

'Yes, I remember, but maybe he doesn't. If he does, he must regret it.'

'You know what? You can go if you want but I'm staying here. I'm not going back there again except to get my things. How many more times are we going to arrive at my mum's house in the middle of the night because we have nowhere to sleep? Or can you guarantee that this won't happen again in a month or a year?'

I waited for an answer, but Robi was silent; for once he had nothing to say. 'This will end with you killing each other in front of your son. Is that what you want?' I asked angrily.

'No,' he said, barely audible.

I'd never spoken to him in that tone before because he would have slapped me but I was not afraid of him now. I felt so strong that if he had hit me, I might have hit him back.

'Have you asked your parents if we can stay here?' he finally asked.

'No, and I'm not going to,' I said, then went to the kitchen to talk to them. 'I've already won the battle with Robi, so I'll deal with my dad somehow,' I thought to myself.

And I didn't ask them, I just announced that we were moving here. My mum was delighted, relieved that we would be safe now, but my dad didn't say a word. He just shrugged his shoulders as if to say that he didn't mind, we could do what we wanted. Maybe he realised that this was not the life his daughter and grandson deserved, or maybe he saw the determination in my eyes. The last time I'd been this brave was when I'd announced that I was getting married. He couldn't talk me out of it then and he couldn't have talked me out of it now.

After breakfast we went back to my father-in-law's to pack our things. I left Zoli with my sisters because he would only have been an obstacle – and he was a guarantee that we would come back here. I didn't really trust my husband; he was unpredictable like the weather. If he was on home turf, he might change his mind and force us to stay there. I couldn't risk that.

When we arrived at the house, we started packing almost without a word. My in-laws had finished breakfast, which for them was not a sandwich and tea but a few glasses of wine. The only thing that had changed since last night was that the table was back in place and the broken bottles had been picked up, though the floor was littered with splinters that we tried not to step on. Perhaps they'd expected me to clean it up as I had done on other occasions.

'They can certainly wait for that,' I thought. 'I'm not cleaning this house anymore, that's for sure! These people don't deserve me to lift a finger for them.'

They had never thought to spend money on replacing that old one-legged table with a normal four-legged one that didn't tip over so easily, but that was their problem not mine.

My father-in-law was very quiet as he watched us pack, but he had no intention of stopping us. It was obvious that he remembered last night and hadn't changed his mind. Finally he said, 'Would you like a glass of wine, son?'

'No,' replied Robi curtly.

Maybe that was his father's way of making up with him before we left; I didn't know and I didn't care. It wasn't until we were done that we realized we couldn't carry everything. True, we didn't have much stuff, but we still had the crib and the pushchair.

While Robi went next door to find a ride, I headed home with two smaller bags. When I walked out of the door, it was as if a weight had been lifted from my heart. It felt so good to think that I was no longer living there and would only visit occasionally.

So that's what I did. Over the next few weeks, I took Zoli to his grandparents a few times because I didn't want to deprive them of their grandson, but they were usually drunk so I didn't push too hard to visit. Robi often checked on them – they were his parents after all.

I heard that they reconciled and were drinking wine together again, but maybe they stopped fighting.

Meanwhile, Christmas and New Year's Eve passed and we entered the New Year. It was 1987; when I think of how many years have passed since then, it's almost unbelievable that I remember those times so well. They say that our brains store up everything that happens to us over the years and we are the only ones who think we have forgotten so much. This book is the proof that this is true. Since I started writing, I have been flooded with memories and I relive them.

I admit that some of my stories have made me cry as my old wounds have been torn open. My memories have become vivid, as if they happened yesterday. The only things I can't remember word for word are the conversations, but I try to write them in a way that makes sense.

I've just made a little detour here and started talking about this because I want to tell you something that happened to me recently. The other day I gave a friend of mine the pages I had written. When she finished reading them, she gave me a rather strange critique: she said my story was so unbelievable that she didn't know if it had really happened to me or if I'd made things up. She said there were too many sad stories in it and maybe I should write happier ones.

That got me thinking. If you remember, I wrote in the introduction that I've led a really interesting, eventful life so far, so how incredible is my story? I don't know – you decide! I think many women have stories similar to mine but they don't talk about them.

The fact that there are too many sad stories here is debatable. I had some good things happen to me in the years before my marriage that I remember fondly, but my twenties were very sad and I can't do anything about that.

I also wrote at the beginning that there was a period in my life that might be too painful and that you might not be able to read my book any longer, but I can't change that either: I can't make what was not a happy time any happier. All the bad things I've been through have only made me stronger, and without my past, my life would not be like it is. I can promise you that I will have happy stories too but you'll have to wait a little longer for them. Like my Nana used to say: once will be better.

I will continue where I left off. It was the beginning of January and my little boy was one and a half years old. He had been in nursery for two months, and although he still cried in the mornings he ran happily towards me when he saw me at the door in the afternoons.

Then one day I walked in and saw him sitting alone on the bench, just like on that terrible first day. This time he wasn't crying his eyes out; he was just sitting there watching the children play. He looked at me, but he didn't run towards me like he usually did. I called his name and waved for him to come, but he didn't.

The teacher went over to him, picked him up and brought him over to me and I knew something was wrong. 'The child was vaccinated this afternoon and hasn't been able to stand up since then.' She handed Zoli to me.

'What?' I shouted. I was scared and very angry at the same time. 'Are you saying that my son might be paralysed and you didn't tell me? I gave you the number of our office – why didn't you call me earlier?' I started crying.

The teacher just babbled on then went back to the other children. I didn't know what to do; if I took him to the hospital now, which was quite far away, it would be night by the time we got home. Zoli would be hungry by then and I couldn't tell Robi where we were. Remember, there were no mobile phones in those days and we didn't have a landline either.

I decided to go home and eat first and then go to the hospital with Rob because I needed his help.

During dinner, Zoli moved his legs and finally stood up. His gait was unsteady at first but later he could run. When his father came home, he was completely well so we didn't go to the hospital that day.

The next morning I took him to the paediatrician; true, there were no signs of what had happened the day before, but I wanted to make sure my little boy was healthy. It turned out that he wasn't and the doctor diagnosed him with pneumonia; she said that was probably why his legs were temporarily paralysed after the vaccination.

As he needed antibiotic treatment, the doctor wanted to refer him to hospital but I could not imagine leaving my child alone there. 'Couldn't we give him his injections at home?' I asked.

'Maybe, if you have a relative or friend who is a nurse,' the doctor said.

Luckily, Robi had an acquaintance who worked in a hospital and made house calls to sick people in his spare time. We paid him well and he came to us every day to give our child his shots. The interesting thing was that Zoli did not seem to have pneumonia: he didn't cough, he didn't have a high fever and his appetite was fine. Maybe these symptoms would have appeared later but, thanks to the vaccination, the problem was detected early.

When we went back to the doctor ten days later, Zoli had no more wheezing in his lungs. He was healthy so he could go back to kindergarten and I could go back to work.

Another few months went by and it slowly turned into spring. Zoli was already twenty-two months old and although he couldn't talk yet, he could explain a lot in his baby language.

At weekends we went fishing in the Latorca river or hiking in the mountains. Our life was a little better than before, and even our marriage seemed more bearable. Of course, there were times when we fought and I got the odd slap in the face, but unfortunately I had got used to it.

Robi continued to put on a good-boy act with my parents because it was important for us to stay there. Since Zoli had stopped crying at night, my dad had no objections but our relationship was not the same and I felt that he didn't really love me or my little boy. But none of that mattered; all that mattered was that we had a roof over our heads.

As much as he'd been against Robi coming into the family, my dad started to like him more and more. Obviously, had he seen my husband beating his father a few months earlier, he probably wouldn't have been so friendly but, as they say, what we don't know can't hurt us. I tried to think as little as possible about those months but I didn't always succeed. I knew we were in the right place and that was the most important thing.

One Friday afternoon my mother was out on the plot with my brother and sisters and the two men were watching a football match on TV. The next day, we were going on a trip to the Carpathians, so I wanted to get my work finished. I had to wash a large load of clothes by hand because the washing machine was broken again. It wasn't even new when my mum had bought it years ago and since then it had been repaired many times.

I sent Zoli to play in the living room so that he wouldn't be in the way, as there was very little space in the bathroom, and I left the door open so I could hear his voice as he played. I was so caught up in doing the laundry and my own thoughts that when I looked up, all I could hear was the sound of the TV.

When I looked into the living room, my little boy wasn't there; the two men were so busy watching the game that they hadn't even noticed.

I went into the kitchen and looked in the front room, but I couldn't find him. I was frightened because he was alone somewhere and I had a bad feeling. When I entered the middle room, I thought I would faint. My little boy was standing on the inside sill of the open window, holding on to the frame with his left hand. When he heard me come in, he looked at me and cheerfully explained something, pointing with his right hand towards the trees.

Believe me, I'm not exaggerating when I say that my blood ran cold. I knew I couldn't run over or shout at him because he'd fall out of the window. The few steps I took from the door to the window were completely erased from my mind; I must have been in shock. All I remember is standing in front of him, grabbing his waist with trembling hands and putting him on the floor.

When I looked out of the window, which I shouldn't have done, I imagined my little boy falling from the fifth floor and his body landing on the concrete. I felt very dizzy, as if I had fallen with him. I quickly closed the window so I wouldn't see that horrible image.

I was shaking and could hardly stand up. Before I collapsed, I slumped down on a chair and began to sob bitterly. It was as if I'd lost my sense of reality because I really believed that he had fallen. I was about to scream in pain when Zoli took my hand. It took me a few seconds to realize that he was there with me and the terrible thing had only happened in my imagination that. I hugged him and rocked him in my arms until we both calmed down.

He was also frightened when he saw me like that because he didn't understand why I was so upset. I don't know what would have happened to me if he hadn't taken my hand and brought me back from that madness.

Only after we calmed down did I look around the room. The window had probably been left open after the morning airing since Zoli couldn't have opened it on his own, but he could have pushed the chair we were sitting on under the window to climb on it. I explained to him not to do that again and we left the room.

The men were still watching the game excitedly and had no idea what had happened to us. I decided to keep it secret from Robi because he would blame me and beat me up for it.

Since I had to finish the laundry, I let Zoli play in the hallway so at least he was in sight. When I was done, I went out on the balcony to hang out the washing, but I couldn't do it. I started to shake and I felt terribly dizzy as if I were falling into the abyss.

That evening I asked Potyi to hang out the clothes for me. My brain reacted to the terrible thing that had happened that afternoon and I was afraid of heights, but I knew I had to overcome it because we had three balconies and I went on them several times a day to get something. I couldn't see a doctor because then Robi would find out what was wrong with me so, I had no choice but to cure myself.

It took me years to overcome my fear of heights. At first, I just looked out of the window or took a step onto the balcony. If I had to do the laundry, I'd hold on to the balcony door with my left hand and throw the wet clothes on the clothes line with my right. A few times Potyi helped me clip the pegs onto the clothes, and eventually I could do it myself.

When you're healthy you don't realise how easy it is to do certain things, but when you're in trouble everything becomes much harder. It took me at least a year before I could go out on the balcony and touch the railing without shaking. I forced myself to look down, at first for only a few seconds then for longer. I held on to the railing so tightly that my fingers were almost white.

Finally the dizziness stopped and the sense of falling disappeared. I don't know whether these symptoms were really those of a person with a fear of heights or not, but the point is that I was cured albeit after a long time. However, I have still not managed to erase the image I saw when I looked down from the window.

I'm really rushing ahead in time, but I shouldn't be because a lot happened to me in the few years that I'm going to tell you about, so let's go back to the day Zoli climbed up the windowsill. Robi never found out what had happened, but I told my family because they had to know that they couldn't leave the windows open.

Another month went by and nothing happened. From work to kindergarten and back home, that was our daily routine. Fortunately there were several shops in our area so we rarely went shopping in the city centre. There was also a grocery store on the ground floor beneath our flat, which had almost everything, and you didn't have to queue for hours like when I was a kid.

Our standard of living improved a lot over the next ten or fifteen years, although I could not say the same for our financial situation. The fruit and vegetables that my mother grew on her hobby farm were very useful in the kitchen, but we hardly saved any money. I was grateful that we could live with my parents but deep down I still longed for my own little apartment.

The Chernobyl disaster had happened more than a year ago, but not much has been revealed since then. The only good news – if it was true – was that the wind after the explosions had not blown the contaminated air towards us. It took days to put out the fire, so nothing was certain; we just hoped that it would not affect us and that we would not get sick.

My brother had been home for a while and seemed fine after his work in Chernobyl; he was probably not infected, but that could change at any time. Unfortunately many people could not consider themselves so lucky; there were already several people from the factory who'd been sent to Chernobyl. Although they were not from my department, I knew some of them quite well.

One of them was a man from the office whom I often met because of my job. It was perhaps only a month or two after the disaster when he was sent to clear the rubble. When he came home he didn't look ill, but after a few months he went on sick leave. It was about six months before I saw him again; if he hadn't spoken to me, I might not have recognised him. He hadn't been a fat man, but now he looked more like a skeleton than a living person. There were big black circles under his eyes and his face had hardly any life left in it. I think he was thirty-five at the time, but he looked at least twice as old.

A few months ago he was diagnosed with thyroid cancer and the doctors said he didn't have much time left. At first he fought it because he wanted to live like everyone else, but soon he ran out of strength.

'I have a wife and two children who need me, but my illness proved stronger than me,' he said sadly.

He had to fight another battle for his family. He filed a lawsuit against the Soviet state for his illness, convinced that his work at Chernobyl had caused his cancer. He said he had been exposed to much higher levels of radiation than the dosimeters showed. Some of the dosimeters turned out to be faulty and it was only days later that they were found to be wrong, so the true readings were not known.

He was sent home early from Chernobyl like many of his companions, but it was already too late; he had probably exceeded the radiation dose limit long before that. The poor man knew he would not live to see the end of the trial but he hoped the state would compensate his family.

We only talked for a few minutes then he left looking very tired. It was a terrible thing to see a colleague of mine who was once a cheerful, kind, vibrant young man like that. I cried when we parted as I knew that was probably the last time I would see him.

What must it have been like to know that he would die soon and his children would grow up without him? After a few weeks the disease defeated him. I don't know how his lawsuit against the state ended, but I hope his family received some compensation. It's true that money can't replace a father or husband but it can make lives a little easier.

Finally the day came when my husband's name was added to the list. I remember that he went to the military and was told that he had to leave in a few days. They said he would be there for two months, though it was possible he could come home earlier. As he was ordered to go, if he refused he would be sent to prison as a deserter.

He left soon after and it was five weeks before I saw him again. It's true that our relationship wasn't perfect but I worried about him. No matter what kind of person Robi was, he didn't deserve to get sick and die like that.

I can tell you honestly, those five weeks were the happiest time for me since I got married. It was so different to come home with my son and not have Robi waiting at home and picking on me. I was always tense and nervous around him as I never knew what to expect.

We celebrated Zoli's second birthday without his father, which was much better than his previous birthday. The only people there were my sister and my son's godmother. There was a very good atmosphere, the lunch was delicious and the cake was eaten to the last slice.

I had no intention of inviting my in-laws to their grandson's birthday party and they were not missed at all. I remembered very well what happened this time last year, so I thought it was better to be at peace. They were in this flat for the first and last time on our wedding day, and they had staggered home drunk.

Since Robi had left, I'd looked in on them a few times but only to see if they were still alive. I didn't love them anymore, and I hated my father-in-law. True, he never hit me, but he was not a good man. My mother-in-law also drank, but the aggression was in my father-in-law. If they had just been alcoholics who drank themselves to sleep every night, maybe their son wouldn't have turned out to be such a bad person. I couldn't change that, but I could make sure that my son would not be like his father.

These weeks alone with Zoli showed me how much better life was without my husband. I was happier and more liberated than I had ever been in my marriage. I would have liked to keep it that way but unfortunately the five weeks flew by. I would love to say that after he returned home Robi's attitude towards me changed, but it didn't. More accurately, it changed for the worse. His jealousy knew no bounds and he was suspicious of anyone who looked at me.

He hardly spoke about what he had been doing in Chernobyl; all he said was that they were cleaning up the rubble, which was obvious since that was why he'd been sent there.

He was with his companions in a ghost town about thirty kilometres from the plant. After the disaster, the surrounding villages were evacuated and the people had not returned. Robi said it was eerie to walk through the deserted streets, past empty shops and playgrounds.

The animals were shot dead in the weeks after the explosion to stop them spreading infection; the only thing they could not deal with were the rodents and the rats in the sewers. That's why, even a year after the disaster, disfigured, bloated rats could be seen running around the abandoned streets. Robi saw one that he thought was as big as a medium-sized dog. It was a frightening situation; a rat is unpredictable and will attack you at any time but luckily it didn't attack so no one was hurt.

I believe that my husband had a much harder time during those five weeks than I did, but that was no excuse for the way he treated me after he came home. I had to report everything that had happened at home since he'd left. He wanted to know where I'd been, what I'd done, who I'd met. He didn't believe that every day except Zoli's birthday was the same as before; he was sure I was cheating on him with someone because he wasn't there to watch me. His jealousy was almost sickening and drove me crazy.

A week later it was still an issue and he said I was keeping secrets from him. We argued and at one point I said to him 'you bastard'. I was really upset and it just came out. I had never said anything like that to anyone, and I would have taken it back if I could have done, but it was too late because he'd heard me.

He slapped me so hard that I saw stars, then came the second and third slaps. I started crying and Zoli started too because he saw what was happening. I quickly picked him up and hugged him, hoping that Robi would stop the beating as he had done before, but it didn't work this time.

He stepped behind me and continued beating me. Finally, he hit me so hard on the head with his fist that I headbutted my little boy at the same moment and the poor child cried even louder. Robi stopped beating me, probably because he didn't want to hurt his son. Finally he put the subject to rest and stopped talking about the past weeks.

That didn't mean that everything was fine between us. The next two-and-a-half months went by with us fighting more than not fighting. He was so distrustful even though I never gave him a reason to be. I did nothing wrong; it never occurred to me to cheat on him. We hadn't had a church wedding but I still took my marriage vows seriously.

It was foolish of me to think that someone who had already been divorced once would do everything to make his second marriage work better. If my husband had been thinking like that, he probably wouldn't have treated me the way he did. He almost took pleasure in keeping me in constant terror and dominating me, but his aggressive behaviour only served to push me further away from him. I knew for certain that we had no future together and it was only a matter of time before our marriage was over.

Autumn arrived; it was the last Sunday in September to be precise. I was cooking lunch in the kitchen, Robi was smoking a cigarette on the balcony and Zoli was playing with Potyi in the room. I had almost finished cooking when I noticed that there was not enough sour cream in the fridge. I told Robi that I would run to the shop to buy some, then went into the room to get changed. You should know that in our family it was the custom that we never went out in our home outfit.

I had just taken the clean clothes out of the wardrobe when Robi ran in and slapped me. 'Tell me, where exactly are you going and with whom?' he asked angrily.

'I'm going to the shop for sour cream,' I said with tears in my eyes.

'Don't lie!' Then came the next slap. 'You must have someone waiting for you? Who is that man?'

'What? What man?' I asked, puzzled.

'He's standing in front of the staircase. Come, I'll show you.' He grabbed me roughly by the arm and dragged me onto the balcony by the kitchen. I only looked down for a moment as I was still dizzy from heights at that time, but I didn't see anyone. 'He's gone.' Robi nodded his head for us to go back to the room.

When he closed the door behind him, he ordered me to sit down. I sat on the edge of the bed and he sat on the chair opposite me, which he pulled so close that our knees were almost touching. I didn't know what he was up to, but I had a feeling that nothing good was going to happen. Then he lit a cigarette and blew the smoke straight into my face; he knew how much I hated that, but that's why he did it. It was strange that he smoked in the room because it was not a habit in our house, but I didn't dare to say anything.

Then he started interrogating me, or rather torturing me. Believe me, I'm not exaggerating! 'So, who was that man waiting for you downstairs?' he asked.

'Don't you understand that I don't know? He wasn't waiting for me!' I said angrily.

What he did next, I was not expecting at all. He held the burning cigarette to my neck and put it out on my skin. To keep from screaming in pain, I put my hand over my mouth. Tears were running down my face from the pain where he had burnt me. He lit another cigarette and smiled at me. I could tell he was enjoying what he was doing and would continue.

'So are you going to tell me who that man was?' he asked again, looking me straight in the eye.

'I don't know. He wasn't waiting for me,' I repeated. What else could I say?

As he was looking at me, he pressed the burning cigarette to my thigh and put it out. My whole body jerked with pain. I wanted to jump up and run out of the room, but there wasn't enough space; I couldn't even stand up. He expected me to try to run away, that's why he sat so close to me.

He relit the rest of his cigarette and continued the interrogation. 'If you're not seeing him, why did you want to get changed?' He pointed to the clothes on the bed.

'Because I'm not going down to the shop in this shabby dress.' I had hardly finished my sentence when I felt the burning pain again. This time he pressed the cigarette to my leg below my knee.

'You're lying!' he said, then stood up and left the room like he'd done a good job.

I was in floods of tears. I simply could not understand how someone could be so cruel. What had I done to deserve this treatment? How could I have been so stupid as to tie my life to such a man? My questions went unanswered; the only thing I knew for sure was that this couldn't go on.

As it was Monday the next day and I had to go to work, which for the first time I didn't feel like doing. Usually work and my colleagues distracted me from my troubles at home but this was different; I couldn't pretend that everything was fine.

Clothes covered my burns, but they were still there and they still hurt. Thinking about the day before brought tears to my eyes and I found it hard to stop myself from crying. Luckily, even when my colleagues noticed that something was wrong they didn't ask questions.

When my working hours were finally over and I stepped out of the reception, Robi was waiting outside the factory. I was quite surprised as he'd never done this since he'd quit. He told me to go straight home because he wanted to talk to me.

'But I have to go to the kindergarten to pick up the child,' I said.

'You'll go after,' he said briefly and started to walk quickly.

On the way home I wondered what was so important that it couldn't wait until the evening. 'Maybe he regrets what happened yesterday and now he wants to apologize to me,' I thought.

He had never apologised before because he never felt guilty; he thought I provoked the fighting and the beatings. Even if he had apologised, I could not forget his cruelty, the smile on his face as he had tortured me.

When we got home and entered our room, Robi got straight to the point. There was no word of regret or apology; he immediately attacked me with his question. 'I heard you have a lover at the factory. Who is it?'

'What is this nonsense again?' I asked.

'Who is it? I want to know his name!' he shouted, then slapped me.

'So yesterday's nightmare continues,' I thought to myself.

'What are you talking about? I have no one,' I replied, crying.

'Don't lie to me,' he shouted, while continuing to slap me. There was no one at home to hear him, so he didn't have to hold back. 'Someone from the factory said you had a lover there. I want to know who he is!'

'Don't you understand that I don't have anyone? Who told you that?'

'What does it matter who it was? I believe him.'

'You believe him and not me? I want to know who told you that!'

Robi stopped slapping me for a moment, as if wondering whether or not to tell me. Finally he said, 'Volodja told me.'

'Volodja?' I wondered at the name.

The next slap came and then my husband pushed me roughly onto the bed. He went to the fish tank on the windowsill and took something out of it. 'Did you know that twine stings more when it's dipped in water?' he asked, laughing.

I didn't understand what he was saying so I turned to see what he was talking about. He was holding a piece of twine, about half a metre long with an L-shaped piece of iron tied to the end. Water was dripping from it as he lifted it out of the aquarium.

I didn't have time to figure out what he was going to do before he struck me with all his might. I managed to roll over onto my stomach at the last moment so I was hit on the back. There was nothing like the pain I felt when he hit me with the iron, and he did it again and again. I screamed as loudly as I could because it was unbearable.

The beating stopped for a few seconds but only because Robi shifted the torture instrument to his left hand, while with his right he pressed my head into the pillow to silence me. As he continued to beat me he shouted, 'Shut up! Stop screaming!'

But I didn't shut up because every single blow hurt like hell. I was screaming into the pillow and I started to choke because I couldn't breathe. Robi released the pressure and I turned my head to the side.

I guess he stopped hitting me because he didn't want the neighbours to hear me scream or he didn't want to choke me to death. Or maybe he got tired, since he needed all his strength to inflict such pain on me.

Unfortunately, that was not the end of the abuse.

'Get up!' he shouted at me. When I didn't move, he started to drag me roughly off the bed by my clothes. My dress tore and he continued to tear it. My husband had gone crazy; he was completely out of his mind.

'Stop it!' I begged him, but he didn't hear me as he hit me again and again.

I don't remember whether I fell or he threw me to the ground, but the next minute I was lying at his feet and he was kicking me like a football. I was no longer crying or screaming; as if I were resigned to my fate, I just lay on the floor and waited for it to be over.

Robi stepped on my back with his left foot as if he wanted to pound me into the ground or stomp on me like a cockroach. His full weight was on me and it felt like he was squeezing all the air out of me.

Before I could pass out, something happened that made him stop: someone jerked the front door handle, which meant that a family member was coming home.

Since there were more of us than there were keys, we signalled to each other to let us in. We had a bell, but only strangers used that. If no one was home, there was a key under the mat, which we left in the lock after we arrived home.

When the handle jerked again, Robi reluctantly got off my back and went to answer the door. My dad had come home from work and, although he had no idea, he probably saved my life. There is no telling how that brutal assault would have ended had Robi not been interrupted in the middle of it.

I realised what time it must be if my dad was already home. I had completely forgotten about my little boy, who was still in kindergarten. I wanted to get up because I needed to hurry but I couldn't. I didn't have the energy to move and every muscle in my body ached, but the thought that Zoli was waiting for me gave me strength.

I managed to stand up but then the room turned with me. I felt dizzy, as if I were drunk, and had to sit down on the bed to pull myself together otherwise I would have fainted. Even sitting down was difficult because my buttocks hurt terribly where Robi had hit me several times with the iron.

While I was sitting, I looked around the room. The twine with the iron on the end was on the floor under the windowsill. Now I could answer the question Robi had asked when he started beating me. 'Yes, twine can sting a lot if it's dipped in water,' I thought. 'I can still feel it on my back.'

He must have brought the L-shaped piece of iron from the workshop because you could see the freshly drilled hole he had threaded the twine through. He probably didn't have anything to do at work that day, so he'd had time to think of a way to punish me. He'd also prepared the pillow on the bed because I'd put everything away in the morning before I left home; he was expecting me to shout, and he'd used it to shut me up. How precisely he had planned everything. I wondered what he would have done next if my dad hadn't interrupted him.

When I could stand up without feeling dizzy, I changed my clothes. I didn't have a lot of clothes and the dress he had torn off me was my favourite. Unfortunately, I couldn't even repair it, so I threw it in the bin.

I was going to the bathroom to wash my face when Robi came back into the room. He looked at me mockingly, then leaned over as if to kiss me. 'This isn't over, we'll continue tomorrow,' he whispered in my ear, then he smiled and left.

I started shaking with fear and burst into tears again. When was this going to end? When he killed me? I headed to the nursery, crying the whole way, no longer caring if people saw me or if I met someone I knew.

'This is not over, we'll continue tomorrow,' I kept repeating to myself. I had to do something, I couldn't let him beat me to death, but how could I protect myself?

As I'd expected, Zoli was the last child in the room, but luckily he wasn't scared, he was just playing alone. When he saw me he ran happily towards me but the teacher scowled. I thought she was going to scold me for coming so late to pick up my son, but she didn't; she saw my tear-stained face and chose not to say anything, just goodbye.

All evening I thought about the next day, dreading what it would bring. It looked like there would be no one home again, so my husband would be free to take out his aggression on me. My dad had the day off but he'd go out to the plot with my mum, and Potyi would still be at work. I don't know where my brother and sister would be, but they hadn't been home today when they should have been.

At night, after Robi fell asleep, I sneaked into the kitchen because I heard my mum was still there. I didn't know how to tell her how much trouble I was in so I just lifted up my nightgown and showed her my back. I begged her to stay home the next day or Robi would continue what he had started today.

My mother was horrified at the sight, her eyes wide with shock. 'How could he do this to you?' she asked.

I shrugged my shoulders and hurried back to the room, lest he woke up. I didn't sleep much that night and in the morning I could hardly get out of bed. I was in so much pain that it felt like a tractor had run over me. I didn't think he had cracked a rib or damaged a kidney, because that would have probably been discovered the day before.

When I got to the factory, the first thing I did was talk to Volodja. After Robi, he was the one I was most angry with since he was the one I blamed for previous day. I couldn't understand why he'd said that I had a lover at the factory as he had no reason to.

People in our department liked me and no one ever approached me with ulterior motives. They knew I was married and most of them knew Robi. Yes, my colleagues teased me a lot, made jokes, but they never crossed the line.

When I saw Volodja, I almost shouted at him, 'What did you say about me to Robi?'

'I said nothing.' he replied with an innocent face.

'You met yesterday and talked about me,' I was so angry, I was prepared to fight with him.

'The last time I saw your husband was about a month ago, but we didn't talk then, we just said hello.'

I could see he was telling the truth and I was ashamed for having attacked him like that, so I left without explaining. Of course they hadn't met yesterday because Volodja was here at the factory; I had spoken to him several times while I was assigning him tasks – and he was the only Volodja we both knew.

And then it dawned on me: Robi was making it all up to hurt me. Maybe the man he said he'd seen outside the stairwell on Sunday had never existed either. Since I gave him no reasons to be jealous, he made them up. Surely a sane man would not do such a thing. That's when something in me clicked.

'ENOUGH! I won't take it anymore!' I had felt the same way when I'd had enough of my brother and thrown the glass cutter at him. You remember that, don't you?

Robi's methods were getting more and more brutal, and he was not going to stop on his own. Yesterday was the final straw. 'I've had enough of this nightmare. If I don't act now, I never will!'

He hadn't even been drunk, so he couldn't use that as an excuse for not knowing what he was doing. On Sunday morning he didn't have a sip of alcohol, and on Monday he was only allowed one or two bottles of beer at work. He had known exactly what he was doing and enjoyed it.

His treatment hurt me not only physically but also emotionally. I was innocent of everything he had accused me of over the years, so what he did me hurt even more. If I didn't do something about it, sooner or later my husband would kill me; he would go to prison and Zoli would grow up without parents.

'No, that won't happen to us. I'm going to raise my son without his father. I must make a move and I have to do it today!' I thought.

I don't know where that courage came from, but suddenly I felt I could stand up to Robi. I had a plan and I was determined to see it through. First I would get him out of the flat, then I would go to court and file for divorce.

I remembered how he had blackmailed me a few months earlier when I was thinking of leaving him: he'd said he would make me look like a bad mother and the court would give him Zoli. At the time he had scared me, but now I was not afraid of him; I felt stronger and more confident than ever before. Something had changed in me that morning and I was ready to fight him.

During the four years since I'd met Robi, I had been happy, blindly in love, disappointed, disillusioned and desperate, but for the first time I could see a brighter future that no longer included him. I felt hope, the hope of freedom. I knew it would not be easy but I was determined. Once I'd said 'enough is enough', I could think of nothing but my new life. We hadn't been married for three years but it was time to get out.

I left work early that afternoon saying that I wasn't feeling well. Although I was still aching and finding it hard to sit down or climb stairs between floors, that wasn't really the reason for my illness: I needed to pack my husband's belongings before he got home so I could send him away. If he was planning on coming to the factory to escort me home again, he'd be very surprised. But I didn't care anymore; I just wanted to get it over with.

When I started walking home, I realised that I was much braver in my mind than I was in reality. I could bump into Robi anywhere on the street and the thought terrified me. I had to pass by his workshop, which was in the basement of one of the two-storey buildings; if he happened to look out of the window, I'd be finished. I didn't dare think what he would do to me if he saw that I'd left the factory early – probably that I was hurrying to see my 'lover'.

My stomach was trembling with nerves, but I couldn't back down. I knew I wasn't safe on the street because that's where I'd got my first slap. I was so scared of meeting him that I ran the last hundred metres. I hoped my mum and dad would stay at home as I'd asked them to, because I needed their help. My husband might not dare raise his hand in front of them, but I couldn't be sure.

When I got home, my parents were waiting for me. I told them I was divorcing Robi and went into the room to pack his things. My dad didn't say anything but I could tell he wasn't happy because he and Robi were friends.

My mum came into the room to talk to me; she hadn't been able to sleep a wink because she was so upset by the marks on my back. She had liked Robi from the first minute and now she was so disappointed in him. She couldn't understand how someone could do this to the wife he supposedly loved.

'Maybe he doesn't love me anymore, or maybe he never did,' I thought.

I watched my mum talking; her face was pale and tired, and there were black circles under her eyes. I was sorry to have bought my own troubles upon her so suddenly, but I'd had no choice. I knew it was a lot for her to take in, but I had to tell her the truth. Even so, I couldn't talk about it even when she asked me what had happened.

It was as if all the pain my husband had caused me was stuck in my chest and I could not tell her what I'd gone through in that room the previous day. I started to cry when I thought that I could have died. I remembered the last few seconds when Robi was stomping on my back, trying to squeeze the last breath out of me. Since then, it had been like a stone pressing against my chest and not letting me breathe.

My mum could tell that she needed to leave me alone for a while, but she asked me anyway, 'Has he done this to you before, or is this the first time?'

'Yes, he's hit me before but never like this.'

'Then why didn't you tell me about it?'

'I don't know,' I said, but that wasn't entirely true.

When I was alone, I wondered why I hadn't admitted to them what was happening. After the first slap, my pride had been greater than the fear: I couldn't tell my dad that he was right and I was attached to a bad person. After I had found out I was pregnant, that had stopped me running home. For a long time, I'd hoped that things could change between Robi and I and we could be as happy as we were the year before we got married. We had weeks when he didn't hurt me and was less pushy, and I naively clung to those days and dreamed of a better future. But it was time to wake up from this nightmare before it was too late.

My hope had long since evaporated, replaced by shame and fear. I hope you are not, or have never been, in this situation, but if you are you will know what I'm talking about. I was ashamed: it was humiliating to be treated like this by the man I had loved so much. Fear had become part of my everyday life, and I was often glad to go to bed at night without anything having happened that day. But now that was changing and my life could only get better.

I packed Robi's things into two large bags and put them outside under the coat racks. As I waited for him to come home, I remember being very nervous because I didn't know how he would react. What if he couldn't control himself and beat me up in front of my parents – or worse, hurt them too?

Fortunately, I couldn't think about it for long because someone pulled the doorknob. 'Unless it's my brother or sister coming home, it's Robi,' I thought.

When I opened the door, he entered the flat without saying hello. He had a mocking smile on his face and he wanted to say something but he didn't, because he saw my parents coming out of the room. He was shocked at first then greeted them with a broad smile. Like a good actor, Robi's expression changed in an instant and he was already playing the role of the good guy.

'Are you all home?' he asked sweetly.

'Yes, we are home,' said my mother. 'What did you expect?' And then she started yelling at him in a way she'd never yelled before. I can't remember every single word she said but I can remember some of the things.

'Did you think you were going to be alone again to do whatever you wanted with my daughter? I brought a healthy child into the world, raised her with difficulty, and you're going to cripple her! We welcomed you into our family and this is how you thank us?' She kept on yelling and yelling.

I'd never heard my mum like that before; she was completely out of control. It's true that when I was a kid she didn't show her love, she didn't hug and kiss me like I wanted, but in those few minutes she protected me like a mother lion protecting her cub. It was only then that I saw how much she loved and cared for me.

None of us expected such a reaction, especially not Robi. He blushed and the gentle smile disappeared from his face. He understood that it was over; he was exposed in front of my parents. My once proud, upright husband shrank and looked like a scared little boy. He was so embarrassed, he started babbling.

'But Mum, but Mum!' he kept repeating.

But she wouldn't let him speak, she just kept saying her piece. I was so proud of her for standing up for me like that; she'd probably been thinking about it all night and now she finally let it out.

I was going to say a few words but I couldn't. I was so nervous that I just stood there, stumbling from one foot to the other.

By the time my mum had finished, Robi didn't want to speak either. It was pointless for him to come up with a story. He looked at me as if he were waiting for my advice about what to do next. I pointed to the bags under the rack and said, 'Leave!' then I opened the door. He left the flat with his head down, without saying goodbye.

My dad didn't speak until then. 'Why didn't you defend yourself? You could have thrown an ashtray at him!'

I didn't answer because I didn't understand how he could ask such a question. If he had known Robi as well as I did, he wouldn't have said such a stupid thing. If he had seen my father-in-law defend himself against Robi, he would have known that it only made things worse. My husband was the kind of man who could only stop himself. But that didn't matter, what mattered was that we managed to get him out of the flat.

The next day after work, I rushed to court to file for divorce. As I wasn't familiar with such matters, I was advised to hire a lawyer to represent me and take care of the paperwork so I did.

At first everything went well, but when the lawyer asked more detailed questions about the abuse I kept quiet. I couldn't talk about what happened: the stone was still weighing on my chest and there was a lump in my throat that made me unable to speak.

The lawyer kept telling me that it was important to talk about the abuse as I had cited it as the cause of divorce. 'I can't,' I said and started crying.

'Is there any evidence that your husband beat you?' the lawyer asked.

'Yes.'

'Then you should go to the police as soon as possible and file a complaint. They will send you to a medical examiner who will write everything down and that paper will speak for you,' the lawyer finally said.

I didn't go anywhere that day as I was in a hurry to get to the kindergarten, but I made the report the next afternoon. Like the court, the police were new to me; I had never dealt with them before.

With the help of a young policeman, I completed the report. It did not require me to give details of what had happened, just the facts, so it was easier. Then they sent me to a medical examiner and fortunately I didn't have to talk much there either, as my bruises gave it all away.

The doctor looked at my back, stunned, and asked, 'Did your husband do this to you?'

I don't know what was visible on my body because I'd got the burns five days earlier and it was four days since Robi had hit me with the iron. The doctor examined and measured every single spot and wound with a ruler and took notes. When he finished, there were two pages of evidence that my husband had brutally abused me.

Nothing happened for a week. Robi showed up at the door almost every evening with the excuse that he wanted to see his son. He always brought him something, especially fruit, which was strange because he hadn't often done that before.

My son was happy to see his father, but I wasn't so happy. I didn't trust Robi. I didn't dare leave them alone so I was usually in the room with them. Interestingly, Robi was more involved with his son during those few days than he had been in years.

I went to the police again a week later because they had received the medical examiner's report but they wanted to talk to me before they continued the case.

'This case went beyond the definition of domestic violence,' they said. 'Your husband could be sentenced to up to three years in prison on charges of sadism.'

'Sadism? Three years in prison?' If Robi went to jail for three years, what could I expect when he got out?

'No, I don't want that. I just want to divorce from him,' I said.

'Then you need to withdraw the charges,' the officer advised.

I withdrew the complaint and the case was closed. The irony was that I used to call my brother a sadistic animal when in fact my husband was the real sadist, as the police had said.

You may think I'm a coward for running away like this, but I think I made the right decision. I'm not saying that Robi didn't deserve to be punished for what he did, but I didn't desire revenge. Him going to prison wouldn't have made me feel any better; it wouldn't have made me forget what had happened. I just wanted to get out of the marriage and live my life in peace. I thought it was enough punishment for him to be alone without a wife and children.

It was late October and Robi and I had been separated for a month. I was feeling much better, even though I wasn't officially free yet. My lawyer said it would be at least six months before the divorce was finalised, and there would be a conciliation hearing as well.

Even though they were trying to reconcile us, I knew what I wanted – or rather what I didn't want. I didn't want to go on living the way I had been living so I had to continue what I'd started.

The constant fear and tension had not only destroyed my nerves but my heart as well. Many times over the last few years I'd felt a stabbing pain or dull pressure in my chest, and sometimes my heart beat too fast or I could barely feel it. After I went to the doctor with my complaints, an ECG showed an abnormal heart rhythm. For that to go away, I needed to calm down, which meant I had to change my life.

One evening, after saying goodbye to his son, Robi turned to me and said, 'Happy wedding anniversary.'

I was surprised but I didn't react, I just closed the door behind him without a word. Yes, that day was our third wedding anniversary, which I had completely forgotten about. But what did it matter? I had filed for divorce a month earlier. Only three years had passed, but it seemed like an eternity to me. I remembered how happy I'd been on our wedding day and how determined I had felt.

In the movies we often see the bride being uncertain on her wedding day, but not me: I'd been sure of myself! I wanted to marry the man I loved and live my life with him. I was sure that I was loved in return because the previous year had been wonderful for both of us. That year was the happiest time of my life and I thought it would last forever.

It hurt to recall how blind and naive I'd been. Love had disappeared and only disappointment and sadness remained. Apart from my little boy, nothing good had happened to me in those three years. Others my age were still having fun and enjoying life, but I had ruined mine. At the age of twenty-one and a half, with a child just over two years old, I was waiting for my divorce.

I think that day also upset Robi. It's true that he sounded sarcastic when he wished me a happy anniversary, but I saw the sadness on his face and in his eyes. I suppose that wasn't how he'd imagined our future together, but it was only because of him that it had turned out the way it did.

The following month was no different from the previous one. Robi continued to visit his son, no longer every day or two days but he came often. On those occasions, he behaved normally and we were almost on friendly terms. He never came to see his child drunk, although neither was he sober. The few bottles of beer he drank during the day were no problem as he never took Zoli anywhere, just played with him in the room.

The day of the conciliation hearing finally arrived. I was very nervous because I knew how difficult it would be to talk about my private life in front of strangers. Luckily there was only one judge and Robi and me, but that didn't make it any easier.

I was so embarrassed that I could hardly answer the questions. Whatever I said, Robi immediately refuted it or explained himself. To the fact that he had beaten me several times and kept me in constant fear, he said, 'It's true that I hit her a few times, but I was drunk, I didn't know what I was doing.'

'Hit me a few times? It was more than that,' I thought, but I couldn't speak. I was so sick to my stomach that my hands were shaking.

'Why did you hurt your wife?' the judge asked.

'Usually out of jealousy,' Robi replied.

'Did he have a basis for his jealousy?' she asked me.

'No, of course not! I never cheated on my husband, he made the whole thing up.'

'Does your husband drink a lot? Is he often drunk?' was the next question.

'Yes,' I answered firmly.

Robi immediately contradicted that too and kept explaining until I finally felt like a liar for making such a claim.

'You said you usually hit your wife out of jealousy, but did you have any other reason?' the judge asked.

Robi didn't answer right away; he had to think up something horrible about me but he finally figured it out. 'My wife is distracted, she can't organise the household,' he said.

'What do you mean?'

'For example, she often starts cooking without having all the ingredients.'

He shouldn't have said that because the judge immediately came to my defence. 'What do you think, that your wife's brain is an encyclopaedia with everything in it? I'm a very experienced housewife, but these things happen even to me.'

Robi gasped then thought it best to keep quiet. The judge gave her conciliatory speech, which was the essence of this trial. She talked about the need to be more patient with each other and that everyone deserved another chance. We had a child who needed both parents. We should try to forget our grievances and forgive each other. It was never too late to start over and change what is not working. Give your marriage another chance; if for no other reason, do it for your child.

That made me feel very uncomfortable. After she repeatedly mentioned the importance of parents in a child's life, I almost felt like a bad mother for wanting to separate him from his father.

'It's a very important decision that you should not rush into. Think carefully about what is right for you and your child,' the judge finished and asking if there was anything to add.

I shook my head, indicating that I had nothing to say. From this whole conciliatory speech, it seemed that I was the evil one who wanted a divorce and my husband was the victim.

I think Robi was thinking something like that too, because it made him feel better. 'Your Honour, I don't want a divorce and I don't want to lose my family.' He turned to me and continued. 'I promise I won't hurt you again. Just give me another chance.'

'I don't believe you,' I said coldly.

'Please, let's try again. I promise I'll never hit you again.' He was almost pleading.

I said nothing; I was completely confused. I wanted to believe him but I couldn't. I was afraid of being disappointed again.

'Give it another try for your child's sake. Maybe this time it will go better. And if your husband hurts you again, give it back to him,' the judge finally said, and ended the hearing.

As I hurried home, Robi ran after me like a puppy. He could see that I was insecure and wanted to take advantage of it. He kept repeating the judge's words that he deserved another chance.

When we got to their street, he was almost desperate, 'I will promise you anything, but don't take me away from my son.'

'Well, that's the thing – you promise something and then you don't keep it. You'll have two glasses of wine or beer and then you'll lay a hand on me again.'

'No, I won't! If I promise to stop drinking and not hit you again, will I get another chance?'

I didn't answer, just stood there looking at him, trying to figure out if he was serious.

'Remember what the judge ended the trial with? She said if I hurt you again, give it back to me.'

Yes, I remembered that but I didn't understand what it meant. Maybe she meant that I should hit back, but surely a judge couldn't say that.

'Here I am, hit me!' shouted Robi. 'Give me back everything I gave you.'

'How can I give you back all the pain you've given me?' I thought, but the next moment I slapped him in a way that surprised him! It even surprised me!

True, Robi had asked me to hit him but he hadn't expected me to do it and neither had I. My palm was red and burning from the hard slap, but I was having so much fun. The tension that had built up during the trial was gone and suddenly I was in a much better mood. Robi took the slap in silence and, since he'd promised not to hit me again, he didn't.

'So now we're making up?' he asked quietly.

'I don't know, I'm still thinking about it,' I replied and left him in the middle of the street.

It was then that I remembered my first slap from him more than three years earlier almost in this same place. It felt good to think that it was the first time *I* had ever slapped *him*.

The next evening Robi came earlier than usual and was completely sober, probably to prove that he really meant what he said. I spent half the night trying to figure out what to do next. A day earlier I'd been sure I wanted a divorce, but the judge's words had made me uncertain. What if she was right, what if we tried again and this time it worked better? If it didn't work out, we could still get divorced later. Everyone deserved another chance, even Robi.

I could see that the separation had taken its toll on him and probably brought him to his senses. He obviously cared about us if he would promise anything so we could be a family again. I hoped his words were sincere and not just an act.

I wondered if he could really give up the drinking and fighting for his son and for me, but if I didn't give him that chance I would regret it for the rest of my life because I wouldn't know what would have happened if we had tried.

For the last two months, Robi has been trying very hard to be a good father to his son, which pleased me. I knew it was hard to change, but with the right encouragement he might succeed.

So I decided to give our marriage another chance. Of course, this could only work if my husband kept his promises. When I told him, he nodded enthusiastically and his joy seemed genuine. Now we just had to figure out where we were going to live.

I refused to move in with his parents and he refused to live with mine. He said my mum had made him get out of the flat and that was why he resented her; that wasn't exactly the case, but I didn't want to argue with him.

My parents didn't know what we were planning yet, but I suspected that my mum wouldn't be happy about Robi moving back in with us. However, there was a third option that would suit us both: Robi's uncle had a new girlfriend, with whom he had moved in a few weeks earlier so his flat was empty. It was the perfect place for us to start again.

The next day my husband spoke to his uncle, who was delighted to hear that we had reconciled. Without a second thought he gave Robi the keys so we could move in over the weekend. We didn't have to pay rent for the flat, just the utilities, which was a great help to us.

Nothing better could have happened to us and it was up to us not to ruin it again – or rather, it wasn't up to me, but I did my best to make the relationship work. However, I had no idea it would be so difficult to start again.

I think I'd changed a lot, which had worked to my advantage. I was no longer the naive, head-over-heels girl who had been swept off her feet by Robi so easily four years ago. I'd been desperate for his love back then, but he never gave it to me, so after our reconciliation I didn't expect him to love me or that I would ever love him back. No, I was no longer fooling myself; those feelings were gone forever. But the pain and disappointment didn't disappear overnight. True, we agreed to start afresh but I couldn't pretend that nothing had happened.

Just over two months had passed since the nightmare and although my blue-green bruises had long since disappeared and my burns had faded, I still couldn't forget what had happened. Every time I thought back to that Monday afternoon, I couldn't breathe and the stone was pressing against my chest again. That and the other horrors of the last three years were very hard to forget. But I tried; I did my best.

Even when we moved into our new home it was not easy. When I entered the bathroom, I was immediately flooded with memories. My eyes welled up with tears, remembering that two-and-a-half years ago, Robi had beat me in this bathroom for allegedly staring at men in the restaurant. I was sobbing on the edge of the bathtub over my ruined life and the following day my precious baby boy was born.

'If the judge is right and our child needs both parents, I'll do this for him,' I thought. Then I pulled myself together, wiped away my tears and went back to unpacking my bags.

The first days of our life together were difficult; the tension between us was palpable and although Robi tried very hard, he wasn't at ease. In the first year of our relationship, when I hadn't yet seen the real him, I had looked up to him, admired him. If I had any problems, he always made them go away and made me feel better. Now we were like two strangers and it was hard to change that.

His efforts to cheer me up seemed so contrived that they were rather pathetic and annoying. I know it wasn't easy for him, but he had no one to blame but himself for putting us in this situation. Playing the role of the good guy was not easy, because I saw through him. But in his defence Robi did his best to make it work; he kept his word and didn't drink, didn't yell at me or pick on me like he had done before.

By the following weekend we were getting on quite well and the tension had eased, mainly thanks to Zoli because we both loved him and he was important to us. We started to live like a normal family where everything was fine. I was happy about that, and I almost believed that it could work between us. Then Robi asked me, 'Aren't you withdrawing the divorce petition?'

'No,' I said firmly.

He got very angry and quickly turned away so I wouldn't notice, but it was too late. His eyes betrayed his anger. As soon as I said no, the gentle smile disappeared from his face and for a moment I saw the aggressive man he really was. When he looked at me again, there was no trace of his anger and he pretended not to be bothered, but I was disturbed and it clouded my belief that we could still live like a normal family.

A few days later when Robi came home from work, he looked rather strange. He looked like he was drunk, but I wasn't sure. I used to notice it right away, and I could smell the beer or wine from far away, but now he didn't smell of alcohol so I didn't question it.

Two days later it happened again and this time I could not let it pass without saying something. When I asked him if he'd been drinking, he denied it. This was quite unbelievable; his face showed that he was not sober, but for some reason he did not smell of alcohol.

The next day he brought home a three-litre bottle of wine, which he quickly took into the pantry. Apparently, it was given to him by one of the residents where he'd been sent that morning to fix the plumbing.

'But why did you take it if you don't drink? Your parents would be happy if you gave it to them,' I said.

'It's almost Christmas. If someone visits, we'll have something to offer,' came the reply.

I agreed that it was okay to have a little alcohol in the house. True, we didn't invite anyone for Christmas, but someone might drop in.

A few days later, when I saw the big bottle of wine again, it was only half full. I got very angry, and when Robi came home I immediately questioned him. He explained himself and took offence that I didn't believe him; apparently the previous day his friends had come by and he'd offered them wine, and today he'd taken a bottle to work. I didn't know if that was true but I didn't want to argue with him so I kept quiet.

Only two days were left until Christmas and I had a lot to do: baking, cooking, cleaning – I wanted everything to go well during the holidays. The next time I saw the big bottle, there was just a little wine left in it. I was so angry because we were saving it for Christmas. When Robi came home and I asked him where the wine had gone, he said almost the same thing he had a few days before. 'My mates came by yesterday and had a few glasses.'

'But we agreed to keep it for the holidays in case someone comes by,' I said. Then I remembered something. 'Yesterday was Saturday and I was home all day. When did your friends drop by?'

He didn't answer; suddenly he didn't know what to say.

'It's all a lie, you drank the wine!' I said angrily.

'Yes, I did and so what? I can do what I want!' he shouted, then raised his hand to hit me.

But I wasn't scared of him. I looked him straight in the eye and waited for him to hit me, but he didn't. He dropped his hand, turned around and walked out of the flat. I was so angry that if he had hit me, I would have hit him back. I wasn't afraid of him at that moment, I felt strong, but Zoli looked scared. He didn't understand what was happening.

During the month we'd lived there, there'd been no fighting or shouting in the flat. I leaned down to hug my son and told him that nothing was wrong, but then I noticed that his forehead was hot. I felt terribly guilty; I was so busy getting ready for the holidays that I hadn't even realised my little boy was sick. There was nothing I could do that night except bring down his fever and put him to bed.

Robi came home late and, as I'd expected, thoroughly drunk. Since he had been caught and no longer had to keep secrets from me, he didn't hold back on the drinking. Luckily he thought I was asleep so he lay down next to me and fell asleep right away. I was wide awake; I was worried about my little boy, hoping he didn't have pneumonia again or anything else serious. 'I have to take Zoli to the doctor in the morning, so I'm not going to work,' I thought.

I had other reasons to call in sick at work. Although Robi had promised me, he still couldn't stop drinking or fighting. It had been at least two weeks since he'd started drinking again but until that day I hadn't been sure. He'd probably eaten something after drinking to mask the smell of alcohol, and he must have been drinking the wine in the pantry at night when I was asleep. But that didn't matter because he'd deceived me and almost hit me.

'Nobody will ever hit me again!' I declared to myself and I meant it.

The next morning Robi got ready and left home. Normally I would have been on my way to the kindergarten with Zoli, but he didn't even notice I wasn't; if he did, he didn't ask me why because he probably hadn't sobered up.

When he left the flat, I immediately started packing. Since I couldn't carry more than two bags, I packed only the essentials. Then I woke up Zoli, who still had a fever, got him dressed and we headed back to my parents' house.

It was only a fifteen-minute walk but it felt a lot longer. I'd just broken up with Robi for the second time, but without him knowing it yet, and that made me very nervous. If he saw us on the street now with two big bags in the pushchair, I didn't know how he would react.

Once I turned into our street, it was just a short section and we were home. As I approached the shop that was under our house, I suddenly saw Robi standing there with two other colleagues, drinking his coffee and looking out at me.

I stopped for a moment, very frightened, then I pulled myself together and started walking straight towards the shop. Robi was staring at us through the window while his colleagues were chatting merrily. When I was quite close to him, we stared at each other, then I turned and continued towards the staircase.

My husband was aware of what was happening but he didn't run after us, try to stop me or talk me out of leaving him. He knew he'd messed up again and there was nothing he could do about it.

After breakfast I took Zoli to the doctor, where it turned out that he had a sore throat, which was why he had a fever. After I got his medication, we went home to unpack and settle back into my old room.

When my dad came home from work and saw that I'd moved back in, he started yelling at me. He didn't want to understand why I'd left my husband, and I couldn't understand when the truth about Robi was revealed why my dad took his side and not mine. He cared more about his friend's fate than his daughter's happiness or safety.

Finally, he made my mum choose. 'Choose! It's her or me,' he said firmly.

'My children come first,' my mother said and that settled the debate. It showed how much she loved us, even if she never showed it.

My dad didn't expect that answer, but he didn't say a word. He went into his room, packed his clothes in a suitcase and left.

I couldn't believe this was happening to us. That morning I'd left my husband and now my dad was leaving his family because of me. At that time my parents had been married for more than thirty years, but this had never happened to them before.

Christmas Eve and Christmas Day didn't go as planned for anyone. I was terribly hurt but I still didn't go back to Robi; our life together was over forever.

Two days later, someone pulled the door handle signalling to be let in. When we opened the door, my father was standing there with his suitcase in his hand. He said he regretted leaving and begged my mother to take him back. Of course, he was welcomed back into the family without a second thought.

When he told us that he'd spent the last two days at his mother's house, my mother said, 'You see, Vili, how life is? When you are in trouble, where do you run to, who do you go to? To your mother in the country. When your daughter is in trouble, she runs to her parents, where else?'

My dad seemed to understand, but nevertheless the coolness between us remained for a long time.

The next day I met Robi on the street. When I said that I would get the rest of my things from the flat, he said no. He wanted me to go back to him or else I would never see my clothes again.

'Why would I go back to you?' I asked. 'You can't promise me anything I'd believe anymore.'

Since I needed my clothes and Robi had decided not to give them back, I went to the police. Two days later, we were summoned, not to the central police station where I'd filed the complaint but to the station in our area.

When I found this out, I did not expect anything good as the district officer was a friend of my husband. Nevertheless I was pleasantly surprised. When I told him that we were going through a divorce and that Robi refused to return my clothes, the officer almost started shouting at him. He said that Robi had no right to my property and that he had to return everything that belonged to me.

Robi started to explain, but the policeman interrupted him even more forcefully. Finally, he ordered him to return everything that belonged to me within twenty-four hours.

Yes, victory! I hadn't even felt this good when I'd slapped Robi in the face on the street. To see his scared face as he stood in front of the policeman not daring to make a sound was a great joy. The big man, the sadistic animal who enjoyed torturing me and who mistreated his elderly parents, was now like a little child afraid of the policeman. The man who had terrorized me for three years was nothing more than a frightened little boy. He no longer affected me; I was no longer afraid of him.

We agreed in front of the policeman that Robi would put the key under the mat at 3pm the next day and he would leave the flat before I arrived for my stuff.

And so it was. With my mother's help I packed the rest of my things. When we were done, I left the key under the mat. That was the end of an era, the end of my life with Robi forever.

Months went by and it turned spring. A trial date had still not been set, even though I'd filed for divorce more than six months earlier.

Zoli and I were doing quite well without his father. Robi didn't miss his son much either, because he visited him less and less often. He would spend an hour with him, sometimes even less, then hurry home as if he had a lot to do. Fortunately Zoli was not very attached to his father and never cried after he left.

What I found a little strange, but in the end I didn't mind, was that Zoli's grandparents never showed any interest in him. They hadn't seen the child in months, but they didn't ask about him. I didn't want to take their grandchild there, but if they had asked me I would have. They loved him in their own way, but they didn't force the meeting; probably alcohol was still the most important thing to them. Thinking back to the days when I'd lived with them made my stomach lurch; I'll never forget the fights, the quarrels or my mother-in-law's wailing. I was glad that my little boy and I were out of it.

Even though I was not officially free yet, I was beginning to taste freedom. I didn't regret giving our marriage another chance because at least it proved that Robi and I didn't work. We'd been living in a flat with no rent and we could have stayed there as long as we wanted. In a few years we could have saved enough money to pay the first instalment on our own flat; not many young couples had that opportunity at the time. All it took was for Robi to keep his promises, but he chose alcohol over his family.

It was only a matter of time before the divorce was granted and then there was custody case. Robi had threatened to take Zoli away from me if I left him. I didn't know how I could have been so scared of him and believed that he would do that. If he said in court that I was an alcoholic, no one would believe him. Given his circumstances and the environment he lived in, he didn't stand a chance against me. He couldn't intimidate me anymore.

There was no point in keeping secrets from my colleagues. When I told them I was divorcing my husband, they received the news with mixed reactions. I was ashamed to admit that he was beating me all the time, so I just said that he was drinking more and more and we were fighting a lot. Some of them were sorry because they thought we made a nice couple, but looks can be deceptive; I knew that better than anyone.

However, some people who knew Robi and his parents said it was to be expected. They'd hoped that I would make him change, because we had such a great love for each other, but in the last few months they'd seen me often come in with tears in my eyes. They said that I deserved better and that I would find the right person one day. I was grateful that they were there for me.

Another month passed and we were already past Easter. Zoli was almost three, so we stopped using the pushchair and walked to and from nursery. I was holding his hand and we were walking home one afternoon when we saw Robi coming towards us in the street. He took Zoli's other hand and walked with us. I didn't say anything because I could tell he was drunk and I didn't want to upset him.

At the crossroads Robi was supposed to turn right, but he stopped and said, 'Zoli, you come with me now!'

'No way! Zoli is coming with me!' I said forcefully.

'The child is coming with me; I have the right.' As he said that, he reached into his pocket and took out a knife. My blood ran cold, but I couldn't let him take my son when he was drunk.

'Let go of his hand!' he said to me threateningly.

My heart almost skipped a beat, but I kept telling myself I was not afraid of him. I looked him in the eye and very slowly but firmly said, 'If you don't let go of his hand right now, I'm going to start screaming so loudly that everyone will look at us!'

For a few moments neither of us moved, then Robi put the knife back in his pocket, let go of his son's hand and walked away.

I needed a few more seconds to come to my senses. I was squeezing Zoli's hand so hard I was almost hurting him. The way Robi saw it, I wasn't scared of him – but actually I was terrified. I was afraid that he would stab me on the street in front of my son but luckily he came to his senses and didn't.

When we got home I calmed down with great difficulty. I wondered whether I should file a complaint with the police. In the end I didn't because I was sure that Robi would deny everything or he wouldn't remember anything – but the fact that he didn't come to see his son for two weeks afterwards proved that he remembered the incident well.

A few days before my twenty-second birthday, the summons for the trial finally arrived. For eight months I had been waiting for this day, for the divorce to be granted and for me to be free. I was much more determined and braver than before, but it was not enough to keep me calm in court.

If I remember correctly, there were four people in the courtroom with the judge, all of them men. This bad marriage had ruined my nerves, which was reflected in my behaviour. My stomach was trembling with nerves and I was shaking like a leaf. I had to talk about my private life in front of four strangers, which was uncomfortable and very difficult.

When asked why I wanted a divorce, I said that my husband often beat me and brutalized me.

'Did you report it to the police?' was the next question.

'Yes, I did. I even went to a medical examiner who noted the signs of abuse,' I replied.

The judge started looking through the papers in front of him but couldn't find what he was looking for. 'There's no report of any kind here, no medical examiner's report.'

That's when I remembered that I had withdrawn the complaint because I didn't want Robi to go to jail. What I hadn't expected was that it wouldn't be included in the divorce papers, and I wouldn't have any evidence of abuse.

When I told the judge that I'd withdrawn the complaint, Robi looked relieved; now it was just his word against mine. He immediately started explaining himself and said almost the same thing he'd said at the conciliation hearing: he had beaten me a few times, but he was drunk and didn't know what he was doing.

The judge seemed to believe him and as I had no evidence, I could not refute him. After being asked if we both agreed to the divorce, Robi said a firm, 'NO!'

NO? What did he expect? That we could still live together after all this, or that we would ever reconcile? Since I still insisted on the divorce, the judge finally ruled. By the end of that day, I was officially free and the nightmare was over.

The whole trial was so humiliating that I fled the court building and went straight home. When I entered the flat, I started sobbing; I was crying so hard I could hardly breathe.

My mother looked at me, frightened, then asked, 'Do you regret it?'

I didn't know why I was crying so much, but I was sure that I had no regrets. I shook my head and went to my room because I wanted to be alone.

When I had cried myself out and calmed down, I got to thinking. I was free at last; I could actually see the prison door opening and me stepping out. The feeling was exhilarating. The huge stone no longer weighed on my chest and I felt light and happy. I thought that only good things could happen to me now; as my Nana had told me: 'Once will be better.'

Chapter 3

Before I continue with my life story, I must make a brief detour. I was wrong to think that the big stone had disappeared from my chest and that I could finally breathe a sigh of relief. It was many years later when I first spoke about the way Robi treated me, but I have never told anyone about the Monday afternoon when he beat me with the iron and nearly squeezed the life out of me until now.

If you recall what I said at the beginning of the book, you'll see what I'm talking about. It wasn't until I read Jacklyn's book that the weight lifted off my chest. I still don't understand why her book really upset me; you can see now that our lives are not alike, yet for some reason I was so affected by her story. If I didn't have that book, and my memories had not burst to the surface, I wouldn't have been truly liberated. I have to thank Jacklyn for encouraging me and keeping me reading.

Just as my mother believed that everything happens for a reason, I now believe the same. If I hadn't dug up my memories and relived them, you wouldn't be holding this book in your hands.

Now let's go back in time, because I have more than thirty years of memories to share with you.

I was a divorced, twenty-two-year-old woman raising her three-year-old son alone. A few weeks after our divorce, I was scheduled for a custody hearing; once that was over, I could start my new life.

Since I knew Robi well, I was prepared for this not to be an easy process. My lawyer said I had no reason to worry because it takes a very serious reason to take a child away from the mother. I hoped that Robi couldn't lie to the extent that he would succeed.

The judge was a woman, which I took as a good sign. She first asked Robi why he wanted custody and he gave two ridiculous reasons that even the judge smiled at: he said I was a bad mother because I couldn't put the child to bed on time in the evening, and

I didn't buy enough toys for our son and hid what I had bought from him.

I didn't expect such accusations, but I was able to explain both.

'Your Honour, the child really doesn't have many toys because I'm not in a financial position to buy him new ones. True, I hide his old worn-out toys, but when I take them out weeks later my son is as happy as if they were new. It's also true that he doesn't always fall asleep on time, but that's only because he's usually most active in the evening and needs more time to fall asleep. I don't think that makes me a bad mother.'

The judge said nothing but looked at me sympathetically. She probably had children of her own, so she knew very well what I was talking about. Then she asked why I thought the father should not get custody.

'My ex-husband drinks a lot and his parents, with whom he lives, are also alcoholics. My son would not be safe there. I can provide better conditions,' I said.

Robi didn't say a word; he couldn't refute my statement because I was right. I was given custody of Zoli. After that, we only had to discuss visitation rights, which we again disagreed about. Robi said he wanted to see his son every other day, to which I immediately said no.

'Your Honour, I did not divorce my husband to see him every other day. We have been separated for months and since then he has hardly visited his son.'

After hearing both of us, the judge made the decision: Robi was allowed to come for his son on the two weekends required by law, every other Sunday from 3pm to 7pm. Only then could he take him, and only if he was sober.

My ex-husband was very disappointed but I could not feel sorry for him. He never felt sorry for me when he slapped me or hit me on the head with his fist. I didn't feel guilty for taking his son away from him because he was the only one to blame for what he'd done to me. I had loved him so much that I'd wanted to spend the rest of my life with him, but it hadn't just been up to me.

That was the first of the three hearings from which I walked away in good spirits; I had expected much worse. Apparently

Robi didn't dare lie about me drinking and going to the pub as he'd threatened; he was the alcoholic and the judge saw it.

It was finally over and I was only going to see Robi once a fortnight. He could no longer stop us on the street to take Zoli – he no longer had the right to do so!

I could finally put the past behind me and focus on the future. My marriage had been very bad but I tried to look on the bright side. I cursed the day I'd got together with Robi, but I'd experienced what it was like to be in love and I'd had a happy year thanks to him.

But that wasn't the real reason why I didn't regret that fate had brought us together. If I hadn't met Robi, I wouldn't have had my baby boy. He was the best thing in my life and I swore I would raise him to be a good man who would not remotely resemble his father. More than thirty years later, I can tell you that I did it!

Talking about fathers, the rift between me and my dad didn't change; in fact it got worse. He continued to be angry with me for divorcing Robi and for years he hardly spoke to me. He said I had humiliated him because divorce was not a thing in our family, but he was mainly worried about what the relatives would say if they found out. Remember that in the late 1980s divorce was not common, at least not in the Soviet Union. But I didn't care; being the black sheep of the family was not a big price to pay for my freedom.

I celebrated the victory of my last trial by buying Zoli a new toy and going to the hairdresser to get my hair cut and have it bleached blonde. Actually, I just got blonde highlights because they was cheaper. I didn't do it because I had extra money or because I wanted to be fashionable, I did it because I had to; for the last four years I'd been so stressed that my hair had gone completely grey at the front. I was only twenty-two but I looked at least twice as old. My colleagues had been asking me for a while why I didn't get it dyed, but I was holding off. While I was married it was out of the question, but as a free woman I could do what I wanted with my hair.

The first Sunday arrived when Zoli was going to his father, and I was very worried about it. He was taking his son to his grandparents for the first time in months and I couldn't be there to look after him. I explained to Zoli what was going to happen, and he was excited to see his father.

When I opened the door to Robi and he saw my new hairstyle he could barely hide his anger, but he didn't dare say anything because he had no right to. I was sure that he was jealous of my imaginary lover, or else he thought that I was spending the child support on myself. But I didn't care: let him think whatever he wanted.

The afternoon that Zoli spent with his father seemed very long and it felt like seven o'clock would never come, but exactly on time Robi was standing in the doorway with our son and I could finally breathe a sigh of relief. He wasn't drunk but it was noticeable that he'd had a few glasses of wine during the afternoon. Because he came home on time and brought my son home safe and sound, I didn't say anything; I thought it best to keep the peace. I wouldn't see him again for another two weeks anyway.

Then something unexpected happened to me at work, something I would never have dreamed of. As I've said many times, we were like a big family in the department. I don't mean that in a pretentious way but people really loved me there; as it is in a normal family, they love you and they care about you.

They could see how much the divorce had affected me and they wanted to help me in some way. My extended family got together, talked to the person in charge and got me a voucher for a beach holiday. When they handed it to me, I was so touched that I burst into tears.

I had already heard that the factory had a holiday resort in Yalta, on the Black Sea, but I had no chance of getting there. It was usually the management, office workers and their families who went on holiday there. Ordinary workers seldom got such passes because the condition was that you had to be a Communist.

In those days, socialism was flourishing in the Soviet Union, and for anything good you had to join the party. If you wanted to get a higher position or a management job, or just a holiday at the seaside, you had to be a Communist. They'd tried to get me into the party several times but I'd always said no. I had enough problems with my marriage so I wasn't really interested in politics.

I don't know how they managed to do it, but the good news was that my colleagues got me a trip to the Black Sea resort. They said I deserved a break; I should relax and have a good time.

After wiping away my tears of joy, I began to worry that I couldn't afford the trip because it would surely cost me a fortune. Since Robi and I had separated, I had to be very strict with my salary. I put aside a little money but it wasn't much. When I found out how much the voucher was discounted, meaning that my ten-day holiday would only cost me ten-days' wages, I couldn't believe it. That included meals, which probably wouldn't be enough for the two of us, but it didn't matter.

I was going on holiday to the sea with my little boy for the first time in my life. The ten days included a Sunday, but luckily it wasn't Robi's visiting day so he didn't need to know where we were going. I was excited but also happy that after all the bad things something good was happening to me.

Finally the morning came when we boarded the bus. We arrived the next morning. I knew we were going a long way and that it would take at least a day to get there, but luckily we stopped often because we had several children with us. As we only had one seat, Zoli sat or slept on my lap the whole time. It was quite uncomfortable, but we managed.

I had only one colleague from our department with his wife and grandson, and I hardly knew the others because they were mostly office workers and their families. We were given a room with three beds, which we shared with two young women who were the daughters of one of the factory bosses.

After breakfast we walked to the beach, which was ten minutes from our accommodation. When we got there I was literally breathless as if I had stepped into another world. The sea really was like I'd seen in the movies or read about in books: endless. You could see only that it met the sky. The view was beautiful. As the weather was scorching, hundreds – thousands – of people were sunbathing on the beach or swimming in the sea. Zoli and I went down to the water and our holiday officially began.

The next few days were incredible and we enjoyed every minute. The sea was very salty but so warm that we didn't want to leave it. My little boy had made friends with my colleague's grandson on the bus, so they played together on the beach. I sat on my blanket and watched them build sandcastles or try to throw the slimy little sea creatures that were washed ashore by the waves back into the water.

My colleague knew the area and the facilities quite well as it was not the first time he had been here with his family. He showed me the market where Zoli and I went almost every day. Fruit was very expensive so we bought mostly melons because at least they were affordable.

One day my colleague and I rented a two-person water bike. I rode with my son, and he had with his grandson on his lap, all the way to the buoys. I can't say I wasn't scared because the waves were tossing us around, but it was exciting and the kids really enjoyed it. In the evenings after dinner we watched subtitled movies on a big screen in an outdoor cinema. I didn't really see any of them because Zoli always fell asleep on my lap, so I took him up to the room. Here he had no problem falling asleep because he was on the beach or in the water all day and it exhausted him. He slept like a log.

I paid for a boat trip one day, which was also very good. Luckily I was pretty good with the money I had so we could afford this trip. We sailed on a huge boat to Odessa where we spent half a day and then came back.

We saw an interesting house, a villa on top of a cliff, which was very beautiful even from a distance. Someone told us that this place was called 'Swallow's Nest' and it was the Prime Minister's residence, so I can say that I saw Gorbachev's 'little house' from a distance. Then we almost saw dolphins, but by the time we got to the other side of the boat they were out of sight. Still it was a memorable trip, and I don't regret paying for it.

However one bad thing happened that overshadowed our holiday. One day a four-year-old boy went missing and all afternoon we heard the announcements over the loudspeaker. I paid even more attention to Zoli and worried about the unknown child. They were still looking for him late into the night, and the speaker kept making announcements. I could hardly sleep that night because I felt for the parents; I hoped that the little boy was still alive and had not drowned in the sea, as many people assumed.

Luckily, he was found in the morning, and apart from the fright and dehydration he was fine. He was supposedly found under a bush but where I don't know because I didn't see any bushes on that stretch of coast. The point is that there was no tragedy and everyone could breathe a sigh of relief.

With only two days left of our holiday, we tried to make the most of it. It would have been nice to get some pictures taken as a souvenir but it was so expensive that I put it off until the last day. Remember that it was the late eighties, when there was no smartphone to take a million pictures or selfies; that's why there were photographers walking the beach, taking pictures of tourists for good money.

Some walked around with an inflatable bear, others with a live python around their necks, then there was a man with a big hump-backed camel on a leash. He was immediately surrounded by people, because it's not often you see an animal like that up close. The braver ones took photos on the camel's back or standing next to it, but Zoli and I were not so brave. One of the children threw sand in the camel's eyes, and it sneezed and spat at those of us who were standing around. We ended up taking a photo with the inflatable bear because at least it didn't spit and wasn't so scary.

Just as everything comes to an end, this holiday unfortunately came to an end too. On the last evening after dinner, Zoli and I went back to the beach to watch the sunset. I heard the view was exceptionally beautiful there, so we couldn't miss it. Like us, many people waited for the beautiful sight as the red-hot sun disappeared from the horizon.

The sky was such a special colour that I can't even describe it in words; I have never seen anything more beautiful in my life. Then the moon and stars appeared, but we continued to sit on the beach. For some reason Zoli was not sleepy and he sat silently beside me, watching the waves. We were both a little sad because we knew we would be gone by this time tomorrow and we didn't want the evening to end. Those ten days were like a dream, like we were in paradise.

I really needed that time off and I was grateful that my colleagues made it possible for me. I made a promise on the beach that I would do anything to make sure that Zoli and I had as many of these experiences as possible.

We went early the next morning to say goodbye to the sea, but I knew it would not be the last time we would see it. I was sure that I had no chance of getting the cheap summer pass again but there were other options. If I could save enough money, we could go to places like this through a travel agent. We could also visit my older sister who was living with her husband's family near the Caspian Sea. I told Zoli about this on the bus and promised him that he would build more sandcastles on the beach. That made him feel better and our journey home was not so sad.

My outlook on life changed a lot in those ten days and I came back from holiday a different person. A new world had opened up in front of me and I wanted to be part of it. I realised that there were other ways to live and it gave me hope. I was full of energy and it made me more confident. I thought I could do anything, I just had to want it. And I had a new goal: to keep my promise to Zoli.

As we lived in the same district as Robi, I often bumped into him on the street. He seemed resigned to his fate, although it couldn't have been easy for him. He knew he no longer had any power over me; I was not afraid of him.

He took Zoli with him every other Sunday and brought him back on time. Then one day it didn't happen that way. They were sometimes a little late, or Robi would just walk him to the stairs and then let the three-and-a-half-year-old child come up to the fifth floor alone. I guess he was drunk and didn't want me to see him like that, but at least he brought our son home.

But that evening they were an hour late and I was getting increasingly nervous. There was no point in waiting any longer; it was clear that something happened and I had to go and get him. I hadn't been to my in-laws' for over a year but, knowing them, I wasn't expecting anything good. I put a pair of sharp-tipped scissors in my pocket in case I needed to defend myself, and called my mum for backup, although we didn't stand much of a chance against the two drunk men.

I remember being very scared again, but I was more worried about my son than myself. When we got there, the lights were on in the house. As the door was not locked, we entered the kitchen. Hearing no loud shouting or fighting, we went into the room. I was not surprised at all by what greeted us. The three adults had drunk themselves into a stupor and were lying on the bed, undressed and sleeping like logs.

Zoli was sitting next to his drunk father, playing with a toy. He was wearing his warm winter coat and boots, just as when he had left home. He wasn't crying but his smudged face and sleepy eyes showed he hadn't had a good afternoon. My heart sank to see him like that, but at least he was safe.

I quickly grabbed my son from his father's side and, with my mom, we quietly left the house. I was in such a state of nerves that if Robi had woken up and tried to hurt me, I would surely have stabbed him with the scissors. Luckily that didn't happen.

For the next two weeks I never ran into my ex-husband, as if he were deliberately avoiding me. I wanted to confront him about what had happened, which would have ended in a fight, so I secretly hoped he wouldn't come for his son for a while.

But it wasn't like that. On Sunday afternoon he stood in the doorway as if nothing had happened. When I told him that he couldn't take his son if I had to pick him up again, Robi looked at me, puzzled. He didn't know what I was talking about and he said he had brought the child home, not me. During our marriage, he had betrayed me many times, but now I would not let him. When I said that my mum had been with me and seen them all drunk and passed out, Robi was embarrassed and kept quiet. He finally admitted that he didn't remember what had happened.

'But I remember everything, and if it happens again you'll never take your son away again!' I said firmly.

I could see how much he didn't like what he was hearing, but he promised me it wouldn't happen again. They came back at exactly seven o'clock. I was in the kitchen, so my sister opened the door for them and Robi went straight to my room, even though he had no business being there. Since we'd separated, he had not been allowed to enter the flat, so what he did was incomprehensible.

I hurried after him, but before I could question him he asked me, 'Where are the toys you bought for the child from the child support money?' He looked at me angrily and that's when I realized how drunk he was. I guess he couldn't digest what I'd made him promise that afternoon, so he wanted revenge.

'Your son needs clothes and shoes, not just toys,' I said. I tried to stay calm, but it didn't really work.

'I want to see how you spend my money!' he said even louder.

'Go home, you're drunk! You have no right to be here!'

'But I have right to know how you spend the money!'

We finally had a quarrel. I hadn't seen him that aggressive in a long time but, although it was scary, I wasn't afraid of him. Suddenly he came closer to me and asked, 'Aren't you afraid I'll kill you one day?' He said it so seriously that I was completely shocked.

I got so angry I yelled at him, 'Get out of my room!'

When he saw that I wasn't frightened, he left without a word and slammed the front door loudly behind him.

After he left, I started to shake like a leaf; that's when the fear really came over me. I was so busy arguing with my ex that I didn't even notice that Zoli was in the room and had heard everything. I don't know what he understood, but the poor child was terrified. He didn't cry, he just looked at me with terrified eyes.

This couldn't go on: I had to do something. If I didn't stop Robi, he would kill me – he would make good on his threat. The previous year, when it was revealed that he was a sadist and could get up to three years in prison, I had withdrawn the charges. Now I knew it was a big mistake on my part, as was my failure not to run to the police in the spring after he'd threatened me with a knife in the street. I'd also forgiven him for getting so drunk two weeks earlier that my three-and-a-half-year-old son was left unattended in the house. It was just luck that nothing happened to Zoli that night. And after all that, Robi had threatened to kill me.

The next day after work, I went to the police station and filed a report. I told them that my ex-husband had threatened my life and it wasn't the first time. True, this time he hadn't beaten me and I didn't have blue-green marks like the last time, but the police took it seriously. A few days later a policeman came to our house and took my statement. I told him everything that had happened that night and he recorded it. He questioned my family members, which was quite unpleasant. We had never had police officers in our home before, so everyone was pretty embarrassed. Because I hadn't told them what Robi had threatened to do, they couldn't tell the police much; they'd heard the argument from the room, but not what it was about.

After we signed the report, the policeman rang the bell of the flat next door to question our neighbours. Well, that was really unpleasant but there was nothing I could do. My father was angry with me for bringing such shame on my family; now the whole block would be talking about it. I started to feel like I had made a mistake again, but there was nothing I could do.

The next time I ran into Robi in the street he said, 'You shouldn't have told the police about me, because they came to my workplace. Now everyone knows what happened.'

'It's okay if they know what kind of person you are. You shouldn't have threatened me, you brought this on yourself! From now on I'll run to the police for everything, and they'll protect me from you.'

Robi must have believed me because he never harassed or threatened me again; I had managed to stop him for good.

After the long, cold months, spring had finally begun. Of all the four seasons, that was my favourite but I'm sure it is for many of us. It's the time of year when we feel the sunshine on our skin, the trees are in beautiful blossom and the birds are chirping everywhere. Nature has woken from its winter sleep, and this filled my soul with warmth.

It was still too early to go hiking in the mountains, but Zoli and I walked a lot in the park or along the Latorca river. I loved this quiet life, the stress-free days with my little boy. I tried to raise him the best I could, because it was up to me what kind of adult he would become. As a single mother, it wasn't easy, but my mum gave me some good advice. She told me to be strict with the child because I wouldn't be able to handle him later, and not to show my love for him because I would spoil him. If Zoli grew up without a strict father, he could easily become unmanageable.

It was only then that I really understood why we were brought up in such a way. Come to think of it, we also grew up without a father as he was not with us most of the year. My mother didn't show her love because she was afraid it would spoil us. She had seven kids in her care, which is a huge responsibility for a parent. It's true that I resented her when I was a child because I felt she didn't love me, but since then I have found out many times that we are her priority and she loves us very much. If she hadn't been so strict with us, who knows what kind of adults we would have become. But she did a good job, so I took her advice.

Luckily, I didn't have much trouble with Zoli; he was a good boy. He accepted, albeit with difficulty, that he had to go to kindergarten, and even made a little friend. He learned the Russian language very well, which made it easier for him to communicate with others.

One day after kindergarten, Zoli and I went to the centre because I had to take care of something. When I was done, we took a different route home. We were walking past a toy shop when he stopped and looked curiously through the window. Then he pointed at a car and asked me to buy it for him. I can't remember what kind of car he wanted, but I do know that it was one of the most expensive toys in the window.

'Zoli, this car is very expensive, I can't afford it,' I told him.

A tear dropped from the corner of his eye but he didn't say a word; he just took my hand and we carried on walking. He didn't scream, he didn't throw himself on the ground like so many kids his age. My smart son understood that he couldn't have everything he wanted.

The truth is, I could have bought him that car with the money I had saved but there were more important things in life. I wanted him to have the vacation I had promised him last summer. I think it would have been a bigger disappointment if I hadn't taken him to the seaside than if he hadn't got a toy. I felt very sorry for Zoli but I was also proud of him for behaving so well.

The extra money I got for the cashier job was good, but I didn't do it just for that. I liked working with money, counting it and distributing it to my colleagues. I gave them some payments in advance in the middle of the month and rest of their salaries at the beginning of the following month. At the end of the day, I always had some money left and, as I didn't have a safe and the cashier's office was already closed, I had to take the money home with me. To make sure I didn't go alone, someone always accompanied me.

One day a guy who had only been working for us for a few months volunteered for this task. Like my son, his name was Zoli and he was the same age as me. We had a nice chat on the way home and when I told him I had to go to the kindergarten, he offered to go with me. It turned out that he lived next to the kindergarten, so after I took the money up to the flat we continued our journey together.

After that it became a habit: he waited for me every day and walked me to the kindergarten. We spent more and more time together and became friends. I enjoyed his company and friendship turned into more.

When he kissed me for the first time, I didn't refuse. I wasn't in love with him but I was attracted to him. I had left Robi almost a year and a half ago and I had no thought of a new relationship with anyone; I needed more time for my wounds to heal. But I wanted to move on, to start a new life. I didn't know if I could ever trust anyone or fall in love again, but it would have been nice.

It's true that I didn't want a new relationship, but Zoli's approach felt good. It was obvious that he was interested in me and I was happy about that. We had been going out for about two months when he invited me to a pastry shop. My birthday was two days away and I thought he wanted to celebrate. On a Friday afternoon after work, we went to the city centre and sat down in a nice pastry shop. I had never been there before as it was well known that it was a very expensive place.

'Never mind the prices, feel free to ask for anything you like,' Zoli said.

In the end, he ordered for both of us because I couldn't choose from the many delicacies. He said it wasn't his first time there and he had tasted almost all the cakes, but the one we ordered was the best. He was right: it was the best I had ever tasted in my life. It wasn't a cake, it was some kind of creamy, meringuey wonder served in a cup, topped with fruit syrup and roasted peanuts.

While I was eating mine slowly to enjoy it as long as possible, Zoli quickly finished his and ordered another one for himself. Finally we asked for the bill because we had to go to the kindergarten. When they brought it out, Zoli started searching through his pockets and then turned to me. 'It seems I didn't bring any money with me. Could you settle the bill?'

I could hardly hide my anger; I was furious. It wasn't the first time he did 'not bring any money', but as long as I only had to pay for a coffee or a soft drink, I didn't care – but this was too much. He had taken me for a complete fool and taken advantage of me.

He lived with his parents in a big house and as far as I knew he had no financial problems, while I was raising my son alone and had to manage all my finances very strictly. How could someone be so cheeky as to invite me to an expensive cake shop and then make me pay the bill? What if I hadn't had any money? What would he have done?

Luckily I did have some money, so I paid for our order and we left. Zoli continued to swear that it was unintentional but if that was true, how could he be so irresponsible? I couldn't believe him, because this was not the first time he'd done this to me.

I told him that this was the last time we would go anywhere together, we had better forget each other. I would not let him take advantage of me and I would rather have spent that money on my little boy than on him. I finally called him stingy and left him high and dry. I was very angry, but my disappointment was greater than my anger; I'd thought he was inviting me to that cake shop for my birthday, but that was not the case. He was just going to eat something delicious and make me pay for it.

Maybe you think that I overreacted and that this was not a serious reason to break up, but in those days if a boy had a girlfriend it was natural for him pay the expenses. It's true that Robi had a lot of faults, but in the year we'd dated I'd never been in that kind of situation with him.

Sunday came and I turned twenty-three. We adults didn't really celebrate birthdays, but Potyi baked me a cake. I wasn't expecting guests, so it was strange to hear someone ringing the doorbell. Much to my surprise, Zoli came to say hello to me. He had both hands full of flowers, beautiful roses. He wished me a happy birthday and then handed me (if I remember correctly) ten bouquets of roses.

I was embarrassed because we'd broken up two days ago, and now he was standing in front of me as if nothing had happened. He said he bought all the roses in the market and now I couldn't call him stingy. Then, to back up his claim, he immediately told me how much he'd paid for them. He didn't realise that this was just another proof of his stinginess, but I didn't say anything.

I was pleased with the flowers and hurried to put them in water. As we didn't have enough vases, I used empty jars instead, but the roses looked very nice in my room. We eventually made up, although I wasn't sure if I wanted to.

The next afternoon we went to the kindergarten together, but before we could turn around, Zoli said, 'I want to talk to you about something. Can I come to your place tonight?'

'Sure, come.' I was curious to know what it was about, but I didn't ask. Then, in the evening, everything became clear.

'Have you heard that a lot of German ethnic families have been going to Germany lately?' he asked.

'Yes, I know about it. There is an agreement between the two countries that Germany will take in the descendants of German people who were resettled at that time. Two families of my father's relatives are arranging the papers for the expatriation,' I said.

'Then you know they will have a much better life there than here?'

'Yes, I'm sure they will, but why are we talking about this now?'

'I want to go too, but I can't prove I have German ancestry.'

I looked at him puzzled, not knowing what he was getting at. Zoli continued. 'Because of your dad, you can easily take German nationality. If we got married, we could go to Germany together.'

I didn't want to believe my ears, but unfortunately I understood what he was talking about. 'So you only started flirting with me because you found out I had German blood and you would only marry me to get you into Germany?' I asked him.

Zoli was a little embarrassed, but finally he said, 'Yes.'

I cannot tell you how I felt when I heard that 'yes'. At least he could have lied or sugar-coated things but no, he was honest with me. That 'yes' hurt almost as much as the first slap I'd got from Robi.

'What made you think I would go along with this? How could you think I'd marry you and help you make your plans come true?'

Zoli could see how angry I was but he was still trying to save the day. He talked about how the German state supported immigrants in every way possible, providing them with housing, paying for language lessons and helping them to start over.

'Stop it, I'm not interested!' I said. 'You never asked me if I want to live in Germany. These are your plans, not mine. I couldn't trust you with my life and my son's. I told you after the pastry shop incident that I won't let you take advantage of me! You'd better go, I don't want to hear any more about you or your plans!'

After Zoli understood that there was nothing more to talk about, he left in a bad mood and I could finally cry. Words cannot express the disappointment I felt. How could I have been so naive again? How could I have thought that he'd noticed me because he liked me? A young, well-off guy doesn't start dating a divorced mum unless he has an ulterior motive. Luckily, I'd found out in time before we got serious.

After I stopped crying, I stayed in the room for a while so my family wouldn't see my teary eyes. The roses were still on the table and the windowsill, but I could no longer admire them. I only saw them as an ulterior motive, not as my birthday present. If I hadn't made up with Zoli, I might never have found out that I was nothing to him but part of a plan.

Since we'd broken up and Zoli will not be mentioned in my book, I would like to make a small digression because I thought you might be interested to know if he finally succeeded in realising his dreams. After a few years, he somehow got into Germany but a month later he was expelled from the country. He allegedly tried to start a new life with forged papers but was caught and sent home. He never came back to work in our factory – he was probably ashamed of what had happened. I wonder how our lives would have turned out if I had gone along with this marriage of convenience. We'll never know.

Once I got over that relationship, life with my son Zoli continued as usual. After his fourth birthday, Potyi and I went to the travel agency and booked a holiday to the Black Sea. Our previous trip to Yalta had gone so well that my sister wanted to come with us. I was happy about that, as two adults and a child would be better than just being alone with Zoli. Our week-long trip was very expensive but in return the agency organised everything for us. Or at least, that's what we thought.

It started at the airport in Uzhhorod, where only half of the group was able to board the plane. Those of us who stayed behind had to wait almost four hours for the next flight. The group was split so unfairly that most of the families with small children were on the second departure so it was not easy. In addition, it was only then that we found out that we would arrive in Yalta with a transfer flight, which meant several more hours of delays.

But finally we arrived. Our plane landed late at night at the airport where no one was waiting for us. Luckily someone in the group had the address of the travel agency, so we headed there. As you can imagine, we were unsuccessful; there was no one there and they were closed.

We stood in the dark, clueless about where to go next. Not only were we tired and sleepy, but we had nothing left to eat. Since we'd left home early in the morning we'd eaten all the sandwiches we'd brought on the trip. Of course, the shops in the area were closed, so we couldn't buy anything.

However, apart from hunger, we were more worried about having nowhere to sleep. We were supposed to get the addresses of our accommodation at the airport but that didn't happen. We had no choice but to wait for the morning on the benches outside the travel agency.

It was a chilly night, so we put on all the clothes we had in our suitcases. In Potyi's bag we found half a packet of biscuits, which we immediately consumed. Zoli fell asleep on our knees, covered with towels, while we didn't sleep a wink on that uncomfortable bench.

The sun finally came up, albeit late, and our man from the travel agency arrived. When we called him to account for what had happened, he just shrugged his shoulders and didn't even apologise for the inconvenience. According to him, it was not his fault that we'd arrived late; once his working hours were over, he went home.

It was pointless to argue with him; the fact that we'd been were homeless on the first night of our holiday could not be helped. But after we got the addresses of our accommodation for the next few days, I started arguing with the organiser. He gave me and Potyi two different addresses, which we refused to accept. We had shared luggage, and anyway we wanted to go on holiday together, not separately.

As we were stubbornly insistent, the organiser solved the problem, but once we arrived at the address it turned out that it had not been resolved. We were given a double room in a family house, but when the landlady saw that there were three of us, she refused to let us have it. I told her that my son would sleep in my bed, but she didn't care. The only way we could stay was if I paid for the extra person's accommodation, which was very unfair as it was a four-year-old child.

I had neither the energy nor the strength to argue with the landlady, so I paid the money, for which I did not get an extra bed or mattress.

Our holiday finally got underway, albeit with some difficulty. The beautiful weather made up for everything and helped us forget the bad things that happened at the start. For the next five days, we sunbathed on the beach or swam in the warm waters of the sea, but we couldn't afford a boat trip or water biking because we were running out of money. As the lady was always in the kitchen, we didn't even go in there, so we had to eat breakfast, lunch and dinner out of the house, which was not cheap. Sometimes we went to the market, but everything was so expensive that we hardly bought anything except melons.

Although we didn't do anything wrong, we didn't get along with the landlady. She was suspicious and watched every move we made with a wary eye. We only came home to shower and sleep, but she didn't like that either. There was no kindness in that woman; for someone who lived off holidaymakers' money, she was not friendly at all.

There was a big tree in the garden of the house full of cherries. One morning, Zoli stood under the tree and tried to pluck a cherry. He jumped up and down, hoping to reach it. The landlady noticed him immediately and started shouting from the kitchen window, 'Leave that cherry alone! That tree was not planted there for you!'

'How can someone be so stingy and malicious?' I thought, but I didn't dare say anything back.

Unfortunately, I wasn't the type to confront a stranger. If that happened to me now, I would certainly go to the tree and pluck a handful of cherries for my little boy, and I'd remind the landlady that I'd paid for extra room and board, for which I'd received no extra benefit, so we deserved that cherry. But since I wasn't like that, I just pulled Zoli out from under the tree. It was already a great achievement of me to get the organiser to find me a room with Potyi, although it wasn't the most pleasant place to be.

Those few days passed very quickly and we were back in front of the travel agency. We didn't regret not seeing the bad-faced woman (that's what Potyi and I called the landlady, rightly so), but it was hard to leave the sea. My sister and I realised that such holidays were not for us, at least not on our budget, but we had a photo taken on the last day as a souvenir and then said goodbye to the Black Sea forever.

As we expected, our journey home was not smooth either. One half of the group, who had started their holiday half a day earlier and didn't have to spend the night on benches with us, were again given priority. They flew home while we got train tickets, which again was not fair on us. We complained in vain, but the organiser shrugged and said it was not his fault.

I can't remember how many hours we spent on the train, but it was certainly a very long journey home. Several people in the group threatened to complain to the travel agency and get their money back, or at least part of it. Their outrage was justified, as we were deceived and didn't get what we were promised. We were told about flights to Yalta and back and about civilised accommodation near the beach, which was a lie. But when a couple told us about their own experience with the agency, I think everyone lost their appetite for complaining.

They had paid for a week's holiday the previous summer and had no problems until they arrived at their accommodation. The agency had rented them an outside shed-like building which had no bathroom. Apart from a rickety double bed, the only things in the room were an old chest of drawers, a table and two chairs. In the corner was a hand basin with a cold-water tap and underneath a bowl for 'bathing'. The toilet, which was nothing more than a hole in the ground, was outside in the courtyard.

Having seen the conditions, the couple went back to the travel agency to ask for alternative accommodation.

They were told by the organiser that there were no other places available, but that he would inform them as soon as there was a room available. Nothing happened for two days, so the couple went to the office again where they were told to be patient and promised again that the agent would take care of the problem. Again, these were just empty promises, so they remained in the outside building.

They were getting used to the bad conditions when it started to rain on their last night. As the roof was leaking in several places, everything got wet. That was the last straw. When they got home, they complained to the local travel agency and demanded compensation for their ruined holiday. The agency denied everything and did not pay them a single rouble for the inconvenience. The couple even hired a lawyer but he couldn't get anything out of the agency.

We were stunned to hear their story and I think we were all thinking the same thing: we were glad we didn't get that accommodation. True, our landlady was money hungry and unfriendly but we couldn't complain about the conditions. Our room was spacious and clean and the bathroom had hot water, which was almost luxury compared to the shed.

Someone asked the couple why they had come back here on holiday after all this, to which the wife replied, 'A year has passed, and we have tried to remember only the good things. As there is no other travel agency in our city, we gave them another chance and paid for this holiday. This time there was no problem with the accommodation but our trip was very badly organised. Sleeping on a bench or being stuck on a train for hours – that was not what we were talking about when we paid them all that money. My husband and I have decided to stop using this travel agency and try to arrange our holidays another way.'

I am curious to know how many of this group (or rather half of the group) used the services of the agency again. Potyi and I certainly didn't because, as it turned out, we really did say goodbye to the Black Sea forever.

We were a little disappointed, but Zoli was not at all bothered by our badly organised holiday. He was happy to tell everyone how much he'd swum in the sea and how salty the water was, which he sometimes swallowed. And I was happy that I kept my promise to him. Although we didn't build a sandcastle on the beach, we enjoyed our time there.

On Sunday afternoon, when Robi came to pick up his son, he looked at us, puzzled, and tasked, 'Where did you get so tanned?'

I didn't have time to answer him, because Zoli immediately said his piece. 'Well, we went to the sea and it was very nice.'

He went on but his father hardly listened; he looked at me angrily. I know he didn't like what he saw or heard, but who cared? I was a free woman, and I could do what I wanted! If I hadn't divorced him, I would never have had such experiences and perhaps I would never have set foot outside Transcarpathia. But I did, and I have no regrets.

A few weeks later, I bumped into Robi in the stairwell on his way up to our place. He said his father had died and he wanted me and Zoli to attend his funeral. Although I didn't love my father-in-law, I was saddened by the news of his death. Still, I didn't think it was a good idea for a four-year-old to see his dead grandfather. I told this to Robi, but of course he had a different opinion.

'Zoli needs to know that his grandfather is gone, and it would be good if you could bring him to the funeral. Don't worry, he'll be fine,' he said.

I wasn't so sure, but I didn't want to argue with him. After he let me know when the funeral was, he left. It was only afterwards I realised I hadn't even asked him what his father died of.

Robi was drunk, but he was still obviously shaken by what had happened. It's true that they didn't always get along and they had several fights, but he was still his father and he would miss him. I found out later from my dad that my father-in-law died of a heart attack, and it wasn't his first one. He shouldn't have drunk so much because it was only a matter of time before his heart gave out.

The funeral was in two days and I wanted to prepare Zoli for what he would see there. I was only a few years older than him when my mother took me to a funeral. One of Nana's sisters died, whom I had never met. It was the custom in the villages at that time (or maybe it still is) to carry the coffin on foot along the main road to the cemetery. Somehow, I got quite close to the coffin and, because it was open, I saw the dead aunt inside. Her skin was a strange yellow colour, and when I looked at her I fainted. She looked so much like my Nana that the sight made me sick and I collapsed in the crowd. I knew it was her sister lying there, yet it triggered such a reaction in me.

But later when my Nana – who was my second mother – died, I was nineteen and pregnant with Zoli. My mum didn't want me to attend the funeral or go to the cemetery with them, which I didn't mind. I had already seen Nana in the coffin as a child and I would never forget it. You can understand why I was worried about Zoli: I just hoped that he was too young to understand what was happening and that he wouldn't have bad memories of that day.

Before we left, I explained that his grandfather had died and we were going to say goodbye. We arrived at the service on time but hardly anyone was there. The open coffin was set up in the middle of the courtyard and only one elderly lady attended the funeral from the neighbours who lived near them. Next to her stood Robi, his cousin and his wife, but strangely I didn't see my mother-in-law.

After the priest said that he could not wait any longer and that he would start the service, Robi rushed into the house to fetch his mother. When she appeared at the door with him, you could see from a distance her black eye and how drunk she was. It was unbelievable that even on this day my mother-in-law couldn't stay sober; she could barely stand. My father-in-law had probably had a heart attack during a fight; although he was already dead in the coffin, the mark of his fist was still on his wife's face.

As the priest said his words, all I could think about was how this man had ruined his life and that of his family. Once upon a time, they had lived a prosperous and happy life surrounded by relatives, friends and good neighbours, of which there was now almost nothing and no one left.

Apart from Zoli, there were only six of us standing beside his coffin, which told us all we needed to know about the dead man. It was all very sad and pathetic.

After the service, a minibus took us to the cemetery where my father-in-law was laid to rest, and we were finally able to come home. Robi wanted us to stay for the funeral meal but I refused. I couldn't have swallowed a bite in the house where my father-in-law had beaten his wife a few days before and then dropped dead.

When I said goodbye to Robi I gave him some money, which he accepted. I was sure he was in debt because of the funeral, so I wanted to contribute to his expenses. He was right about Zoli, because seeing his grandfather like that really didn't hurt him. The child wasn't really attached to him so he wasn't upset by what happened and didn't miss him later.

In the following weeks and months not much happened to us. On weekdays I was at work, Zoli was in kindergarten, and on weekends we went mushroom picking, walnut or chestnut picking in the mountains.

I don't know how it all started, but at some point I started organising bus trips from the factory, or rather I helped the head organiser to organise them. Transcarpathia is a very beautiful place, so there was always somewhere to go. Once we figured out the destination, I would collect the money from the applicants, the main organiser would book the bus and the driver, and off we would go. Not only my immediate colleagues and their families could come on these trips, but anyone else from the factory. I always took Potyi with me, and Zoli who had a great time with the other children.

Usually we went for a day, but once or twice it happened that we left on Saturday morning and came back on Sunday afternoon. This cost a bit more because we had to pay for accommodation and meals, but it was worth it.

On one occasion the destination was a ski resort in the mountains. Several members of our group could ski, so they rented skis while we took sledges and slid down the smaller hills.

When I saw how confidently the skiers were gliding down the high hills, I was inspired to learn or at least to try it. But before I could rent skis an accident happened right in front of me, which immediately discouraged me from even trying. A man not far from me fell so hard that he broke his leg and an ambulance took him to hospital.

After that I changed my mind, but I wanted to remember this idea. I strapped on the skis borrowed from a colleague and pretended to ski for a photo. It was fun.

Some of us sledders went up one of the higher hills to get a better view of this beautiful landscape. A cable car took us up there, which was scary but exciting. Even though I had managed to overcome my fear of heights by then, I was still worried that I would get dizzy or that Zoli would be scared by the high altitude. Fortunately, there were no problems. We even got caught in a blizzard as we reached the top of the mountain, but it quickly passed.

Once the sky cleared and the sun came out, we were breathless at the sight around us. The mountains and hills were covered in thick snow, so everything was almost blindingly white. In the wooded areas, the snow-covered pine trees looked even more beautiful than in summer.

The scenery was dazzling, but we didn't have long to admire it as the wind picked up and another snowstorm seemed to be on its way. As the downhill slope was only for skiers, we took the footpath for pedestrians. We agreed to go up the mountain again the next day, but it didn't work out. On Sunday morning the weather was so bad that they didn't even start the cable cars. Nevertheless, we were not disappointed because we didn't miss anything.

In the spring we organised a pig roast with a small group. Years ago, when Robi and I had got together, he had included me in his circle of friends who were also our colleagues. We spent a lot of time with Peti and his wife, and the forever bachelor Ivan. Fishing and hiking were a shared passion, so we went out together almost every weekend. After Robi and I split up and he left the circle, I remained friends with them. This was good for everyone because Peti and Ivan were my immediate colleagues, while my ex-husband found new friends at his workplace.

The idea of the pig roast was supported by many people and a good team came together. The meeting place was at the edge of the forest closest to our town, which was about forty minutes away from us on foot. As it turned out, the pig was not that small (around forty kilos), so it and the equipment were taken there by car. Some people were busy preparing the spit, while the others gathered dry wood in the forest for several hours of roasting.

When the roast was finally ready, the fire was extinguished and potatoes with their skins were thrown into the hot ashes to cook. Perhaps it was because the pig had been marinating for a week, or maybe we were just really hungry, but I've never had a more delicious roast. The meat of the pig roasted on the spit was crumbly and tender and the skin was crispy. The ash-fried potatoes were a bit burnt but nobody cared. There was so much meat left over that everyone took some home. The fun company and the incredible food made that day memorable for me and I wanted to share it with you.

So that is how Zoli and I lived our little life together. My mother often told me that I should find someone for myself, that I couldn't stay alone forever. She thought Zoli needed a father, and I needed a man I could count on to help me raise my child. I didn't want to think about getting married again, so my mother's words went in one ear and out the other. I had too many bad memories about marriage and I didn't want to experience any more disappointment. At the age of twenty-four, I thought I was capable of bringing up a child on my own.

Zoli was a sensible, obedient little boy but sometimes he would get stubborn about something or throw a tantrum. I would slap him on the bottom and he would come to his senses. I know it's called cruelty nowadays, but in the seventies and eighties it was part of bringing up a child to sometimes give a smack or a slap. Even teachers were not afraid to discipline, saying that if a parent didn't teach their child manners they would. We respected them for that and would never have spoken to them the way today's pupils do.

I was a good kid but sometimes I got a slap with a ruler on my fingernails – and in the third grade I was even slapped by my form teacher for skipping class with my sister. If the teacher hadn't been so strict with me, I might have done it again and would have finished school as a failure. I wasn't a fan of hitting kids, but I thought a little slap sometimes wouldn't hurt them if they deserved it.

I remember when Zoli was about one-and-a-half-years old, I picked him up in my lap and he punched me in the face. I slapped his little hand and scolded him that he shouldn't do that. The poor kid cried, but he remembered it and never hit me again.

I've already written about how I enrolled Zoli in nursery school when he was sixteen months old and, as a Hungarian-speaking child, he found it very difficult to fit in. For a year he went into the classroom crying in the morning and came running out in the afternoon, but slowly he got used to the place, learned to speak Russian, and made a friend.

At the age of five he had problems again in kindergarten, not with the children but with one of the teachers. She was a middle-aged woman who had never married, had no children of her own and had obviously chosen the wrong profession.

She was always nervous and impatient with the children, always yelling at them. Many of the parents complained about her, but the only explanation they got was that she was like that.

Zoli mentioned several times that the teacher hated him, but I thought he was exaggerating because he was a sensitive child. Then it got to the point where he didn't want to go to kindergarten when the teacher was on duty. Sometimes I let him stay home with my mom, but he couldn't do that all the time.

One morning when the evil teacher was on duty again, Zoli went to kindergarten in a bad mood and came home in an even worse one. It turned out that not only the teacher but also his friend had been mean to him that day. They had quarrelled over some toys and got into a fight, which made him feel very bad.

I tried to reassure him that they would make up tomorrow, but he was not comforted. He was grumpy and hysterical all evening so I lost my temper several times. He wouldn't listen to me, so I finally slapped him on the butt.

Zoli looked at me with those big eyes and said, 'Mommy, are you fighting too?' He was so disappointed and so sad that my heart was about to break.

That's when I realised what I had done: not only had he fought with his friend but I, his mother, had hurt him too. The poor child was crying so much I could hardly calm him down. When I put him to bed and we said our evening prayers together (as Nana had taught me), I stayed by his bedside for a while. While I was stroking his hair and waiting for him to fall asleep, my little boy looked up at me and said with a very serious face, 'I wish I had never been born!'

That was too much for me; I felt like I was being strangled and suddenly I couldn't breathe. I was sobbing so hard that I had to run out of the room so Zoli wouldn't see me. I rushed straight to the toilet, put my hands over my mouth so that no one would hear me, and I cried.

I felt so guilty, I can't even describe it. How could I have treated him like that after he'd had such a bad day? What kind of mother did that? How could I not see how much he was suffering if he could say something like that to me? How could a five-year-old wish he'd never been born? I cried so hard I could hardly stop. I swore I would never hit my little boy again; I would be a better mother and not disappoint him anymore.

When I went back to the room, he was sound asleep but the sadness was still present on his face. The next day Zoli made up with his friend and everything was fine again. He managed to forget about that day and what he had said to me that night, but I will never forget it.

After a week or two, the teacher was the topic again and by then I was sure that Zoli was not exaggerating. I don't think I mentioned before (or did I?) that my brother had been living in Hungary for a while. He had been there as a Soviet soldier and after he was discharged he continued to work as an interpreter for a few years. When he came home on leave, he always brought us goodies and sweets.

One morning Zoli took some sweets to give to his friend but the evil teacher noticed and immediately took the package away. According to my little boy, when she saw that they were Hungarian sweets she shouted at him even more and then gave the sweets to the other children. As if that wasn't enough, she called him a mocking nickname for the rest of the afternoon.

It was obvious that the teacher hated Hungarians, which is why she hated my little boy so much, but calling him a name was too much. I remembered when my mother sent Potyi and me to summer camp and the Russian kids called us Hungarian goats because they didn't understand our language. It hurt that we were ostracized, though we didn't care that much because we were only with them for a short time.

Zoli, on the other hand, had to go to kindergarten for another year before starting school. And if the teacher (the teacher!!) mocked the child, sooner or later the others would start mocking him too. I couldn't let that happen; I had to protect my son.

The next day I left my son at home with my mum and after work I went to the nursery to talk to the director. I didn't get anywhere with her; she just told me what she'd told all the other parents who complained, that there was nothing wrong with the teacher, she was just a bit rude.

After that, I thought it was best to ask for Zoli's papers, collect his indoor clothes and never take him to kindergarten again. I'd talked to my mum the night before and she'd agreed to look after him until he went to school. From then on, she took him to the market, the hobby gardens and even to the cemetery to clean the graves of Nana and Grandpa. I don't consider myself a bad person but at the time I wished that the teacher would get fired and stop making the children's lives miserable.

Later that summer, Robi and his mother moved to a small apartment in our street. I don't know how he managed to make such a good exchange because the apartment was obviously worth more than the house they were living in. He certainly didn't have the money, but it was none of my business so I didn't ask him.

We were living across the street from each other and we could have seen each other's windows if it hadn't been for the little park between us. It was uncomfortable because my ex-mother-in-law was always sitting at the window watching people walking down the street. I could never go to the corner shop without her noticing me. I would wave my hand in greeting and she would wave back if she was sober enough to recognise me.

Once Robi invited me in to show me around their new home. The one-bedroom apartment was in very good condition, with a nicely renovated bathroom. Since they had left a lot of junk behind and brought only the furniture they needed, they had decorated the room quite well. The beautiful pictures painted by his uncle back in the day were in the hallway. I thought that Robi could give one of them to his son as a memento, but I said nothing. That was the last time I saw the paintings because someone told me later that Robi had been slowly selling them and spending the money on alcohol.

At first Zoli was taken and returned by his father at the appointed time but after a while, because we lived so close to each other, he went by himself. He was big enough to play with the children downstairs, so it was no problem for him to go to his father's place on his own. Our street wasn't busy; because of the cobblestones, cars drove slowly and Zoli had been trained to cross the road, so I let him go with a calm heart.

There was nothing wrong with that for a while. Every other Sunday at three o'clock I sent my little boy to his father's place, and Robi sent him home on time. Then one day Zoli came home early, running in and crying, saying he would never go to his father again. He told me that his father had given him a military jacket and then Robi and his friend had laughed at him. They told him to roll around in the long jacket and that made them laugh even harder.

The poor kid took it very badly, so it was understandable that he freaked out and didn't want to see his dad anymore. I guessed both men were drunk, but that didn't give Robi the right to humiliate his son.

If he was such an idiot, he would suffer the consequences; I was certainly not going to force my son to go to his father's house. I told Robi the same thing when I met him on the street a few days later. He looked at me blankly, as he had done so many times before when I accused him of something. He thought nothing had happened that would upset Zoli like that.

'You mean he ran home crying over nothing? Or were you so drunk you didn't even notice?' I asked angrily.

He finally admitted that they had a little too much to drink (I wonder how much?) and it seemed like fun to put that military jacket on Zoli.

'It may have seemed like fun to you, but your son felt very bad that you laughed at him. If you knew your child better, you'd know how sensitive he is to such things.'

With some reluctance, Robi finally admitted that he'd made a mistake and that he would talk to his son when he came for him next time. But Zoli still didn't want to see his father; when he heard the doorbell, he locked the bedroom door and did not come out until his father had gone.

All I could advise Robi to do was to leave Zoli alone for a while and then, when he calmed down, try to approach him again – but that never happened. Zoli avoided his father; if he saw him on the street, he hid or ran straight home. He even refused to go to the corner shop for bread because his grandmother would see him from the window.

I told him that his father regretted what he had done and that it would never happen again, but my little boy was adamant. There was nothing Robi could do about it; if he went to court to assert his rights as a father, he might be even worse off. If I was asked, I would tell the truth, which would not be in Robi's best interests. The fact that he was never sober when his son visited, and once drunkenly passed out leaving his three-and-a-half-year-old child unattended, would certainly not be appreciated by the court and they might even take away his visitation rights.

Robi didn't take any chances but he blamed me for everything. According to him, I said bad things about him to his son and incited the boy against him, which was why Zoli didn't want to see him.

'I could say many bad things about you, but I don't,' I said. 'Face it – your actions have consequences! You drove me away and now you've done the same to your son. It's easy to blame others for what happened but you have only yourself to blame.'

I don't think Robi gave my words a second thought. He tried a few more times to reconcile with his son but it didn't work, and he gave up. He gave up on Zoli as he had given up on his son from his first marriage, whom he hadn't seen since he was a baby. His new friends, his drinking buddies, offered him consolation and compensated for his lost family.

I don't want to sound insensitive but I don't regret it. I was grateful that Zoli hadn't been harmed by his drunk father or witnessed the horrors I had. My father-in-law had died but I don't think the fights stopped in that family. Robi was probably still aggressive and beat his mother, which fortunately my little boy didn't have to see.

Life went on. With Robi out of the picture, I had to pay even more attention to Zoli's upbringing. I wanted to make him a good person so I couldn't make any mistakes.

Zoli didn't want to hear about reconciling with his father, and I couldn't blame him, but what did surprise me was how a child of almost six could be so stubborn and persistent. I really hoped that my mum wasn't right about him growing up without a father and becoming unmanageable. So far he'd been fine except when he refused to go down to the corner store.

Zoli made friends with a boy two years older than him who lived next door, and often went over to play with him. In good weather they spent a lot of time downstairs with the other children, which I didn't mind because at least my son had company. Our back yard wasn't an exciting place but the boys always found something to do to keep them from getting bored.

In order for my little boy to hang out with the others, he had to follow the rules. He was not allowed to go outside the back yard or the small park, and he had to come home before dark or when I called him. Zoli did not break these rules but I still kept an eye on him from upstairs.

One time when I looked down from the balcony, I didn't see him in the back yard with the other children. I thought maybe he was playing in the park with his friend, although they rarely went there because of his father. I started shouting his name but there was no response; I went from one balcony to another and kept shouting but nothing happened. Slowly it got dark and the back yard emptied and the children went home, only Zoli was nowhere to be seen.

I was terrified, panicking. Where could he be? What could have happened to him? Perhaps he'd run into his father and made up with him, and now he was at his place and hadn't noticed that it was dark?

If I went to Robi's and Zoli wasn't there, I'd have to listen for years about what a bad mother I was. Then it occurred to me that maybe the boys had come up earlier and now Zoli was in the flat next door, but it turned out the other kid wasn't home either. That actually made me feel a little relieved because they were somewhere together, not wandering around in the dark alone.

I was very nervous, but my neighbours reassured me that they would turn up soon. I couldn't understand how they could be so calm while I was so nervous. If I'd known where those two kids were, I would have gone after them – but they could be anywhere, so I figured I'd better stay home and wait, which wasn't easy.

I don't know what time it was when Zoli finally jerked the door handle. Before I could even open the door, he was crying in the hallway because he knew he was in trouble. His clothes were covered in dirt, as were his face and hands, but at least he was in one piece. I wanted to hug him but I didn't; I sent him to the bathroom to wash. In my heart I was glad that he was safe and sound, but I had to be strict with him to make sure it didn't happen again. If I didn't punish him now, he wouldn't learn from his mistake.

When I asked Zoli where they'd been, he remained stubbornly silent, which made me even more angry. I gave him a good scolding and then I put him in a corner of the room. Having sworn to myself that I would never lay a hand on him again, I devised that punishment to make him understand what he had done. I even put a large pot of stinging cactus in front of him so he couldn't sit down or come out when I wasn't in the room.

After a while I asked him if he was hungry and he nodded his head. I handed him a plain piece of bread and he immediately started to eat it. I couldn't stand it and ran to the toilet again to cry; I wanted to be strict with him but it was so hard. It was cruel of me to do what I did, and it hurt me so much, but I had no choice. He'd really scared me by not coming home on time and I didn't want to go through that again. He was everything to me and if anything happened to him, I would never forgive myself. I had to be strong, even if it was hard.

After an hour or so, I let Zoli out of the corner because I thought we had both suffered enough. I told him how worried I'd been and made him promise never to do it again.

After dinner, he told me that he and his friend went to the railway depot where they were climbing on an old locomotive. It couldn't have been a more dangerous place for these two kids to be, and we were lucky there wasn't a tragedy. Our neighbours worked for the railway and had probably taken their boy with them several times, so the child knew the way. Since he was Zoli's best friend, I didn't want to keep them apart; I just hoped that my punishment had been a good lesson for him. I explained how dangerous what they were doing was and that children should never be in such places.

At the time, the punishment my son received seemed cruel, but over time it proved effective. Fortunately it was the first and last time he had to stand behind the cactus in the corner. After that, Zoli was always home on time and never went to play with his friend at the railway station again.

Even though I tried to raise Zoli strictly, I began to doubt I could do it alone. I started to believe that my mother was right: my son needed a father. I felt sick to my stomach thinking that one day he might grow up to be a man like Robi but unfortunately it was possible because he might have inherited his father's genes. I wanted to be proud of my son when he grew up, not ashamed of him.

If he had a stepfather who was a good influence and someone he looked up to, maybe his future would be different. Even though my mum had been so strict and yelled at us a lot, we didn't always listen to her, but my dad only had to raise his voice once and we obeyed immediately. He was the head of the family, the man of the house, and although we were a little afraid of him we respected him and looked up to him. I started to defy him when I fell in love with Robi, but as it turned out I should have listened to him.

I felt inclined to reconnect my life with someone because of Zoli. My mother already had a prospective husband for me, Ivan from our group of friends. My parents had known his family for a long time and thought well of them. According to her, I didn't have to be afraid of him because he wasn't aggressive and would never hurt me. I was aware of that because I had known him for a few years, but I was still afraid of him.

I knew he was a good man; I could count on him for everything and I liked him as a friend, but I wasn't in love with him. Then I thought about the fact that my Nana wasn't in love with my grandfather when they got together, yet they lived happily together for more than thirty years. Why shouldn't I?

Maybe in time Ivan and I would fall in love and live happily ever after. My marriage, based on a great love (at least from my side), ended up being a huge disappointment, so I would not make that mistake again. I would only marry Ivan or anyone else if our relationship worked. I needed to live with my partner for a while to see if we had a future together.

When I told my mum, she was a bit surprised by my decision but didn't try to talk me out of it. Nowadays it's normal, but in the early nineties people who lived together were criticised; such a relationship was called a 'wild marriage'. Since I was the black sheep of the family because of my divorce, a wild marriage could not tarnish my reputation.

And now I have come to a part of my life story that I cannot remember. No matter how much I try to remember how the conversation about moving in together with Ivan went, I can't recall it; probably it was so unpleasant that my brain erased the whole thing. But I do remember that Ivan agreed to live with me; he just asked me to go to his house so we could tell his parents together. It seemed like a good idea because if we were moving in together, it would be good to get to know his family first.

Unfortunately, the meeting did not turn out as I expected. I already knew Ivan's younger brother because he was a classmate of my sister's, but I had never met his older brother and his parents. I was surprised when I walked into the house and saw them.

Ivan was half a head shorter than me, while his brother and father were huge next to him and it felt like we were standing next to two giants. Ivan, his younger brother, his mum and I were miniature compared to them. I felt uncomfortable around them from the first minute and it got worse later.

Telling the parents together did not work because Ivan did not dare to speak. His father kept asking me questions, which made me more and more uncomfortable and tense, but I pulled myself together and told them that I was moving in with Ivan soon.

Although it was the first time he'd met me, Ivan's father started shouting at me and his older brother joined in. They were so outraged that we wanted to live together without being married that I could hardly speak after that. I was surprised and scared by their behaviour; I had not expected such a reaction from them.

Ivan, his younger brother and his mother remained silent so I had to defend myself. I don't remember exactly what I said to them, but I ended by saying that we were grown-up people and we could do what we wanted.

The father kept saying his piece, but I got up and left. I felt bad that my future partner didn't protect me from his father and brother, or at least prepare me for their reaction. He probably knew there would be a fight, yet he had let me talk to them.

My parents thought they were nice people but I didn't agree. I didn't think it was normal for them to yell at me like that when they didn't even know me. What could I expect later if I became part of this family? It was obvious that you had to do what Ivan's father and brother said and others had no right to say anything.

I'd known Ivan for almost eight years, but I'd had no idea he was living in such a repressive home. We often went hiking and fishing together, but he hardly ever talked about his family; that was understandable because I wouldn't have boasted about such a family either.

My mother was disappointed when I told her what had happened. She said the parents should have been happy that someone was finally moving in with their thirty-five-year-old son. Just like Robi, Ivan was ten years older than me and, as far as I was aware, he had never had a girlfriend.

'If it's up to me, he won't have one,' I thought, and that was the end of the matter.

I was a little annoyed but in a way I was also relieved because I hadn't been totally happy about moving in with Ivan, though I'd thought it was worth a try.

Much to my surprise, the next day at work Ivan told me that everything was fine and we could move in together. I was surprised that his father was 'allowing' us to do that after the way he'd acted the day before. I didn't know whether to be happy or not, but it was too late to back out so I agreed.

We started planning our life together, which included finding a place to rent. I was sure that, despite their big house, I would never live with Ivan's parents but I didn't want our future to start in my home either. Luckily for us, Peti's grandmother had a small building in her courtyard that was vacant. After Peti talked to her, we went to see it and moved in over the weekend.

Our new home was just a twenty square-metre room that was a kitchen, living room and bedroom. It was similar to the studio apartments we have nowadays, except that it didn't have a bathroom: we used the toilet in the courtyard and went home to our own families to bathe. That was not a problem because our rented home was only a few minutes away.

The old lady was very nice to us because she only asked for a small amount of rent, which we could easily pay. We agreed that we could stay there until late autumn as the little house could not be heated in winter; that was fine because five or six months would give us time to see whether the relationship worked or not.

A few days later, Ivan confessed that his father had allowed us to move in together because he'd promised that we would get married soon.

'He allowed us?' I thought I would explode with rage. 'You are thirty-five and I am twenty-five – why do we need parental permission to live together? We are adults, not teenagers! Besides, why make promises you're not sure you can keep? If our relationship doesn't work out, are we still getting married because you promised your father?'

Ivan always stammered a bit, probably because of the circumstances at home, but I tried not to notice. Now he was so embarrassed that he just babbled and couldn't say anything meaningful. In the end I felt sorry for him; I shouldn't have pushed him so hard because it was the only way he could get his father to let us move in together.

Ivan and I had known each other for a long time so I thought that our life together would be smooth but it wasn't. It must have been a very smart and experienced person who said, 'You will only get to know each other by living together.' As long as we were just friends there was a lot I didn't know or could ignore, but as his partner these things started to bother me.

I had a vague picture of each of them. Peti was the genius who knew everything and was right about everything (in his opinion); Robi was the one who would comment on everything and was always arguing that he was right, and Ivan was the nodding man. He didn't have an opinion of his own and he never argued with anyone.

I didn't think about it at the time and I didn't look for the reason why he was like that, but in the first few weeks of living together I realised why he behaved like that – and I didn't like it. Unfortunately, Ivan didn't care about anything. I didn't expect him to be political or to watch incomprehensible political programmes, but I wanted him to be informed about what was going on around us.

In our family it was normal for my dad and I to watch the evening news to find out what was happening in the country and the world. Before the internet, that was how we kept up to date with what was going on around us. Back then, the news was real news, not just about who had been murdered or whose house had burnt down. I would have liked to introduce this habit to Ivan but it didn't really work out. Ivan sat with me for the half hour that the news lasted but it was obvious that he didn't care or understand what it was about.

The same was true for newspapers. Like my dad, Robi and his dad had also read the papers (provided they were sober enough) because it was a natural thing to do. I didn't have time for that, so I mostly flipped through the headlines because I was interested. I tried to make Ivan curious, to get him interested in something, but it didn't work. Even though I bought the newspapers and he supposedly read them, he couldn't recall anything when I asked him.

Once I entered the house to find Ivan sitting at the table with a newspaper in his hand. I was so happy that he was finally interested, but when I approached him I saw that he was holding it upside down. That's when I gave up; I didn't push him anymore because there was no point.

It may seem that these things were not as terrible as what I'd endured with Robi, but that's not how I experienced it. It was important for me to talk to my partner about more than what was for dinner or lunch the next day. It also bothered me that Ivan had to be controlled, that he didn't have a will of his own or an independent thought.

My mum said it was fine; the important thing was to live with a good person and accept him for who he was. She said I couldn't change him so I should be content with what I had, but I couldn't be.

I think the problem was that I wasn't in love with him so it was hard for me to overlook his faults. Our relationship as friends was not going to develop any further; in fact, we were backing away and becoming estranged. Even though we seemed to be getting along, without emotions our lives were empty.

I was happy that Ivan and Zoli got on well together, and I am not exaggerating when I say that he got on better with my son than with me. One of the reasons was because Ivan had a motorbike with a sidecar that Zoli loved to ride in. I don't know how legal it was for me to sit with the child on my lap in the sidecar, but we were never stopped and fined by the police. We only went to the nearby lakes by motorbike and still took the train to the mountains for mushrooming or hiking. Peti also had a motorbike, and so did Robi at the time (if you remember), but he had an accident and crashed it.

Summer came. As the weather was getting better, we spent most weekends outdoors. Peti was with us all the time but his wife came less and less often, which I found a little strange. When they did come together, there was often a noticeable tension between them, and they argued in front of us, which was quite unpleasant. They probably had problems that they didn't share with us and we didn't want to get involved. The truth is that I didn't mind when his wife didn't come with us because Peti was different then. As I mentioned, he was the genius in the group: he was knowledgeable about history and politics, as well as other things that came up.

He could talk for hours about interesting things that were impossible to get tired of. He was like a university professor, and I listened attentively; no teacher at school could keep your attention the way Peti did.

I don't know where he got this knowledge from because he didn't go to college or university, yet he was much smarter than anyone else I knew. When I told him that he was wasting his talents as a factory worker when he could do so much better, he just smiled. He loved his job and had no desire to go anywhere else. I was certainly glad to be part of his circle of friends and listen to his 'lectures'.

Ivan wasn't such an enthusiastic listener; although he kept nodding, it was obvious that he wasn't paying attention. He paid more attention to Zoli and let me listen to Peti because I was interested in what he had to say.

Then one day Peti had some other business to take care of, so we went fishing without him although we shouldn't have. We didn't catch any fish because of the heat, but that wasn't the main reason why I regretted going. I was so used to Peti being there with us and talking all the time that I missed his company. I loved his lectures so much that I'd become addicted to them and the day was boring without him. I couldn't talk to Ivan because he cut every single topic short, and it was obvious that we were not on the same wavelength. Then I wondered: if we were so mismatched, why did we want to spend our lives together? In the summer we managed to get by because we were always going somewhere and usually not alone, but what about the long winter days?

Ivan was a good man, which I should have appreciated, but he was not for me. The more I got to know him, the greater the gap between us grew and I was getting irritated by his behaviour. By then we had been together for three months and I was beginning to realise that we were not going to have a future together. Fortunately, he hadn't mentioned marriage again because I think he was afraid. Neither had I met his 'nice' family since the quarrel, but that was fine. I'm sure they would have urged us to marry but they didn't get the chance.

After a few days of the boring fishing, his brother unexpectedly came to visit us. He just said hello to me, then ignored me. After all the shouting we'd had with his father about a wild marriage, I wasn't surprised.

He put a bottle of wine on the table and sat down without being invited to. Ivan quickly took out two glasses and poured the wine. They didn't offer me a drink, not that I would have accepted it.

I continued to prepare dinner and was glad not to have to chat with our unexpected guest, but as we were in the same room I could hear what they were talking about. The conversation was one-sided because Ivan barely spoke, just hummed and nodded.

The subject was their childhood, which I would have enjoyed listening to if it hadn't been presented in the way it was. What I understood was that Ivan's brother must have been a real bully back then, always picking on his two brothers; that may be why Ivan had started stuttering.

I was sure that this bullying behaviour hadn't changed because the brother was teasing and taunting his brother at the table. Perhaps it was the tension, or maybe the two glasses of wine had something to do with it, but Ivan suddenly burst into tears. I had my back to them and I turned around to see what was happening. Yes, Ivan was crying like a little child.

His brother was sitting opposite him, so pleased with himself that it was disgusting. When I looked at him and saw the smirk on his face, I wanted to slap him. Even though he was twice my size, I wasn't afraid of him and I started shouting at him. 'You came here to humiliate your brother! Aren't you ashamed?'

Of course he wasn't ashamed, but at least the grin was gone from his face. He really didn't like my tone, but he didn't say anything. He just looked at me angrily, then got up from the table and left without saying goodbye.

Ivan still did not move from his seat. After he stopped crying, he could not look me in the eye; he was ashamed. He was in a bad mood all evening; he didn't want to play with Zoli and after dinner he went straight to bed. But I stayed up late thinking about that afternoon, thinking that my partner cried like a little child was so pathetic. I'd had to stop his brother because he couldn't defend himself.

How could I live with this coward? What would he do when he needed to protect me or my son from someone? Would he hide behind my back? For me, a man should be a man, not a crying child.

I would have liked Zoli to have a role model, a foster father to look up to, but it would not be Ivan. After what I'd seen I was sure that I had to end this relationship, and I had to do it as soon as possible. I would rather stay alone and raise my son the best I could, but I would not be the wife of such a man.

Ivan must have had a difficult childhood because of his father and his brother; that had affected his adulthood and I felt sorry for him, but pity was not enough to tie my life with him. For days I had been feeling that it wasn't going to work between us, so why should we pretend? I wasn't happy in the relationship, and I didn't think he was either, so what was the point? Why were we wasting each other's time?

The next afternoon I didn't pick up Zoli from my mother's because I wanted to talk to Ivan alone. The night before, I'd figured out what I was going to tell him that wouldn't hurt him or make him feel guilty. He didn't have any self-confidence; if this breakup went badly, he might never move on and remain a bachelor forever. I wanted his life to go well and for him to be happy with someone. By then it was clear that someone wouldn't be me.

That afternoon I said things like, 'It was a mistake for us to move in together because we don't suit each other at all. If we couldn't make each other happy in three months, we won't be able to do it later. For us, being friends worked better than living together so it is better to part.' Then I encouraged him to find a partner he was happy with because he deserved to be happy.

Ivan took our breakup much better than I expected. I had chosen my words carefully so as not to hurt him. He was a little sad, but perhaps my encouragement had given him hope to move on.

Then he asked me something that absolutely took me aback. 'Will you hook me up with someone?'

'No,' I said bluntly, then turned so he wouldn't see how disappointed I was.

It was a very inappropriate question but he didn't even notice. How could he ask me that? We were separating at the weekend, which meant we were spending two more nights in the same bed, and he was asking me that? I had tried to make our break-up as bearable as possible for him, but I didn't expect him to get over me so quickly! His words made me feel bad, but that was okay because in two days I'd be free again and that made me feel good.

As the evening wore on, Ivan's only worry was what he would say to his father when he got home.

'Just what I told you, because it's the truth,' I said.

Actually, it was only a half-truth but if I had told him everything I thought about him it would have hurt him. I wanted us to separate peacefully and remain friends but our relationship was not the same afterwards because the void that had formed between us over the three months remained and we slowly drifted apart. Ivan still went on the factory outings I organised, but we no longer sought each other's company.

A few days after Zoli and I moved home, my sister invited us to her place by the Caspian Sea. Since she'd got married, she and her two sons had only come home twice to visit, but now she had a daughter and another son so travelling had become a problem. A few years earlier when the youngest child was born, my mother and my younger sister had spent a month there helping her. Now it was mine and Potyi's turn to visit, and my mum and Zoli couldn't stay at home either.

The plane tickets were very expensive, so we tried to get to Dagestan by train and bus. It took four days and was terribly tiring but it was worth it because we had a very good two weeks with my sister and her family. Zoli also had a great time because the children treated him like a brother from the very first moment.

We went to the beach a few times but the water was so cold that we couldn't swim. It was very hot and that's why I couldn't understand how the water in the Black Sea could be so pleasantly warm and the Caspian Sea so cold. Some people didn't mind and went into the water but we weren't so brave. If we weren't sunbathing on the beach, we walked around with the kids or shopped at the market for lunch.

The two weeks flew by and soon we were on our way home. Unfortunately the way back was no shorter than the way there, but at least we knew what to expect. We travelled by sleeper train, then by normal passenger train, then by bus and finally by high-speed train. As we waited hours for connections, one of our suitcases was almost stolen at the Kiev train station.

The journey home took four days, but we managed. Today I would definitely not take a six-year-old on such a long trip, I would save up for a plane ticket instead. Luckily Zoli didn't complain and he took the ordeal much better than I expected. All in all, our holiday went well and we also helped my sister so she could relax a bit too.

Zoli wasn't in kindergarten any longer. Because he'd turned six two months ago, I enrolled him in primary school. My little boy was in first grade and, as he was the youngest and one of the smallest children, I was a little worried about him. Luckily we got a very nice, retired teacher who promised to take good care of him. Thanks to her, Zoli settled in quickly and enjoyed going to school, unlike kindergarten.

During the autumn I continued to organise the factory trips; they were not very frequent, they were better than nothing. Strangely enough, Peti and his wife never came with us though Ivan never missed a single one.

One day, luck smiled on him and he met a woman who was new to the factory who came on a trip with us. After that they spent all their free time together and a few months later they got married; as far as I know, they had two children. I was glad that Ivan had found a partner who saw the goodness in him and accepted him for who he was. When he moved away from home his 'nice' family could no longer control and bully him.

Ivan's life turned out well but I still hadn't found my partner – not that I was looking for one. I longed for love, but since that didn't happen I resigned myself to my fate. That autumn I enrolled in a tailoring course because I wanted to sew clothes for myself. I could use our hand-folding sewing machine at home for minor repairs but I didn't have the skills for more serious work.

The course was held twice a week and started right after work, so my mum or Potyi fetched Zoli from school. I had been there for a few weeks when two guys started to take turns to accompany me. They were both mechanics in the factory and my only contact with them was to tell them when a machine broke down in our department.

I had known them for years but they'd never shown any interest in me. This went on for about three weeks and, although I was puzzled by their approach, I liked their attention so I let them accompany me. It was as if they were both flirting with me but they never asked me out on a real date or for coffee.

I started to feel uncomfortable when one of them confessed that they'd discussed who would walk me to class and who would walk me home in the evening after the course. Then the truth came out, which I was not happy about at all: their group leader told me that the guys had a bet on who would get me first.

'They made a bet on me? What am I, a horse?'

They didn't care about me, they were just messing with me and laughing at me behind my back. I felt so bad that I cried and several of my colleagues asked what was wrong. I was ashamed to tell them what those two guys had done to me because it was so humiliating.

When I had pulled myself together, I went to the mechanics' room and told them that they'd lost the bet because neither of them would ever get me. I was very angry with them but even more angry with myself because I hadn't realised what was going on around me. Why was I not suspicious that they hadn't noticed me before and now suddenly both of them were interested in me? After that I walked to the course alone until I finished it.

Meanwhile, spring had arrived and the trees were in full bloom, but I couldn't enjoy my favourite season as much as before. In fact, I couldn't enjoy anything because I was always grumpy and impatient. I missed my old life – not my marriage to Robi, but the life before and after that period. I missed my friends with whom I could go fishing.

When I remembered how much fun I'd had with them last year, how much I'd laughed and how interested I was in Peti's 'lectures', my heart sank. I had broken up with Ivan nine months earlier and I hadn't been fishing since.

I didn't regret that we'd split up because at least one of us moved on and found the one who made him happy, but our circle of friends no longer existed. Everyone was living their own lives and I couldn't find my place. I became more and more depressed.

Then one Friday afternoon Peti sat down at my table and we started talking. That was the first time he brought up his marriage and told me how bad it was. He said they were fighting a lot and it was getting worse, but he didn't want to leave his wife because he would lose his little girl.

I knew that his son from his first marriage would not talk to him, so it was understandable that he was clinging to his current family. His daughter was only two years older than Zoli and she adored her father. It was bad to see Peti so sad and sorry that he and his wife ended up like that.

Over the years we had gone hiking and fishing together a lot, but somehow his wife and I never had never become friends. She'd always made me feel that she was better than me as she came from a better of family, graduated from university and was now an office worker in a factory on a good salary.

I didn't mind that there was a distance between us; the main thing was that I was in that circle of friends. The group had fallen apart, but it turned out it was not only me who regretted it but also Peti. He said that he had been fishing a few times that year, but it was bad going alone. Then we got nostalgic about the good old days, which made me miss that life even more.

'Why don't we go fishing tomorrow, just the two of us?' Peti asked unexpectedly.

'Let's go,' I replied without thinking.

After discussing where and when to meet in the morning, Peti got up from the table and went to work, then he looked back and winked, making me blush. I was embarrassed and confused. We were just friends, so why did I feel like he was hitting on me? In the eight and a half years we'd known each other, that had never happened before – so why now? True, his marriage was on the rocks but I couldn't imagine him cheating on his wife, especially with me.

I tried to shake the thought away; I had probably imagined wink meant more than it really had. I told myself we were going fishing alone because there was no one else to go with. But why was it so hard to tell my mum where I was going the next day, and why did I hide who I was going with? I knew it wasn't right but I was so eager to get outdoors that I ignored my intuition.

It was still half-dark when I left early in the morning, but even so I immediately recognised Peti standing next to his motorbike. Probably because of the wink and because I was thinking about him too much, my heart was pounding and I blushed as I approached him.

Peti kissed me on the lips instead of greeting me, then he put the helmet in my hand and got on the bike. I was so embarrassed that my hands started to shake and I could barely buckle my helmet. I got behind him, put my arm around his waist and knew at that moment that I was lost. From that moment on, the two of us were no longer just friends.

I fell in love with Peti; I shouldn't have but I couldn't control my feelings. I had deluded myself into believing that I didn't need anyone, that men had only disappointed me, but that wasn't the case. I was longing for the love of a man who understood me and with whom I felt comfortable.

I never expected in my wildest dreams that this would be a married man. Maybe subconsciously I had been in love with Peti for a long time, but those feelings only surfaced with that wink and our first motorbike ride together.

Months passed and we were very happy, only secretly. I had found my soul mate and I wanted to tell the world but I couldn't. We had too much to lose; if our affair came to light, I couldn't have looked my parents in the eye, and if Peti's family had fallen apart because of me I couldn't have forgiven myself. So I had to keep secrets and lie just to spend a few happy hours with the man I loved.

What I didn't consider was my remorse, which was slowly consuming me. I was an honest person and I had never lied to my family before, but now I was forced to and it was destroying my nerves. When Peti and I spent a day together, we were the happiest people in the world, but on other days I had a terrible guilty conscience. I found it harder and harder to lie to my mum about who I was going fishing with, and I deliberately said the names of people that she couldn't run into on the street the next day.

I was bad at keeping secrets from Potyi, but Zoli was the one I had the most trouble with. When he asked me why I never took him with me, I could hardly look him in the eye. 'We're leaving very early when you're still fast asleep,' I replied, which was only partly true. The reason we were going so early was to avoid running into people we knew.

'Sometimes you could go later and then you could take the kid with you,' my mother commented.

'It's not up to me,' I said and my stomach twisted at the new lie.

'Yes, it is up to me! I have to say no and break up with him,' I thought, but I didn't. The next day, when Peti and I met and I got on the bike behind him, I forgot about everything. I wanted to be happy, and I was.

That happiness came at a price: I could hardly eat or sleep because of the constant stress and I couldn't cope with the guilt. By not allowing Zoli to come fishing with me, I had disappointed him and it upset me. I felt like a terrible person and a bad mother, yet I did nothing about it. I convinced myself that Peti and I had no future together and that I had to end the relationship as soon as possible, but I just couldn't do it.

By mid-summer my nerves were completely shot. I couldn't live this double life because it wasn't like me, it wasn't who I was. I had to find the strength to break up with Peti, but I couldn't when I saw him every day at work. I needed distance and a clear head to make this difficult decision, so I took all my leave and went to a rehabilitation health centre for a whole month. I took Zoli and Potyi with me on this 'holiday' to make up for the missed fishing.

The institution was in a very beautiful place in the middle of the forest in the Carpathians. Since we had bought the cheaper tickets, we were accommodated in a small wooden house barely a few square meters but it served its purpose. It only had two beds, a table with two chairs and a chest of drawers for our clothes. The toilets and showers were in another building, which we shared with other people who were staying in similar houses. There were no cooking facilities, but we didn't need them as three meals a day were included.

Since we were surrounded by forest, we walked for several hours a day in the fresh air and picked mushrooms, which we dried in the sun. We discovered a meadow with a small stream nearby where we went to sunbathe.

Not only did the staff provide recreation but also entertainment. Every evening there was music and dancing in a large pavilion. Potyi and I didn't go, we just listened to the music as we sat in front of our little house while Zoli slept inside.

Time passed very slowly in the health centre and the days seemed to be long. It was a peaceful and relaxing environment, which was just what I needed. Maybe it was the fresh air and long walks but I slept better at night and my appetite returned. I felt stronger and that helped me make the decision to break up with Peti as soon as I got home.

A week before the end of our 'holiday', we were walking back to our house from the canteen when a motorcyclist stopped beside us. My heart missed a beat when I saw it was Peti. I was bewildered. He said he'd been in the neighbourhood and thought he would pay us a visit. Then, turning his back on Potyi and Zoli, he faced me and said almost soundlessly, 'I missed you.'

I'd missed him too but I only realised it when he was standing in front of me. I loved him too much to break up with him.

My life hadn't changed at all but Potyi's changed radically. She met a guy in the rehabilitation centre with whom she later had a serious relationship. Pisti seemed to be a nice, decent person, so everyone in our family liked him. The situation was not so clear with Pisti's family: he was still young when his parents divorced and his father remarried and started a new family. They immediately took a liking to Potyi and were genuinely happy. Pisti's mother, on the other hand, was against their relationship from the very first moment. She'd never married again and was angry with the whole world because of her own unhappiness. For her, none of the girls her son introduced her to was good enough.

But Potyi and Pisti loved each other and wanted to be together, so they went to the local registry office and secretly requested marriage. Of course, it was no secret to us because we were happy to welcome him into our family.

The rings were bought, the wedding dress was chosen but with only a week to go until the wedding something happened that no one expected: Pisti unexpectedly came to our house, broke the engagement and asked for the ring back. It turned out that his mother had found out about the wedding (maybe he was the one who told her) and she was furious. She could not bear the thought of her son, whom she had raised alone, leaving her and moving in with a girl in another town. She threatened to kill herself the day they got married.

At the end of the argument, she gave her son a choice between her and Potyi. Although Pisti was a good man, he was also weak and dared not stand up for his love; he chose his mother instead.

A few months after they broke up, Potyi was standing in front of the mirror combing her hair while we talked. Suddenly I noticed something, something I hadn't noticed before. 'Have you gained weight? You look like a pregnant woman,' I laughed.

Instead of laughing with me, she replied seriously, 'Because maybe I am.'

Sure enough, my sister was pregnant and her belly was already showing.

'Does Pisti know?' I asked her.

'Yes,' came the short answer.

So he knew about it and he'd still chosen his mother. A week before the wedding, he gave up not only his love but also his child.

If I noticed, sooner or later others would find out Potyi's secret, so we decided to talk to my mum and she would soften up my dad. I was sure that my mum would not let Potyi down just as she'd stood by me when I was in trouble, but my dad was different. His daughter having a baby without being married was as much a disgrace to him as my divorce. Again, he was concerned about what people would say when they found out.

'Every miracle lasts for three days,' my mum said, 'People talk about it for a while, then they find something else to talk about.' As my dad couldn't respond to that, the family discussion came to an end.

A few months later, something happened that affected me too, but now I'm going to jump ahead in time. At the beginning of May, Potyi gave birth to a baby girl whom she named Leda. For some time, we'd hoped that Pisti would have a conscience and show up to see his baby but unfortunately that never happened; he wasn't interested in his child.

I don't know why, but after a while my dad changed a lot for the better. A very special relationship developed between the little girl and her grandfather. While he had no patience with his other grandchildren and would often shout at them, Leda could do anything and he didn't mind. When she could walk, they walked around the neighbourhood for several hours a day and tried every swing on their way. My dad always had a few coins in his pocket, which he used to buy a treat for the little girl.

Leda didn't have a father to take her to the playground so my dad probably wanted to fill that void. He did it so well that she adored her grandfather, and the feeling was mutual.

Now I'm going back again in time to when Leda was still in her mother's tummy and I was still in love with a married man. Sometime in the spring I was told at the factory that if I paid a certain amount of money, I might have the opportunity to own a two-bedroom flat. I couldn't believe my ears or my luck. I had completely forgotten about this scheme, which I'd signed up for nine years earlier when Robi and I got married. Although we got divorced, we were still on the list, and eligible for a flat.

I didn't have the money, but I wanted that flat so much. I wanted to change my life and this seemed like a good opportunity. Having my own place meant freedom and independence, so I had to do everything I could to make my dream come true.

In previous years, the government had eased regulations and opened the borders to Hungary. In the past Ukrainians were only allowed to travel there as tourists or to go shopping but now, with the right documents, we could also get a work permit. The rumour was that if someone worked hard, they could earn much more in a short time than at home. As I needed the money badly, I saw no other way out: I had to go too.

I contacted a friend of a colleague who was recruiting people for a sewing company in Hungary. After he told me about the conditions and the salary, I immediately entrusted him with arranging my work permit. I calculated that, if all went well, three months should be enough to earn the money I needed. That was only the down payment on the flat; the rest would be deducted from my salary in instalments once the block of flats was built.

As the deposit was urgent, I borrowed money from my two brothers. Unfortunately this was not enough, so one of my colleagues made up for the shortfall.

For the next few weeks while I waited for my visa, I practised sewing after work in a nearby workshop to get some experience. Then the day came when I left Zoli in the care of Potyi and my parents and went to Hungary to try my luck. I knew that three months would be a long time without Zoli, but I felt that it was not a big price to pay to make my dream come true.

Chapter 4

When someone says they want to work abroad, what comes to mind is a foreign country where people speak a foreign language, but for me Hungary was like coming home. Born in the Soviet Union, I had learned to speak Russian but otherwise I had nothing to do with Russians. I had German blood in me through my father, but I'd always felt Hungarian in my heart.

When Hungary had been partitioned, my grandfather and the others had no say in the annexation of Transcarpathia to Ukraine. Fortunately they continued to live their lives as Hungarians. We were born into it, so it was our mother tongue and we tried to preserve Hungarian traditions. I'm sure many Hungarians like me from across the border felt the same as I did when I arrived in Hungary. Home!

When we arrived, the administrator took me and three other women to the sewing factory in Budapest. It was a private company that was trying to expand with foreign workers, and when it turned out that I spoke Hungarian, the owner was very pleased. The few women they had hired so far only spoke Russian, so they needed an interpreter – which was me.

After we had seen the workshop, they took us to the workers' hostel a few minutes' drive away. Upstairs there was a long corridor with many rooms and only one kitchen, which, as I recall, had only one gas stove. We had to queue if we wanted to cook, as well as if we wanted to take a shower. I'd lived in worse places, so I thought I could manage for three months.

Work started in the sewing factory that afternoon and continued almost non-stop for three months. Only Sundays were free; on the other days we worked ten or twelve hours a day, sometimes more, which was exhausting. The constant pushing, hunched in front of the sewing machine, was physically exhausting and the interpreting was mentally tiring, but the worst part was that I missed my little boy so much that I felt almost a physical pain when I thought about him.

Zoli turned eight and I couldn't be there for his birthday. I knew he was in good hands because my family was looking after him, but I was still very worried about him. I had also made life difficult for Potyi, as she already had Leda who was less than a month old when I'd left home. Although my mum helped, it was not easy for Potyi to have two children to look after.

During sleepless nights, the only comfort and strength I had was the thought that when the three months were up I would have my little boy with me again.

Unfortunately, things didn't happen that way. In the first month I received almost half of the promised salary, which was a big disappointment. They deducted my accommodation, travel from my home to Budapest and the cost of my work permit.

'But we already paid the administrator for the permit,' I said indignantly to the payroll clerk.

'No, that was just his working fee,' came the reply.

I felt betrayed, but there was nothing I could do about it. The next month, only the accommodation and the compulsory taxes were deducted, but the money was not much more.

To our indignation, the owner told us that we had to work harder if we wanted more money. Harder – but how? We were in the sewing room from morning till night and sometimes we were called in on Sundays for half a day if they had an urgent order. 'How many hours do we have to work for the money we were promised?'

It wasn't until the third month's payment that I realised we'd been scammed; we would never get paid as much as we'd been promised. It was still a lot more than my salary at home but not enough to pay back what I owed, so I decided to do another three months in the sewing factory to get rid of my debt for good.

When I went home and cashed in my Hungarian forint, I was shocked at the amount I got for my money: it was only enough to pay my colleague what I owed him, and my brothers had to wait for their money. We didn't know it at the time, but the Soviet Union was falling apart and Russian money was inflating at an incredible rate. For some time, we'd been buying groceries on a ticket system and they were getting more and more expensive; some goods disappeared from the shelves completely. It was quite a scary situation, but we were hopeful that things would improve.

When I visited the factory, I had the feeling I'd been gone at least a year rather than three months. My colleagues were so happy to see me that I was completely bewildered.

I noticed Peti looking at me; I could see that he was happy to see me, but he didn't come closer, didn't greet me, just listened from a distance to what I was saying to the others. I could barely answer their questions; when I said I was going back, they were sorry that things hadn't worked out as planned.

After my boss signed another unpaid leave, I went to talk to Peti. 'Are you angry?' I asked him.

'No, I'm just disappointed. Will I see you somewhere else?'

'I'm only here for a few days, and I want to spend that time with Zoli. But I'll be home for Christmas.'

'I understand,' Peti said briefly, then went on with his work.

After paying my colleague and leaving the factory, I felt almost relieved. It was not how I'd imagined meeting Peti, but I'd expected him not to be happy to see me leave again. I still felt something for him – my heart beat faster when I saw him – but something had changed between us. I'd thought about him a lot while I was away but I didn't miss him as much as I missed my little boy. It was as if I were sobering up from that love – but that was what I wanted, wasn't it?

The few days flew by and I said goodbye to my family again. Zoli took the fact that I was going back quite well, probably because I promised to bring him goodies again. I said goodbye to him with a heavy heart; it would be a long three months without him.

And it was long! Time went by much slower than the last time; everything was so monotonous and only the letters I received from home brightened my days a little. Then, two weeks before I was due to return home, I received a letter from Potyi that made me so sad that I cried. She wrote that they'd called a meeting for the future homeowners and told them that they'd run out of money. The amount we'd paid as a deposit, wasn't enough because of the increase in the price of building materials; they needed another deposit, and not a small one, to continue building.

At the meeting, where my mother represented me, there was an outcry when it was announced that anyone who did not pay would be taken off the waiting list and would probably not get their money back. The amount they were asking us to pay was a lot, so, I wouldn't be able to pay back what I owed. I told the sewing company that I would come back after the New Year because I needed more money.

After I cashed in the Hungarian currency and paid the next deposit for the apartment, I still had enough to pay back some of my debts to my older brother – but my younger brother had to wait for his money.

After I was given the address of our new home, Zoli and I went to see how the building was progressing. The nine-storey block was being built in a rather remote part of the city, far from the centre, but there was public transport.

As the building was not fenced in and I saw no security guards, we ventured inside. The building was semi-finished, with windows and doors not yet installed, so we walked freely around the site. I wanted to see the home I would own one day. The two-room flats, like the one I would have, had two balconies: one from the kitchen and the other from the living room.

I imagined how everything would look when the house was finished and I was delighted. Zoli was also interested in how I was going to decorate his room and where his bed and desk would be. I needed a lot of money to make it happen, but I couldn't give up; I wanted to make my dream come true.

I was a bit nervous when I went to the factory because I didn't know whether I would get unpaid leave or not. My boss was understanding, but said that if I didn't return to work after Easter I would have to resign. Peti, on the other hand, was no longer so understanding and could hardly hide his anger. When we were alone, he said he wanted to talk to me and asked me to meet him the next day at the Latorca river. I was hoping he would break up with me, but that wasn't the case.

He was waiting for me in a place on the riverbank where we were unlikely to run into anyone we knew, but if we did it would seem like we'd met by chance. Peti did not hold back; he was angry at me for leaving again. We started arguing, or rather fighting, for the first time since we'd met. I kept saying that I had to go because I would never get the same salary at home as I got in Hungary. He said I didn't have to do it alone, he'd help me.

'This will be my home and my problem,' I said. 'Do you think it's easy for me to leave Zoli and stay away from my family for months? If you do, you are wrong. But I will do it because I need that flat.'

We finally made up and he seemed to accept that he couldn't make me stay. Before we went our separate ways, Peti looked around to see if anyone was coming then kissed me quickly. It was as if he wanted to show me how much he missed me and wanted me back. Then he said softly, 'I want to live with you and your son.'

I was so baffled that all I managed to say was that I had to go back, and I left quickly.

'What does he mean by all of this?' I thought. 'Is he going to leave his wife to live with us? No, I don't want that, I never did! I can't be happy when others suffer because of me! How am I supposed to look in the eyes of his wife or his daughter? No, this cannot happen!'

When I returned home, everything became clear and I knew what I had to do. Peti's feelings for me might not have changed, but I'd become estranged from him over the last six months. I was no longer in love with him, which is why it was scary that he would leave his wife for me. I decided to break up with him after Easter before it was too late.

New Year came and I had to go back to Hungary. My parents wanted to accompany me to the border, so they waited in the corridor while I said goodbye to Zoli. It wasn't as easy as the last time because my son hid behind the wardrobe and refused to come out. I could no longer bribe him by promising him sweets; he was not interested in anything. I left home without saying goodbye, without hugging him and kissing his face.

My parents and I sat silently on the train to Csap, not in the mood to talk. All I could think of was how much pain I'd caused Zoli by leaving him again. I started to cry so bitterly that I think everyone on the train was looking at me, but I didn't care. If I was feeling so bad, what could that poor child be feeling? How could I do this to him?

I cried and cried, my heart almost breaking from the pain. My dad was sitting across from me and even he became emotional and his eyes filled with tears. After I calmed down and stopped crying, I thought that this would be my last three months and I would never go back – but that didn't turn out as I planned.

With new staff coming into the sewing factory almost every week, the owner took on more and more orders. Before Easter we were up to our necks in work, so we were told that no one could go anywhere. There were several of us who were looking forward to leaving but no matter how much we complained and begged that we had families waiting for us at home, the bosses didn't care. They treated us like slaves who had no lives of their own. They said we had signed an employment contract, which meant that they determined when we could go on leave or return home for good. If we didn't follow the rules, they would revoke our permits and deport us; apparently then we could never come back to Hungary and we did not want to risk that.

We had signed every piece of paper they'd put in front of us without reading them and we were not given copies, so we did not know what the truth was and we believed the bosses. We were promised that if this big order was completed we would be allowed to go home, but that didn't happen either the next month or the month after.

I missed Zoli so much that I hardly ate, and I slept very badly. One day Potyi wrote to me that my aunt had installed a landline phone and if we arranged a time in advance I could call them. We arranged a time for Sunday, so I was really looking forward to that afternoon to finally talk to my little boy. I called them from a phone booth and was so happy to hear my mum's voice on the other end of the line.

I asked her to put Zoli on the phone but he didn't come: he didn't want to talk to me. I heard my mum calling him several times but he still didn't come to the phone. I heard what sounded like crying in the distance but by then I was crying too, so I could hardly understand what my mother was saying.

After that I felt even worse; I was sure that it was not only me who was suffering so much but also my little boy. My roommates tried to cheer me up but they were not successful.

On our days off, we sometimes went downtown, walked along the Danube and admired the buildings, but that didn't bring me out of my depression. On Saturdays, there was a disco in the hall of the workers' hostel, where the residents could let off steam after a week's work. My roommates couldn't get me to come down with them. Disco wasn't my thing; I'd never learned how to dance and I'd never had chance to practise.

My twenty-eighth birthday was on a Saturday and the girls ganged up on me. They said enough crying, I had to go down to the hall with them and have a good time.

I made excuses but there was no escape. I borrowed clothes from one of them and someone else put make-up on my face. When I looked in the mirror, I found I was beautiful.

We went down to the disco and I had a really good time, which I hadn't expected. Although it was my first time in a place like that, I picked up the rhythm pretty quickly and learned to dance. I needed to relax, and I didn't regret the girls talking me into it. For the first time in months, I didn't think about Zoli: it was just me, the music, and the dancing.

That night something changed in me. I wanted to have fun, to enjoy life. Disco became like a drug I couldn't get enough of; I couldn't wait for the working week to end so I could dance again on a Saturday night.

At the age of twenty-eight, I threw myself into the nightlife and I really enjoyed it. I felt I had to make up for everything I had missed in my life. I still thought about Zoli a lot and I missed him, but I cried less because I had something to distract me. I bought some cheap clothes in good condition at the market, the girls dyed my hair blonde, and we went to the disco every weekend.

I could usually get by all night with a soft drink but occasionally the guys would buy me a drink, the 'price' of which I soon found out. When they whispered their room number in my ear while I was dancing or showed me the key to go up to their room with them, I quickly left. True, I wanted to have fun and enjoy myself, but I swore I would never get involved in bad things.

There was a young woman called Andi who worked in the sewing shop and she got involved with a much older Arab man.

Her family didn't like it, so they kicked her out of the house – or so she told us. As she had nowhere else to go, she came to live with us in the hostel. The following weekend we ended up in her Arab friend's group.

Andi's lover was a businessman who ran stalls in the nearby market, and you could tell from his nice car and expensive suit that he had no financial problems. The two men he called his friends were probably his employees, because they called him boss and treated him as such. Our new friends took us to a fancy nightclub, something I had never dreamed of. Although it was a full house, they let us in.

I think it must have been the boss's regular spot because everyone knew him and we got special treatment. It was like being in the company of a celebrity whose every wish was granted. Several people came up, shook his hand and exchanged a few words in Arabic or English, which I didn't understand. One man didn't leave my side all evening. He spoke Hungarian very badly, but he kept complimenting me and repeatedly told me how much he liked me. He called me his princess, which was flattering although I couldn't take him seriously.

We danced until dawn and had a great time, but it was time to go. I'm sure it was just the drink talking but my admirer finally confessed his love for me, which made me laugh out loud. I must admit it was nice to have his attention and for the first time in my life I really felt like a princess. I was no longer a little grey mouse that the boys didn't notice but a young, pretty woman who had charmed this Arab man.

I finally got rid of him by giving him the phone number of the sewing shop, which I 'accidentally' wrote down wrongly so he never called me. I had an incredible time that night, but that was all I wanted. No more relationships or one-night stands.

For about two months I didn't miss a single occasion at the disco; I became an addict and my only regret was that I hadn't start partying earlier. As I stood in front of the mirror and put on my lipstick, I looked at myself with satisfaction. My long nose, which had made me feel ugly, didn't look so long anymore, and my blonde hair matched my blue eyes. True, I was thin but the black miniskirt with black tights looked great on me.

Then I thought, what would Robi say if he saw me like this? He wouldn't even recognize me. I'd changed so much since I'd separated from him that I was starting to not recognise myself. An independent, confident woman looked back at me in the mirror and I liked it.

On one occasion, our friends said they wouldn't come out until later, so the girls and I went down to the hall to party without them. It was a good night, and when the boss and his mates arrived they joined us on the dance floor. There was a new face among them who was standing right across the circle from me and kept looking at me while I was dancing.

Suddenly I noticed the stranger nod in my direction then look questioningly at the boss who shook his head indicating no. That gesture made me shiver. We heard tales of girls disappearing from discos, then being kept in an apartment for days and raped and beaten until they agreed to become prostitutes. Maybe that was not the case here and I just misunderstood, but I had a very bad feeling.

These people said they were our friends, but who were they and what did they do? If they worked in the market, why had I never seen them there? What if the stories were true and I had just been singled out to become a prostitute? I didn't really know them, yet the other day I'd got into their car and let them take me to a nightclub and I'd had no idea where it was.

In that moment I realised how dangerous what I was doing was; at any moment I could disappear into the night and find myself on the street selling my body.

I was so scared that I started shaking like a leaf. Even though the boss had signalled no with his head, I still didn't feel safe. As soon as we finished dancing, I went up to my room with a headache. That was the last time I went to the disco; I was done with partying for good.

The next day, when I told the girls what I had seen and how it had scared me, they shrugged their shoulders. They said I must have misunderstood the situation, and besides they could look after themselves. But I didn't take any chances; it wasn't worth it.

As my desire for fun faded and I no longer had anything to distract me from my problems, I became depressed again. I got the news from home that the construction would stop if we didn't pay a certain amount of money again. Would this never end?

I was hoping to pay my brother back when I got home and still have some savings. I no longer had a job at home; my unpaid leave had expired a long time ago so I'd had to leave the factory. What if they asked for more money later and I couldn't pay? How would I ever have a place of my own?

Then came the news that my sister had moved from Dagestan with her husband and four children, so the four-room flat was full without me. I didn't know what to do. The best solution seemed to be to stay in Hungary and work there until the house was completed and the keys handed over to the owners. Maybe it would only be a few months, half a year at the most, but what would happen to me and Zoli in the meantime? How could I go on without him for so long? I'd left home more than a year ago, and in that time I'd only seen my little boy twice; I didn't even see him on his ninth birthday. If I was finally allowed to go home, how could I tell him that I had to go leave again? I was exhausted at the thought of the pain I was causing my child, but I had no choice.

Then I thought: what if I don't spend my holidays with him at home but brought him to Hungary for a few days. We could go to the amusement park, the zoo and other places that might be interesting for him. It would make up for the past few months and maybe he would accept more easily that I wouldn't be with him for a while. My mood brightened and I started planning our 'holiday'.

I knew I couldn't have Zoli in the hostel with me, and I hated living there anyway. The fact that I often ate buttered bread or tinned food because it was almost impossible to get into the kitchen didn't bother me, but I was fed up with drunken men brawling in our corridor every week or two. These incidents always upset me because I remembered the things I had experienced with Robi.

One of these fights turned into a stabbing, and when I had to walk past a pool of blood in the corridor in the morning I decided to move out. One of my colleagues, who had recently come over from Transcarpathia, was looking for a flat and a roommate because she didn't want to stay in the hostel either.

We found a room to rent in a family house, which was not cheap, but it was worth it for us to live in peace and quiet. The host allowed Zoli to stay with me during my holidays, which I was very happy about. I wanted to make those few days memorable for him, so I planned where we would go and what we would see. A dear colleague of mine, who was born in Pest and knew the city well, helped me. She gave me a map on which she marked the places that would interest a nine-year-old child.

I got my two weeks' holiday and finally got on the train. I hadn't seen my son in over eight months, so I couldn't wait to hold him. I didn't write to Potyi to let her know when I was arriving because the letter would have arrived later than I did, so they weren't expecting me.

After I pulled the doorknob, I stood outside our front door with my heart pounding. My mum opened the door for me in surprise, followed by my dad. Potyi came out of the kitchen. Then the door to the little room opened and a child came out shyly. He looked like my godson, but he wasn't...

'Zoli, is that you?' I asked him when he looked up at me. Of course, it was and I hadn't recognised him! What kind of mother was I?

He was at least a head taller than the last time I'd seen him, and his hair was longer. He looked like my godson but it wasn't him, it was my little boy. How could I have doubted it, if only for a moment? What kind of a mother doesn't recognize her own child? I started crying so hard that I felt sick and had to sit down to keep from fainting. I sat Zoli on my lap and cried and cried.

I never wanted to feel that way again and I never wanted to leave my little boy alone again, but I had no choice. That evening I told my family what my plan was and they agreed with me. Zoli was sad that I wouldn't stay at home with him, but when I told him that we would go back to Hungary together and that he would be with me for ten days, his eyes lit up. He was curious about the places I was going to take him and excited about the trip.

I only had two days to get everything done and visit my brothers and sisters, so I went to the factory the next morning. As I'd expected they'd hired someone to replace me. It was nice of my boss not to fire me after my unpaid leave had expired at Easter. Instead, he'd extended it and he let me resign.

I spoke to my former colleagues, who were sorry to see me go and wished me good luck. It was all so strange, so different, even though it had only been a year and two months since I'd left. Even my desk, where I'd sat at for ten years, was somehow strange, as was the woman who was now doing my job.

As I was approaching Peti to say goodbye to him, my heart wasn't beating as fast as it had done before. I had changed; I was no longer in love with him and that was the way it had to be, the right thing to do. We said goodbye like two good friends and then I left the factory. That was the end of another era in my life.

I remembered when I was seventeen and got a referral not to college but to this factory. I hadn't wanted to come but I'd loved my job, I had a big family who took me in, gave me confidence and helped me. It was here that I fell in love with Robi and then years later with Peti. It was nice to think back to the bus trips I'd organised that had gone so well and the weekend fishing trips with friends. They were good memories – and I'd seen the sea for the first time in my life thanks to my colleagues. So much had happened to me in those ten years and I was a little sad that it was all over, but as they say: when one door closes behind you, another one opens in front of you.

When I found out that I was still entitled to the apartment, even though I'd quit my job at the factory, I paid the amount requested. But people in the office could not tell me when the construction would be completed. Due to the increase in prices, more payments would be needed but the house would be finished sooner or later. I was hoping to get more specific information, but they did not give it to me so I had to settle for that.

I went to my younger brother and finally paid off my debt to him. I asked him to come to Budapest to pick up Zoli and bring him home at the end of my holiday because that was the only way I could spend ten full days with him. Luckily, my brother was fine with that as he was going to Hungary at the end of the month anyway.

A day later, on the twentieth of August, Zoli and I were on the train on our way to great adventures. I chose this date deliberately, as it was a national holiday that ended with a huge fireworks display. A year earlier, I had enjoyed it with my roommates on the banks of the Danube, and now my son was going to see it too. I remember how nervous I was because the train from Záhony was running quite late and I was afraid we wouldn't get there in time, but luckily we arrived at the last minute so we didn't miss anything. The fireworks were even more beautiful than the previous year and Zoli loved them.

Everything went as planned – even better. We went to the amusement park where we tried out a lot of rides, and Zoli and I ate a big candy floss for the first time in our lives. At the zoo my son was lucky because he won a nymph parrot in a raffle, which I had to buy a cage for but it was still a great joy.

One day we took the cogwheel up to a part of Buda from where we could see almost all of Budapest. We took photos at the Fisherman's Bastion and Buda Castle, then went to an open-air performance where clowns entertained the children and a famous actress sang children's songs. At the end, the organisers offered everyone scones and fruit drinks, which were very nice in the heat.

The next day we toured Margaret Island and, much to our surprise, discovered a small zoo in the middle of the island. We had ice cream while walking along the banks of the Danube and watching the boats passing by. On the last day we took the cable car up to Mount János, from where the view was amazing.

Our little holiday went well, and we enjoyed every minute of it, but the ten days were soon up and Zoli had to go home. In the morning on the bus to the train station, my little boy was so sad that it almost broke my heart. I sat beside him speechless, not knowing what to say or how to comfort him. The next time we would meet was Christmas; that seemed so far away, it was useless to promise him anything.

The train arrived on time and was only at the station for a few minutes, so we had to hurry. After the passengers disembarked and boarded, I handed the bag and cage with the parrot to my brother who was standing in the doorway. I turned to Zoli to hug him and say goodbye but he wouldn't let me; he got on the train so quickly and hid behind my brother that I was speechless. He was angry at me for leaving him again and he wouldn't let me say goodbye.

The train started to move slowly and I thought I would die of pain. Tears were streaming down my face and my legs were collapsing. Unable to move, I had to sit on a bench to pull myself together. The sewing shop was only ten minutes away from the station, but I didn't have the strength to walk that far.

I don't know how long I sat there, but after a good cry I went to work. The shift started at six o'clock and I couldn't be late. I had no idea at the time what a long day was ahead of me.

Early morning, the group leader told us that we had a big order of blazers and we couldn't go home until they were ready. We worked hard, which I didn't mind because it took my mind off Zoli. At six in the evening the local Hungarians went home because no one could force them to stay, but we continued working all night, hoping to finish by the morning.

At dawn, the women fell asleep one by one and laid their heads on the sewing machines. Our group leader also disappeared for a while; I think he slept in the medical room for a couple of hours. It was just me and one other girl pushing the pedal until morning, but we still didn't finish the blazers. In the morning they brought in another batch of fabric, which was also urgent, so we kept working non-stop all day.

Not only were we tired, but we were also hungry as we hadn't expected such a long shift and all our food was gone. Someone brought bread and butter from the shop, so that was our breakfast and lunch. At 6pm we were working on the last of the blazers when the team leader brought more material to be ready by the morning. When I saw it, I was completely freaked out.

By then I had been sitting in front of the sewing machine for thirty-six hours and I was so exhausted that I couldn't control myself. I started shouting so rudely at the group leader that the poor man was babbling and panting in his bewilderment.

'That's enough, we are not your slaves! Fuck this sewing office and fuck the management!' I shouted at him and then I burst into tears.

I had never spoken to anyone like that before. My nerves had given up and I had a tremor that was frightening. I slumped down in my chair and tried to hold down my trembling knees with my hands but I couldn't. I was a nervous wreck. Shocked, the others watched the scene then one of them brought me a glass of water. After drinking it I felt a little better. I got up and left the sewing room without a word.

I knew something was wrong with me and I needed help. What I'd done was not normal, and my outburst could result in me losing my job. First thing on Monday morning I went to the GP, who sent me straight to the psychiatrist. It quickly became clear that I was having an incipient nervous breakdown which, if left untreated, could become more serious and I could end up in the basement.

I wasn't going to risk that, so I agreed to medication. I had to take a very strong sedative three times a day, which slowed me down and made me sleepy all the time but it helped. I was given a week's sick leave; on the advice of the psychiatrist, I did a lot of walking in the park or reading a book outdoors.

Fortunately, I was not fired from the sewing factory; the team leader probably did not report the incident to the management. When I went back to work I was a bit embarrassed, but the girls acted as if nothing had happened so it didn't feel awkward. I had to go to the psychiatric clinic every month for another dose of medication, but I didn't mind because I needed it. Maybe I should have seen a doctor earlier, as my nerves were already shot from constant fear during my marriage. I hadn't got treatment for my fear of heights, and then I hadn't dealt with my depression.

Leaving my little boy and only seeing him three times during fifteen months was too much for me, and the thirty-six-hour shift in the sewing room was the last straw. I'm not keen on taking medication – I only take painkillers when I really must – but I couldn't have survived that difficult time without the sedatives.

The following month the landlord told us that his mother was moving in with them and they needed the room. We were given two weeks to look for a new sublet, which was not easy before the internet and smartphones. We finally found a room to rent from an elderly lady, which was more expensive than the previous one and further away from the sewing shop so we had to pay for commuting. After a ten-day holiday, I had hardly any money left; on top of that, my sick leave had reduced my salary and the extra expenses had not been good for my finances. When I went home at Christmas, I had hardly any money saved.

Construction had been halted indefinitely in mid-autumn due to lack of funds. People could not afford to pay more so it was doubtful whether the house would ever be built. It was as if I had thrown my money into a bottomless pit and my year and a half of work had been for nothing. Had I wrecked my nerves and hurt my little boy for nothing? No, I couldn't let that happen. It was time to take control of my destiny!

Over the past year and a half I had experienced life in Hungary and it had made me think. What if Zoli and I tried to make a living there? As I had Hungarian nationality I could apply for a residence permit, and in time I could become a Hungarian citizen and we would stay there forever. If my plan succeeded, with hard work I could give Zoli a better life and a better future.

I never gave up hope that one day that property would be built and I would be a homeowner, but I couldn't imagine us living in that apartment: I would rather sell it and buy a smaller house or a cheap apartment in Hungary with a bank loan. I set that goal and started planning my future with Zoli. It all seemed so simple but if I had known then what difficulties I would face, I might never have started. I didn't know what was waiting for me, I just hoped that everything would work out the way I wanted it to. I believed that after all the bad things, things would get better – and if that meant starting a new life in Hungary, I would do it.

Chapter 5

I needed more money to carry out my plan because if Zoli was living with me and going to school in Hungary, my expenses would be much higher. I needed to work as many hours as possible in the next few months, but unfortunately, it was not up to me.

When I went back to the sewing room in January, we had hardly any orders so we didn't work overtime or weekends. The pay I got that month was disappointing; after I'd paid the rent and bought the bus pass, I had hardly any money left for food.

I heard from someone that they were looking for night cleaners at one of the train stations and I applied. Unfortunately, they did not arrange a work permit so they could not officially employ me as I was a Ukrainian citizen. However, they offered me the opportunity to work illegally, but there would be no holidays or sick pay and I would receive my salary in cash.

This suited me perfectly so I started the next day at ten at night. The shift lasted until six in the morning, but my shift at the sewing room started at seven, so I had an hour to get there. Despite three- or four-hours' sleep, I managed the nights quite well at first, but then the two jobs became more and more exhausting. We had to work very quickly to get the trains cleaned in time, so I was tired and sleepy when I caught the bus to the other side of town in the morning. As there was little work to do in the sewing room, I went to the dressing room several times a day and slept for a few minutes with my head on the radiator.

I did that for ten days, but when I fell asleep while standing on the bus at six in the morning I knew I couldn't go on and I gave up. I needed the money, but not at that price.

As the months went by, we had problems with the landlady. The nice old lady whose house we were staying in was no longer nice to us; she told us off if we took a shower for more than five minutes and wasted water, or if the light in our room stayed on for longer than it should have done because we were wasting electricity. We only used the washing machine once a week but she didn't like that either because she thought that was too often.

When she came up with the idea that we should collect rainwater in the spring and use it to wash our clothes, my flatmate and I decided to move out. When I was a child, my mother used to wash clothes in the Latorca river – but collecting rainwater for washing in Budapest twenty years later was too much for us! On top of that, she wanted to raise the rent because she thought we weren't saving enough on the utility bills.

We secretly started looking for a new sublet, one where I could bring Zoli later. We found a room advertised and went to see it at the weekend.

It's amazing what people will come up with to get money! They had turned a garage into a room, which was locked from the outside with a padlock. Inside, where the car used to be, there was a double bed, a table with two chairs opposite and a wardrobe in the corner. There was an electric cooker on the table, so that must have been the 'kitchen'. The garage had no windows, so you either had to leave the light on all day or live with the door open and people passing by staring into the room. Not to mention it was much colder inside than outside, but the owner proudly pointed to the electric heater.

'I'd rather collect rainwater than live in this cold garage,' I thought. In the end, we didn't take the room, saying that I would soon have my son with me and the three of us wouldn't fit in there.

Then the owner thought of something that might interest me. He had a friend called Feri who was bringing up his two children on his own; he didn't need a lodger but rather a babysitter. He lived in a house with a garden in the countryside and there was plenty of room, so I could certainly take my son there. Before I could reply, he quickly wrote down his friend's phone number and gave it to me.

I was interested, but I was reluctant to call the man. A man without a wife and raising two children on his own might want more than just a babysitter – but if I didn't talk to him, I would never find out the real reason.

The next day, at the end of my shift, I called him from work. Feri's voice on the phone was very confident, while I was shy and could barely speak. It turned out that he worked as a security guard in a factory in the same neighbourhood as the sewing shop.

As he was still working when I finished my shift, we arranged to meet at his place of work. I wasn't expecting to see him that day so I was as excited as if I were going on a date. The truth was that Feri piqued my interest. I was curious about him and I wanted to hear his story.

A security guard in his forties stood at the entrance of the factory, cigarette in hand. 'Feri?' I asked uncertainly.

'Yes, it's me.' He chuckled then opened the gate for me.

Over the next two hours I learnt all I wanted to know about him as he went on and on about himself. He didn't ask me anything about myself, which didn't bother me because at least I got to observe him properly.

He must have been about ten years older than me, or maybe more, and his hair, which was slightly long, was grey in places. He looked good with a black moustache and a goatee, but that also made him look a bit pretentious. We'd never met before, yet I felt as if I knew him from somewhere or he reminded me of someone.

Then he said something funny and started laughing out loud, which gave me the creeps. Not only his laugh but his whole attitude reminded me of Robi, and that put me in a bad mood. Feri didn't notice the change in me and kept on talking about himself and his children to impress me more.

He told me from the beginning that he didn't need a babysitter but a partner to help him raise his children. I said goodbye to Feri with mixed feelings; although we had agreed to meet again, I wasn't sure if I wanted to.

If it hadn't been for his strong resemblance to my ex, I would have agreed to this relationship without a second thought, but it didn't work out that way. As a teenager, I'd read a lot of novels about orphans, and I always felt the urge to help them in some way. Now the opportunity was there and I was unsure. My heart told me that I could love these two children and be a good mother to them, but if I listened to my wits I would avoid their father by a long shot. It was obvious that Feri wasn't Robi, and not all men are sadists, but why did that laughter make my stomach turn? It had been seven and a half years since Robi beat me with an iron and almost killed me, and I still couldn't get over it. How could I live with a man who reminded me of that terrible thing?

I decided not to see him again but I changed my mind very quickly after the landlady warned me again for taking too long in the shower and said that she was going to raise the rent next month. It wasn't hard to talk myself into another meeting; I figured that if I got to know Feri better I might suppress that bad feeling and things might work out.

We met twice more that week. I'd be exaggerating if I said I fell in love with him, but I was starting to like him. The fact that he didn't abandon his kids when his wife left suggested that he wasn't a bad person. He said it wasn't easy with them but it never occurred to him to give them up, unlike Robi who had given up on Zoli several years ago and stopped contacting him.

However, the more time I spent with Feri, the more obvious it became that I was going to be a grey mouse again. Just like my ex-husband, Feri loved to be the centre of attention; he was always the topic of conversation and my life was of little interest to him.

Then he came up with the idea of me going over to their house at the weekend and meeting his kids. I thought it was a bit soon, especially as I didn't know where I stood with him. On the one hand, I liked him because he was interesting and never boring to be around, but his similarities to Robi scared me. I finally let myself be talked into it because it was supposedly the kids' idea: they wanted to meet me.

The Sunday lunch and the whole get-together went much better than expected. The kids were shy for about ten minutes then eased up. They kept asking questions about me and Zoli, which I was very happy about. Since they were interested in me, they learned more about me in that short time than their father had learned in a whole week.

After lunch and clearing the table, we sat down in the living room to talk. Suddenly the little girl came up to me, sat on my lap and put her arms around my neck. She told me she had just turned eight and her mother hadn't even sent her a birthday card. The sadness in her voice touched me but it wasn't the only thing that helped me make the decision. The way she put her arms around my neck gave me a motherly feeling I hadn't had in months.

This childlike embrace melted my heart and seemed to ease the pain of Zoli's absence. The little girl completely swept me off my feet and I could not say no to her father. I wanted to be the mother of the two children, but only if Zoli was with me. Feri was very happy when I told him that.

'If you get on well with my children and they like you, you can bring your son and we can live like in a fairy tale,' he said.

It sounded great; we just had to discuss when I would move in with them. My rent was due the following weekend, but then I'd have to stay with the old lady for another month.

'If you've already decided to move in with me, why wait another month?' Feri asked. 'Move here next weekend and I won't have to pay the babysitter anymore.'

My head knew that we shouldn't be in such a hurry, but I followed my heart because the children needed me and I needed them. Once I saw how much their father loved them and the relationship between them, I was less worried about tying my life to someone like Robi.

When I told my landlady I was moving out, she refused to return my deposit because I hadn't told her sooner. There was no contract stating that so I thought it was unfair, but there was nothing I could do about it.

I moved to the countryside at the beginning of March and spent money on train and bus fares instead of rent. The children seemed to blossom on my arrival and were very happy to see me. Thanks to them, I settled in quickly and we were almost like a real family. Almost, because Zoli was still not part of it but I hoped that he would be with us soon.

I started a new life in Hungary two months before my twenty-ninth birthday. The twenty-one months I had spent in the country had never felt like a new phase in my life just a temporary one, all about work and earning money. Now I knew that my life had changed a lot and maybe things would finally get better. I was full of hope, and I believed that I could do it now.

I immediately became fond of the children and they liked me, too, but although I tried hard it was not so easy with their father. I can't say that I was less bothered by the similarities between my ex and my new boyfriend, but I tried not to notice them and accept him for who he was. Then again, they say you get to know someone by living with them.

Feri turned out to be quite a drinker and liked to spend his free time in the pub. The first time he came home drunk I was really scared, but luckily he wasn't aggressive. I could see that the children were not bothered; it was probably not the first time they had seen their father in such a state. In fact, they were happy about it, because then they could do everything that they weren't allowed to do at other times. They wrestled with their father then sat on his back and rode around the living room. Finally, the little girl put all her coloured headbands in her father's hair and Feri had a good laugh when he saw himself in the mirror.

This drunken, loud laughter made my stomach cramp and it didn't go away for the rest of the evening. Needless to say, I didn't sleep a wink all night while he slept soundly beside me, snoring occasionally. Why didn't I know this about him before? I'm not sure if Feri was an alcoholic, but the fact that he presented himself to me like that just a week after I moved in said a lot about him.

A week earlier I'd had such high hopes for this relationship, but they had begun to evaporate. I regretted writing to Potyi about Feri and the children, but she had to know my new address. Perhaps I had given Zoli false hope, because what if it didn't work? I had made another bad decision but, despite blaming myself for it, I couldn't change it. I had nowhere else to go and I wouldn't turn my back on the children. Feri was not aggressive and was no threat to any of us. Maybe my bad marriage made me too hard on him? I decided to try to change my attitude and not see the bad in everything that was not so bad.

The following weeks were very similar to the first. I looked after the children and did everything in the house except the cooking. We agreed at the beginning that the children were used to their father's cooking, so it would continue to be his job. In return I baked cakes every weekend, which everyone enjoyed. Feri often had friends over on his days off and sometimes the drinking went on until dawn, or he went to the pub and came home drunk.

What I noticed – and I saw this as a positive thing – was that he never drank alone. He liked to be the centre of attention and for that he needed people who would listen to him. I didn't even like to go to the shop with him, because he was a real attention seeker. I was embarrassed by his behaviour, especially when he argued with the shop assistants about something trivial, and I often felt ashamed of him. But I loved his children very much and that compensated for everything.

It was only when I received my next monthly wage that I realised how little I was earning. Either my salary was very low, or commuting was costing me a lot of money, but it wasn't right.

It was again possible to work overtime in the sewing room but I couldn't because of the family. However, my earnings were not enough so I decided to start an hour earlier and stay an hour longer because it was more than nothing. To get to work by six I had to get up at four in the morning, and I only got home from work at half past six in the evening.

One day later that week the train was delayed, so I missed the bus and the next one didn't come for an hour. Luckily the kids weren't alone because their father had the day off, but I was still worried – as it turned out, rightly so.

Before I even stepped through the door, Feri started yelling at me. 'How dare you come home so late? If I was on duty today, who would be with the children? Do I have to pay the babysitter to look after them again?'

Then he called me irresponsible and he was right. Even though the children were independent, they could not be left alone for so long, so before I really started working overtime I had to stop.

Feri's company paid eighty per cent of his travel expenses and he thought I should get that too. After I got my next salary, which was also ridiculously low, I asked my boss about it.

'Nobody asked you to move to the country and commute to work. We don't pay travel expenses here and if you don't like it, you can leave! Three people are willing to take your place,' was the answer.

So that was it; they didn't need me anymore. They couldn't make me work all day and night like they used to so they sent me away instead.

I became jobless at the beginning of May, which didn't mean that I was bored: I had plenty of work at home. Feri was doing nothing but cooking so all the other work was waiting for me. Because of the spring rain the courtyard was full of weeds, not to mention the big garden. I didn't know much about gardening because I'd lived in a flat since I was a teenager, but luckily the old lady who used to babysit the children gave me some advice. She showed me how to dig up the garden, hoe, weed and sow.

I tidied up the yard and, being a city girl, I really enjoyed the work. I bought seeds and bulbs and lots of tomato and pepper plants and planted them. I did a lot of shopping for lunch and stocked the fridge when needed, so I was slowly running out of money. My neighbour mentioned that I could go to work for the Producer Organisation and pick fruit, but the problem was that it was on the other side of the village. It wouldn't have been a long distance if I could cycle but I couldn't.

Normally it is the parent who teaches a child to ride a bike, but in our case, it was the other way round. At the age of twenty-nine, my two foster children taught me to ride a bike in the school playground at weekends. Thanks to them, I could go anywhere in the village on their father's bike.

When I applied for the fruit picking job at the local PO, I was accepted immediately and started the next morning. The job was to sort cherries for several weeks for a private trader, followed by the plum season. It didn't pay much but at least it was local and we could buy the fruit cheaper than the market price.

I took the opportunity to make jam or compote every weekend, which the kids loved. I enjoyed making them and was delighted to see the pantry filling up with jars. But somehow, I couldn't please Feri no matter how hard I tried. Then one day I found out what his problem was with me.

'It's time to contribute a bit towards the bills,' he said angrily.

'But I have no money,' I replied.

'Our deal wasn't about you living here for free! I could invite a stranger from the street who'd be willing to live with us happily. You're taking food away from my children,' he yelled in my face.

'But don't I work enough to be here?' I asked, almost in tears. 'What I earn, I spend on us. How many times have I gone shopping, bought seedlings, sugar for jam. It all costs money. Am

I taking food away from your children?' I repeated his words, then started sobbing so he turned around and walked out of the kitchen.

How could he be so unfair? I may not have contributed to the utilities but I was his babysitter, his housekeeper, his gardener and his lover. I spent all my time making them happy and this was the thanks I got. I had thought we were doing well and now it turned out we were not.

I had a little money that I had put aside for the trip to pick up Zoli, but I couldn't give that to Feri. Luckily, the children didn't notice my tears when they came in from the courtyard and their father pretended that nothing had happened. I, on the other hand, couldn't forget Feri's cruel words and started fasting that evening.

In order to avoid eating his children's food, I ate only half a bowl of soup every evening and took a slice of bread and butter to work for breakfast and lunch. Feri even counted the peppers in the garden and forbade me to pick any of them. The fact that they were my seedlings and I was taking care of them didn't matter; they were in his garden, and I watered them with his water.

A few days later, Feri's mother phoned to say she wanted to visit her grandchildren for the weekend. I had lived there for almost five months but only met my 'mother-in-law' once. I knew that mother and son were not that close, but I didn't expect what Feri told her on the phone.

'You can come down for the weekend if you want, but bring some food with you because I'm not feeding you too.' When he hung up, he looked at me to see if I'd got the hint. Yes, I understood; I had failed to convince him that I deserved to eat. In the end his mother didn't show up, perhaps resentful that her son was depriving her of a Sunday lunch.

It's been a month since I'd found out I was nothing more than a stranger to Feri. I was skinny from starvation and the stress also played a part in the weight loss. The tranquilizers my psychiatrist prescribed every month had run out in the spring, and since I didn't pay my social security I couldn't get any more. So far I hadn't needed them because I'd had a new life, a family and I was comfortable with them, but now that had changed I was not well, especially because school was about to start and the plan was that Zoli would start fifth grade here.

Feri did not comment, as if he had forgotten his promise. The children were on holiday at their grandparents from their mum's side until the end of the month, so it seemed like a good opportunity to go home and finally bring my son. When I mentioned this to Feri, he said something that took me a few seconds to comprehend. 'You stay here and raise my children and your son will be raised by your parents.'

'What?!' I asked angrily. I couldn't believe my ears. 'So I'm good to raise your children and Zoli will grow up without me? No, that's out of the question! I'd rather go home!'

Feri didn't say anything, just shrugged his shoulders. How could he do that to me? As much as I loved his children, I would never give up my own child! Six months ago, Feri had promised me that I could bring my son and we would live a fairy tale life, but he had lied.

For the last month I hadn't been sure if it was a good idea to bring Zoli here because then it would be two of us taking food away from Feri's children, but if I had a decent job and salary I could contribute to the expenses and our relationship would go back to normal. I had hoped for that but to no avail because he didn't want my child.

How was I supposed to go home and tell my son that he would not be living in Hungary after all? How disappointed would he be when he found out? It had been over two years since I'd left him and this was supposed to compensate, but my time here had been meaningless. In my letters I had promised him a better life, but I only gave him false hopes. How was I supposed to look him in the eye now?

I was very depressed and didn't sleep a wink that night. The next morning when I went to work, my eyes were red and I had bags under them. My friend immediately noticed that something was wrong and started to worry about me. We had sorted fruit opposite each other from day one, and over the months we developed a good relationship. She had a ten-year-old daughter she was raising on her own and she was very supportive of me and Zoli. We thought that our children would probably be classmates as they were both going into fifth grade in September.

During the morning break, I told her tearfully what Feri had said the night before and she cried with me. She knew how much

I wanted to bring Zoli over for good, so she wanted to help me. She said she wouldn't let me give up and go home but would rather set me up with someone who would take me and the child.

She told me about a woman who had been hospitalized a few days earlier and was dying; her elderly husband and son were going to be left on their own. My friend asked me to wait a day or two while she talks to the guy and then we'd see what happens. His name was Karcsi, he was thirty-four and a bachelor, so I had a chance with him. Under normal circumstances after Feri had deceived me like that, I wouldn't have thought of hooking up with a stranger but I didn't have much choice. It was the last straw I had left to cling to because I would have done anything for Zoli, as long as I didn't cause him any more pain.

As promised, my friend arranged everything for me; I just had to meet Karcsi in person before I went home to Ukraine. My plan was to stay at home with Zoli for a few weeks, get myself together, then come back without him and he would join me the following month. Even though I was starting a new life in a strange place, I was sure that I wouldn't wait another six months to have my son with me. If they needed me, they could accept me with the kid or forget the whole thing.

At the end of my last day of work, with my last pay cheque in my pocket, we drove to Karcsi's house in my friend's car. Only his father was at home and he couldn't tell us where his son was. We were there for maybe a minute or two, but that was enough time for me to see my new home, and it was disheartening and shocking.

It was not the poverty in which these people lived that bothered me but their lack of standards. They must have been hoarders because the courtyard was full of junk and scrap. To the left of the gate was a small house – or rather a hut – which was completely ruined. As it turned out later, Karcsi's father lived there and that was fine with him. There was a building in the middle of the courtyard that must have been a summer kitchen; it looked okay from the outside but inside everything was shabby and very dirty. Opposite it was the 'big house', the door of which was closed so I couldn't see in, but the crumbling plaster and the paint peeling off the doors and windows suggested that the people who lived there didn't care. I grew up in poverty and lived with Robi's parents for a while, but the conditions here were much worse.

When we left there, my friend saw my shock and tried to console me. She told me that Karcsi's mother had been an alcoholic for thirty years and had completely neglected her family. She was hospitalized because she drank poison to try to commit suicide and was going to die soon. The two men needed me because they had no one to look after them.

'Does Karcsi drink too?' I asked.

'Well, he drinks, but he's not an alcoholic.'

Suddenly we saw a man coming out of the pub. My friend pointed at him and stopped the car. 'There he is, that's him.'

'He's not an alcoholic yet we meet him on the way out of the pub,' I thought but I didn't say it out loud.

Karcsi was very shy when we approached him and he didn't say a word after we were introduced. I was embarrassed too, but I told him that I was going home the next day and would be back in a month. I had a ten-year-old son whom I wanted to bring with me the following month.

'Okay,' said Karcsi briefly.

We agreed on the day I would arrive. He would come to Feri's and help me move in with them.

'Okay,' Karcsi repeated.

'Well, he's not a talker,' I said to my friend after we'd said goodbye.

By the time Feri came home from work in the evening, I had all my things packed and ready to go. When I told him that I was leaving the next day, he didn't try to stop me leaving. Ever since I'd found out that he would keep me but had no interest in my son, we had hardly spoken to each other.

He was surprised when I told him that I would leave some of my things there because I would be back in a month to go to another place. 'Where are you moving to?' he asked curiously.

''Does it matter to you? Away from here.'

I sat on the bus to the train station in the morning with a heavy heart, but somehow I was also relieved. I was glad that the children were not at home because at least they wouldn't hear the bad news from me, and their father could tell them what he wanted. I was going to miss them a lot, but it would be nice to be able to meet them in the village and see them whenever I wanted to. I was disappointed that we hadn't manage to become a real family, but it wasn't up to me. Zoli belonged by my side; I had already wasted too much time without him.

The month with my loved ones in Ukraine flew by very quickly and then I was back on the train to Budapest. I managed to put on a few kilos but I was still thinner than I should have been; however I felt much better because the time I'd spent with Zoli was the cure for all my problems.

Saying goodbye wasn't so painful this time because I could finally tell him that I'd be back soon to take him with me. From what I'd seen at Karcsi's I knew it wouldn't be easy, but I was hopeful. I thought that in time I could change the circumstances and give my son a better life.

It was evening when I got off the bus and I walked straight into the house. Feri didn't remember what day I was arriving, only that I would spend one more night there and leave the next day. The kitchen and living room were empty, then I heard voices coming from the bathroom. Feri was crouched on the tiled floor fixing something on the bathtub drainpipe and the children were standing over him, watching.

'Hi!' I greeted them and all three turned to look at me.

The girl and the boy called my name and ran straight into my arms. They were so happy to see me that I couldn't stop crying. I hugged them tightly and we stayed like that for a while. I loved these two children very much and I'd missed them.

When I looked at their father with tears in my eyes, I could see that he was touched, too. But I also saw something else in his eyes that I didn't expect: he had missed me. Although he didn't come closer and kiss me on the lips like before, his eyes spoke. Maybe the past month without me had made him realize that I was more to him than a stranger. That didn't matter anymore; any feelings I'd had for him had faded; now he was just a stranger to me.

During the evening, I realized that the kids didn't know that I was leaving the next day. They kept talking, interrupting each other to tell me what had happened during their holiday, and they asked why I hadn't brought Zoli with me since school had already started. Their father had never been so tight-lipped as he was at that last dinner.

Not wanting to spoil their mood, I decided to tell them the bad news in the morning. That evening I put them in bed, kissed them goodnight and stroked their backs until they fell asleep. The boy was over the age of eleven but even he demanded a pat on the back; perhaps it reminded them of their mother. Tears started to run down my cheeks, but luckily the children were already fast asleep and didn't notice.

I lay down in bed with Feri with a broken heart. 'Why didn't you tell them?' I asked him.

'You tell them you're leaving them,' he said. Then he added, 'But you can stay if you want, and you can bring your son.'

'It's too late,' I said briefly and turned my back on him.

Even though I was exhausted from the journey, I hardly slept. I was in a difficult situation and Feri had made it even harder. The reason for leaving was no longer relevant, as he had changed his mind and would allow me to bring Zoli. Not that I thought that I would change my decision; it was out of the question. I'd respected him for not abandoning his children, but he had expected me to give up mine. Did he really think I would choose his children over my own? Had he misjudged me so badly?

But what should I tell his children? How should I say goodbye to them? They were too young to know the truth and I didn't want to besmirch their father because he was all they had. In this story I was definitely going to be the evil stepmother who abandoned her foster children.

As I expected, there was a crying fit the next morning when I told them I was leaving. I told them something along the lines that their father and I no longer loved each other and so we couldn't stay together. I comforted them by saying that I wasn't moving far away and we could see each other anytime, but all three of us knew it would never be the same. I broke their little hearts and it broke mine to cause them such pain, but there was nothing I could do: I had to go.

At ten o'clock, the bell rang and Karcsi was standing at the gate exactly as we'd agreed a month ago. He had even called his friend who had a car to help.

When Feri saw him, he started to laugh out loud. 'Are you moving in with him?' he asked contemptuously.

I didn't answer, just started carrying out my bags. The children stopped crying, stood sadly beside their father and watched me close the gate with the last bag in my hand. Karcsi packed everything into the boot of the car, and we set off for my new home.

Chapter 6

The first week with Karcsi and his father went relatively well, although it was not without its problems. His mother's funeral had been a few days earlier, so I hadn't had a chance to meet her.

At first, I thought it was because of grief that the old man (as Karcsi called his father) wasn't happy to have me there, which he made no secret of. The place was even worse than I remembered. There seemed to be more rubbish in the yard than the last time, though that didn't bother anyone but me.

The house consisted of only one room, a kitchen and a long pantry. I wasn't surprised that there was no bathroom but I was surprised that there was no water; apart from the garden tap, there was only water in the summer kitchen, which came up from a pipe sticking out of the ground. In winter this pipe froze and in the morning they burned newspapers under it to melt the ice. Water was brought into the kitchen in a bucket for cooking and washing up, and the dirty water was poured into the yard because there was no drain. When I asked how they bathed, Karcsi took me to the building at the back of the house and showed me the 'bathroom'.

It was in a decaying wooden shed; judging by the bad roof, it often flooded with rain. In the middle of the room was a long table with a metal tub on it, rusted in places. In the absence of a boiler, water for bathing was heated in a cauldron in the courtyard and carried to the tub.

'How can you take a bath here in the winter at minus ten to fifteen degrees?' I asked Karcsi. I couldn't see a stove in the room.

'The water warms you up,' he laughed. Well, I couldn't laugh at that because it sounded more pathetic than amusing.

Entering the house I was struck by a musty smell, which I thought was due to the lack of ventilation, but I was wrong. Because there were no foundations, the mud walls were absorbing moisture and mould, which was spreading to the furniture next to them. There were no gutters to drain off rainwater, so the walls were soaked from the outside. The front door was cracked beyond repair from the summer heat and rain and a simple coat of paint would not have helped. It was obvious that nothing had been touched in twenty years. After the comfort of Feri's house I felt as if I had slipped into another world, but I was not discouraged.

After Karcsi showed me around, I didn't regret moving in. Despite the bad conditions, there were a lot of good things that made me happy. In the front garden behind the summer kitchen was a big pear tree, which at that time, September, was full of sweet pears. Further along I saw a cherry tree, two plum trees and a mulberry tree, and between the farm buildings there were two more mulberry trees.

The old barns and cobbled huts at the back of the farm looked ugly, but they turned out to be very useful. In one of them, two pigs were being fattened for the December pig slaughter, and in the other rabbits were kept, also for meat. A little further away in a taller adobe building were goats that provided fresh milk, and there were hens and young chickens running around so there was no shortage of eggs.

The back garden was separated from the farm buildings and stray chickens by a rickety fence. I didn't know how big this garden was, but it certainly seemed very big and to a city girl like me it seemed like paradise.

Right at the front were three big walnut trees full of nuts, one after the other, and behind them were two long rows of grapevines. The big black bunches of grapes smelt delicious as we passed. To my right I saw redcurrant and blackcurrant bushes that I wouldn't have recognised by their leaves alone, but because no one had picked them in the summer the currants were still there. There were apple, plum, apricot and several varieties of peach trees – but don't think of it as a tidy orchard. According to Karcsi, most of the trees had grown from seed; they were wild and he'd grafted them. On the other hand, the dozens of table-grape vines behind them had been planted by the old man many years ago and he had looked after them ever since.

On the way back from the garden, I couldn't resist the juicy grapes. I was hungry for fruit, especially this delicacy, so I tore off a bunch and started eating them. When I got to the yard, the old man saw the grapes in my hand and got really angry. 'These grapes are not for eating!' he said loudly.

'Then what are they for?' I asked.

'For wine.' To emphasise his anger, he thumped the pavement with the walking stick he always carried.

I was taken aback; I hadn't expected such a reaction from him. In the end I ate the grapes because they were not going to make wine anyway, but they didn't taste so good anymore.

In the evening I had another argument with the old man, or rather he argued with me, after which it was obvious that life here would not be boring. I saw a lot of eggs in the summer kitchen – there must have been forty of them in the basket – so I made us scrambled eggs for dinner.

When the old man saw that, he started yelling at me again. 'Don't waste eggs, they have to be rationed,' he said angrily.

'But there are enough, aren't there?' I asked, startled.

'When the weather cools down and the hens stop laying, there won't be enough!'

'It's all going to go off here,' I thought, but I didn't dare say it out loud. Later that night the basket of eggs disappeared; the old man had hidden them from me so I wouldn't waste any more.

Karcsi was present on both occasions but he didn't say a word, just let his father shout at me. I didn't blame him but it would have been nice to have him on my side.

Fortunately, apart from those two unpleasant things, something good happened to me on my first day. After lunch, Karcsi's mum's sister came to see us; she wanted to meet me. She was very nice to me and so direct that I liked her immediately. She knew that it would not be easy for me to settle in the house, and she came to help. My clothes needed space in the wardrobe so Auntie started sorting them out.

Her dead sister's clothes were put in a bag and then on the fire to light the fire under the cauldron. While the water was warming, we changed the linen and sorted all the things in the wardrobe that were still usable and could be saved by washing.

The old man felt bad when he saw us burning his wife's clothes, but he didn't dare tell his sister-in-law. Seeing the look on his face, I felt sorry for him. It would never have occurred to me to get rid of these things in this way, but the aunt was not bothered. But when I got angry with the old man in the evening about the eggs, my sympathy disappeared and was replaced by something else.

It didn't take long to realise that the old man couldn't stand me. He found something wrong with everything and he yelled about it. Although I tried hard to please him, nothing I did was good enough. His offensive words hurt me badly, so I often complained to Karcsi, but he just shrugged it off. 'Never mind, he'll calm down.'

I hoped he would, because it wasn't good for either of us in the long run.

It was two or three weeks after I moved away from Feri when I met his children again. The girl was in third grade and went to lower primary school, which was not far from the Karcsi's house. One day I was coming home from shopping and saw her playing in the school yard. She noticed me and started to run towards me, as she had done so many times when I'd picked her up from daycare. She suddenly stopped in front of the wire fence, as if she had just realized that there was no exit, and looked at me so sadly that it almost broke my heart.

Her hair was hanging messily in her face; even though it was braided in the back, it was obvious that I hadn't braided it for her. I tried to talk to her but she hardly spoke, just looked at me with sad eyes. It would have been nice to hold her and comfort her but I couldn't. I told her that she and her brother should come to my house after school, and she immediately felt better.

An hour later they were both standing at the gate waiting for me to let them in. I was very happy to see them, because I'd missed them so much.

Karcsi, seeing my little guests, hurried to the corner shop and brought them ice cream, rather expensive ones. It was a nice gesture and I was grateful. I thought that if he was so nice to these two children who were strangers to him, he would be nice to my son too. The old man watched us with a wary eye but he didn't know what to make of it all, so he said nothing.

The kids couldn't stay long as the babysitter was waiting for them, so I quickly showed them our pets, picked some pears for the road and off they went.

'Come again!' I told them at the gate after I said goodbye.

But they never came again, it was the first and last time they visited me. Their father found out that they had been to see me and banned them from my house to punish me for leaving them.

Fortunately, they didn't miss me for long as I was replaced by a new mum. Later that year, Feri met a young woman who took care of his children. I sometimes ran into them in the village or saw them riding their bikes on the road, but there was no longer any contact between us; we completely drifted apart.

A day or two before I went home, another friend visited me and shared some good news. I had also met her during the fruit picking and our friendship had continued after I left. She knew I was looking for a job, so when she heard that a businessman was opening a sewing shop in the village she told me right away. We were both seamstresses, so we went together to apply for the job and we were hired.

The owner promised to arrange my work permit in time, but until then I had to work for him without a contract. This was not a problem because I was on a visa that was valid for a month and I had to leave and return once a month to renew it.

I finally felt lucky because things were starting to go well. I had a job that was local and I didn't have to buy expensive train and bus tickets to get to work and back. I had a roof over my head; although I was not satisfied with the circumstances, all that mattered was that Zoli would soon be with me.

I remember sitting on the train on my way home and thinking how long it had been since I'd first crossed the border and left my child at home with Potyi and my parents. It was exactly two years and four months, a very long time without my little boy, but it was over now. In a few days my life with Zoli would be completely different – but I had to take care of two things before that. One was about the flat, and the other was getting Robi's permission for Zoli to travel abroad. I felt that the latter would be no problem as Robi hadn't been in contact with his son since he was five, so he couldn't stop me from taking him. But when it came to the housing, the situation was different and I didn't know what to expect.

Construction had halted a year earlier and there was little chance of the project ever being completed. It was time to give up my dreams and realise that I had failed. I had invested all the money I made in the sewing shop in Pest in this flat and it had ended in nothing. Even if by some miracle they continued building, I could not spend any more money on it, so I decided to get out of the queue before it was too late and let the money I had paid in so far go to waste.

It turned out that I had some debts and until I settled them I would not be taken off the list. Fortunately the amount was not large so I paid it on the spot and I gave up my title. The person in charge promised that once the house was finished and my flat sold, I would get my money back. Needless to say, that was an empty promise. I got nothing back.

I was right about Robi: I gave up alimony and he gave up his son in return. After he had signed the papers and I had paid the hefty notary fee, we left the office together. Typically, Robi was not interested in the kind of life Zoli would have where I was taking him.

On the way home he told me about two friends who were in the same shoes as him: both had given up their children so that their ex-wives could take them abroad, but one of the women had left her house to her ex-husband and the other sold her car and gave the money to her ex. I was stunned to hear the two stories (which may or may not have been true) because I knew what he was getting at.

'I have no house to leave you, no car to sell. What do you expect me to do?' I asked angrily.

'Nothing. I'm just saying.'

'Of course, you are just saying that,' I said, annoyed.

He walked me all the way to the staircase and, even though he had changed the subject, I was still angry. Then I took out my purse and put all my money, even the change, in his hand. 'This is all I have,' I said and left without saying goodbye.

Robi mumbled something – maybe he was thanking me – but I didn't want to hear it. I felt so uncomfortable but not because I'd given him my last money; it wasn't much, maybe he could buy a few bottles of wine with it. That was not what bothered me; it was the cost of my son's freedom.

I had thought Robi would never disappoint me again but he'd done it one last time. Never mind: the papers were signed and I could finally start a new life with Zoli, away from his father.

With the money I borrowed from my mother, we finally made it to Hungary in the evening and arrived at our new home. Karcsi was waiting for us with dinner and he seemed happy to see us, but the old man only made spiteful comments. He could not hide his dislike and there was nothing I could do about it.

A few days later, during an argument, I found out what was his problem with me. 'Karcsi could have found someone better than you!' he shouted. 'Someone without a child!'

He said the word 'child' in such a strange tone, so mocking, that I immediately lost my temper. 'But he didn't!' I shouted back. 'What has this child done to you?'

He didn't answer, just stomped off thumping his walking stick. Fortunately I was working during the day and Zoli was at school so he could only tease us in the afternoons or at weekends – which he did.

My relationship with the old man didn't improve. But what about Karcsi? I couldn't figure him out, but I realised soon enough that he was afraid of his father and so I couldn't count on him for help. They had almost daily arguments and fights, but eventually Karcsi always gave up and the old man came out as the winner. I promised myself that I would not be like that and would confront him if he hurt me or my child.

Other than the fact that he did not protect us from his father, I had nothing against Karcsi. He went to work, had a beer or two after work or went to the pub, but he came home on time and not drunk. He tried to get along with Zoli; although he didn't buy him expensive ice creams, he seemed to be trying. This idyllic state lasted for four weeks.

I remember it so well because it was the first time Zoli and I travelled home to extend our visas. So that he wouldn't miss school, we left on Saturday and came back on Sunday with the new stamp in my passport.

I strongly suspected that this weekend would be enough for the old man to fill Karcsi's head full of nonsense and turn him against us – or rather against my son. Karcsi was still normal with me but he had started to hurt Zoli, not physically because I would have scratched his eyes out for that, but the teasing and malicious remarks became more and more frequent, and I couldn't let them pass. This was partly due to the fact that he no longer drank one or two beers a day and started his weekends with beer instead of breakfast. In December, when the new wine was almost ready to drink, Karcsi often went to the cellar to 'taste' it.

I was beginning to feel that I'd made another bad decision and tied my life to an alcoholic again. The huge difference between my two relationships was that Robi was aggressive with me when he drank while Karcsi raised his voice instead of his hand. In the first days I had told him about my ex-husband's actions (not the worst ones) and that I'd sworn that I would never let anyone hit me again.

'What if I do?' Karcsi asked, laughing.

'I'll hit back!' I said firmly and I meant it.

In the seven and a half years since my divorce, I had changed a lot and it had served me well. The abused, bullied woman who was almost killed by her husband no longer existed. I felt strong and would have done anything to protect myself and my child. I hoped that wasn't the only thing that stopped Karcsi from laying a hand on me because I saw the good in him, but unfortunately that side of him rarely came out.

Christmas arrived. As usual, I baked and cooked; I wanted to celebrate this intimate holiday. A small plastic Christmas tree and its decorations in a box were taken down from the attic. After Zoli and I had decorated it, my boy sat down on the edge of the bed and gazed sadly into the distance. 'What's wrong?' I asked him, puzzled.

'What is Leda doing now?' he asked quietly, then began to cry bitterly.

I looked at my sobbing child and realised what I had done: Leda was like a little sister to him, and I'd torn them apart. Selfishly, I'd thought Zoli belonged with me and it never occurred to me how much pain I was causing him. The two children had been raised together for almost two and a half years so no wonder he missed his little sister. I felt so remorseful that I cried too.

'We'll go home soon, and you can see her then,' I told him, but it was little comfort to him.

To have our visas extended, we travelled home every fourth weekend and spent less than half a day at home, which was better than nothing. But once I got my work permit, these frequent trips will stop and we would visit only once or twice a year. We were in a difficult situation but in order to have a better life in Hungary, we had to make sacrifices. How was I supposed to explain that to a ten-and-a-half-year-old child?

That winter the old man called me a thief so I had to change my routine. He accused me of going into his house and stealing his money, which was not true; I did go to his house, but only to collect his laundry. I didn't touch his money – I didn't even see it. I told him that, but he didn't believe me.

'I don't want your money!' I shouted at the old man.

'Sure, you do! You must have needed it for beer!' he said.

'For beer? But I don't drink beer.'

'I'm sure Karcsi didn't drink all that beer himself!' The old man pointed with his stick under the table in the summer kitchen, where the empty bottles were lined up.

'What's that got to do with me? So I'm not only a thief but also an alcoholic?'

No one had ever humiliated me like that before, and I was so angry that I almost exploded. What would come next? That day I swore I would never set foot in the old man's house again. I made Karcsi collect his laundry and take in his evening meal and tried to see him as little as possible to avoid such accusations. The old man didn't deserve my care, but I had no choice. When I moved there, I'd taken it upon myself to do so.

Later that winter another incident happened that I'll never forget and I don't think Zoli will either. After work I went to a parents' meeting to the school and got home quite late. In winter, because of the cold and the lack of an entrance hall, we entered the house through two doors that led straight into the kitchen. I had already opened the outer door and my hand was on the handle of the inner door when I heard a cry for help.

'Help!' Zoli screamed in terror.

That frightened voice is etched in my mind forever; it still gives me goosebumps when I think of it.

Entering the kitchen, I was struck by a dreadful sight. Karcsi was lying on the floor unconscious, convulsing violently, his mouth foaming as he kept banging the back of his head against the stone floor. He was having an epileptic fit, which had probably begun seconds before I entered the house. Zoli was standing over him, shaking like a leaf.

I was very frightened too and I didn't know what to do. Many years earlier, I'd seen an epileptic woman collapse in church, but there was help there so I didn't go near her. Now I didn't have anyone and I had to help him.

Then I remembered the old man. I ran to him with Zoli following me. 'Come quickly, Karcsi is unwell!' I shouted.

Karcsi was still on the floor but his convulsions seemed to have subsided a little. The old man gasped then tried to lift his son, but it was impossible. I don't know what he was thinking: Karcsi's muscles were tense and his whole body was in spasm, so it was impossible to move him.

The only thing I could do was to put a blanket under his head so he wouldn't hurt the back of his head on the stone tiles. Then I remembered that epileptics could swallow their tongues during a seizure and suffocate, so I tried to reach into his mouth and grab his tongue but I couldn't. His teeth were chattering so wildly that I was afraid he would bite off my fingers.

Then, from one moment to the next, the spasms stopped and Karcsi came to. He looked around, not understanding why he was lying on the floor. I helped him to his feet and without a word he went into the room and fell asleep. I think he realised what had happened to him and was ashamed.

The old man was still in the kitchen and I snapped at him angrily, 'Why didn't you tell me your son had epilepsy?'

'I didn't know, I didn't know.' He hesitated. 'That was the first time.' Then he quickly left the kitchen so I wouldn't question him any further.

Zoli was sitting on the edge of his bed. Although the fire was burning in the tiled stove, he was shivering. I sat beside him and put my arm around his shoulders, trying to calm him down, but I was shaking too.

'Mummy, let's get out of here.' The poor child was almost begging.

'Zoli! Karcsi is sick and I can't leave him here. He needs me.'

My son said no more. I stayed by his side until he was completely calm and asleep.

I didn't sleep a wink that night. Karcsi ground his teeth loudly and sometimes twitched so violently that my heart almost jumped out of my chest. I was afraid he would have another seizure and suffocate in bed beside me while I slept.

I couldn't stop thinking about what had happened that night. I didn't know a great deal about epilepsy, but it was a terrible thing to see my partner in such a state. I was angry at the whole world, but especially at those who'd known about Karcsi's illness and didn't warn me, like my friend who'd hidden this 'little thing' away from me and arranged for me to come here. If I had known about his illness I might not have moved in, or at least I would have known what to expect. I was angry with the old man, too, because I was sure he'd lied to me; he hadn't been as scared as me and Zoli, so this wasn't the first attack he'd seen.

'Let's get out of here!' Zoli's words would not let me rest. But how could I leave a sick person? How could I look in the mirror afterwards? I regretted moving there a thousand times, and after every fight I thought we should leave, but I couldn't do that now not even for Zoli's sake. I couldn't live with my guilty conscience if I left Karcsi because of his illness.

So we stayed and got on with our lives. I brought up the subject several times but Karcsi didn't want to talk about what had happened that night; he was completely closed off. My friend didn't know about his illness and I believed her, but Karcsi's friend told me the truth. Yes, he had been having epileptic seizures for some time, but he wouldn't listen to anyone or go to the doctor. When I asked why he hadn't told me earlier, the friend said, 'I think it's your business, not mine. You two talk about it'.

He was right. Karcsi was ignorant about his illness and refused to talk about it but although he never fell ill in front of us again, at least I knew it could happen any time.

Spring came and I threw myself into work. Luckily there was no wine in the cellar so Karcsi was less drunk and I could count on his help. He dug up the front garden for me and I planted seeds and various seedlings. This time the lady next door helped me and gave me some good advice about sowing. Of course, the old man always followed me around and criticised my work. I tried to control myself, but he always got his way and managed to make me very angry.

As the weather improved, we took down the outside door and asked Karcsi to make a mosquito net door in its place, which came in very handy in the kitchen in the evenings. The old man frowned upon this too but when he saw me sanding the old paint off the windows to repaint them, he was absolutely furious.

'Why do you have to do that? Don't you have anything else to do?' he shouted. 'It's fine the way it is!'

'It's fine for you the way it is, but not for me!' I shouted back and continued with my work. When I had finished, I moved on to the door, even though it was in such bad shape that it would have been better to replace it than to repair it. We didn't have money for that, so I went to the shop where I bought the paint and asked for advice. In the end, I saved the door by sanding it down, filling the gaps with glue and then applying two coats of paint. For someone who was doing it for the first time, the end result was pretty good and I was proud of myself.

Why didn't Karcsi do this not-very-feminine job instead of me? Because he was always worried about what the old man would say – and I think that was just an excuse for him not to do anything.

When I brought up the idea of having the water brought into the kitchen, he used that excuse again.

'I don't care what the old man says!' I replied. 'Every normal house has water these days, but not here. If he starts shouting, you can blame me. He fights with me all the time anyway. One more or less doesn't matter!

Later that week, the old man went to a friend's house and told his son that he would be away all day on Saturday. That was music to my ears because I knew it was the right time to do it! Fortunately I didn't have to nag Karcsi for long because he understood that I only wanted to do what was right for us.

He secretly bought the materials and we set to work as soon as the old man put his foot out of the gate on Saturday morning. As there was water in the summer kitchen, we just had to transfer it from there to the other kitchen. Karcsi dug a trench from one room to the other, laid the pipe and covered it up to hide our tracks. In the back, among the rubble, I found a used but tolerable sink that served the purpose. There was no drain, so I put an empty bucket underneath to collect the dirty water. That didn't bother me too much; the main thing was that I finally had some water in the kitchen.

Even the old man couldn't spoil my joy – and believe me, he didn't mince his words when he attacked me that evening. I was a trespasser and a beggar who hadn't been invited, then he accused me of trying to cheat them out of the house.

'This is not your house and it never will be!' He shouted in my face.

'I don't want your house. I just wanted some water in the kitchen!' I shouted back but he didn't hear me, he just kept on shouting.

Karcsi left when he saw the old man enter the kitchen and did not return until the storm had passed. I couldn't blame him because we had agreed that I needed water in the house and I would take the blame for him. I can't say that the old man's words went in one ear and out the other, or that my blood pressure didn't rise at what I heard, but it was worth it.

Though it was difficult, things began to change as I did my best not to be ashamed of our living conditions. I slowly carried the rubbish from the front yard to the back and put it out of sight, although the old man would occasionally bring some back. The area between the house and the pavement, which must have been about eight or ten square metres, was full of weeds and rubbish, but I cleared it thoroughly and planted flowers. I got most of the seedlings and bulbs from my neighbours and my friends, so by midsummer I had a beautiful flower garden. The tall dahlia bushes covered some of the crumbling plaster on the walls and made the house look less ugly.

In the meantime, I got my work permit so I could start organising our settled status. The council administrator gave me a long list of documents I needed to obtain, and some good advice. She said that as a single mother with a minor child, there was little chance of me getting a residence permit unless I had a very good salary.

'But I am in a civil partnership,' I told her.

'That doesn't count. Immigration only accepts a marriage relationship.'

'Well, this will be interesting,' I thought on the way home. 'Could I be wasting my time and money unnecessarily because they'd end up rejecting my application?'

I entered the kitchen worried, and when I saw Karcsi I just said, 'Let's get married.'

'Okay,' he said without thinking.

'Really?' I asked in amazement.

So that was the proposal, although later Karcsi would often tease me that I proposed to him.

We only told the old man a few days before the wedding because we knew what to expect from him. We weren't disappointed because he was his usual self. He was totally freaked out and to prove how much he was against the wedding, he didn't even come to the ceremony.

We went ahead with it anyway. Karcsi's sister and her husband were our witnesses, and their two children, Zoli and Auntie were present. When we finished at the local government office, we went home and had lunch to celebrate. My family were not invited because it would have been expensive to travel and accommodation would have been a problem. They knew this and just sent a congratulatory card. So, just after my thirtieth birthday and eight years after my divorce, I got married again. I wasn't sure that this wasn't another mistake, but what could I do?

I had already started to get the documents I would need and had them translated from Ukrainian into Hungarian at a nearby translation agency for a small fee, but the clerk told me that the immigration office only accepted documents from the National Translation Office in Budapest. I had to go back to the capital and pay a lot of money for the same documents to be translated again.

It is easier now, but in the mid-nineties getting a residence permit in Hungary was a nightmare and a financial disaster. I won't bore you with the details, and I don't remember everything, but I will tell you one thing to make it clearer: Zoli and I had to go for an AIDS test, a simple blood test that cost more than my monthly salary. Don't you think it was robbery that time?

Having learnt over the years to budget what little money I had, months later I eventually managed to pay for everything and tick the last item off the list. Once I'd submitted the application, it was only a matter of time before it was processed.

Shortly afterwards I was called to the immigration office. I'd heard that it could take months to get a response to my application, but maybe this time I would be lucky.

Confidently, I travelled to Budapest, stood in the two-hour queue at the office and the clerk at the window read me the order. While she read the text without batting an eyelid, I understood only two sentences: 'I am being deported from the country' and 'I am ordered to leave Hungary with my son within twenty-four hours'.

I couldn't say anything. Suddenly I was in such a fit of tears that the administrator looked up at me in horror and stopped reading. I was in a state of shock, sobbing almost uncontrollably. She saw no point in continuing, so she handed me the documents without another word, signalling that we were done.

I turned and walked towards the exit, passing the people queuing behind me. Although they had no idea why I was crying so bitterly, they looked at me with sympathy.

I was so distraught that I couldn't stop crying all the way to the station. How could I be so unlucky? I had lost more than three years of my life and all the money I had earned. I had no home, no residence permit and we had been expelled from the country. We could go home tomorrow morning empty-handed and empty-pocketed, if I had the money to pay for the two train tickets. And what were we going to do at home? We had no place to live; since my sister had moved home with her husband and four children, all the rooms had been taken. There were eleven of them in that flat and no room left for Zoli and me. How could this happen to me? How could my Nana tell me that once will be better? It was not true; it would never get better!

After my tears subsided and I calmed down a little, I read the order I received. The reason given for the deportation was that we did not have enough income to live on.

It was true that I had only given them a statement of my income because Karcsi wasn't working at the time, at least not officially. I had deliberately not mentioned what he did for a living because he often changed jobs. I'm not saying my husband avoided working because he usually found a new job within a week or two, he just didn't stay long. He was good at farming but those were seasonal jobs and they didn't last long. He also worked in a timber company and supervised the sprinkler system in the fields, but those jobs didn't last long either, because he was sent away from one job and quit the other for some reason.

Unfortunately, Karcsi didn't care about being legally employed and entitled to holidays or medical care. When I needed his payslip, he was working on the black market for a local businessman. What made me angry was that on paper I was the one supporting my husband and child but I was the one being deported. How unfair was that?

I read the order several times and suddenly it dawned on me: all was not lost, because my work permit had not been withdrawn, which meant that I could continue to work in the sewing shop. I'd been expelled but not banned from the country, which meant I could come back to work at any time. I hoped I was right because it was my only chance.

The next day we travelled home using the little money I had, and the day after that we travelled back using the money we'd borrowed from my mother. There were no problems at the border and they let us through.

The following day I was in the office of Karcsi's employer, where I explained our situation and he promised to take care of everything. Within a few days I had my husband's payslip in my hand, which I attached to the documents I had collected so far. Some of them were only valid for a month (perhaps the one with the AIDS test), but I was lucky enough to submit them the day before they expired so I avoided wasting any more money.

The authorities re-evaluated my case. This time everything was found to be in order and I finally got my permanent residence permit. With some difficulty, I had achieved my goal and I started to believe again that things would get better. Well, they didn't get better that winter, that's for sure.

The grape harvest was quite good and although I often made sure there were fewer grapes left for wine, they still produced a good amount. Karcsi was always going down to the cellar to drink so our quarrels became more frequent. Not only did the old man suck my blood but I had to fight with my husband to protect Zoli or myself.

One night I became very ill and the next day I wasn't any better. I felt a terrible pain in my belly and I couldn't stand up because of the constant cramps. My friend drove me to the hospital where I was diagnosed with appendicitis and had surgery that night.

The doctor said that the inflammation could have been caused by stress because nothing was found in the appendix that could have caused it. I'd had plenty of stress in those last few months, – but come to think of it, the last few years hadn't been exactly stress-free either.

The next day Karcsi visited me in hospital and brought Zoli with him. I could see from the door that he had downed a couple of glasses of wine before they arrived, and I hated seeing my son with my half-drunk husband while I lay helpless in my hospital bed.

While we were talking, they brought my lunch. Zoli looked at the plate with such hungry eyes that I immediately held it out to him and he began to eat greedily. My eyes filled with tears. Looking up at Karcsi, I saw that he was also staring hungrily at my food and it made me very angry. He was a grown man but he'd forgotten to feed my child and probably only had wine for breakfast. How could he be so irresponsible? I wanted to scream at him, but I was ashamed in front of my roommates.

When they left, I couldn't take it anymore. I pulled the blanket over my head and started to cry. How could Karcsi do this to my boy? Why couldn't he take care of him when I was not around? Suddenly my roommate pulled the blanket off my head and spoke to me forcefully. 'If you want to help your son, stop crying! You'll only get a fever and then you can't go home. Pull yourself together so you can get out of here.'

She was right: I had to pull myself together because Zoli needed me.

They kept me in hospital for five days because I had another operation. About two months earlier I had developed a ganglion on my right wrist from the strain, which was causing me more and more problems. It looked like a bone growth, but it was actually a big lump with a jelly-like substance inside. The doctor said it could have gone away on its own if I had rested my hand for a few weeks, but because we were sewing big, heavy coats in the sewing shop and I had to do my chores at home too, the lump kept growing and my wrist got more and more sore.

Two days after my appendectomy I had an operation on my hand, so that problem was also solved. Those five days in hospital seemed like the longest period of my life because I was so worried about my son. I could only be sure that he would have his lunch at school, but I had no way of knowing whether he had breakfast at home or dinner before going to bed and it drove me crazy. I'd left some money for Karcsi to buy food, but I had no idea whether he bought bread or cigarettes instead.

Zoli hadn't been with me for more than two years, but I hadn't worried about him as much as I did during those few days. My parents were poor but I was sure that my son never went to bed hungry because they'd looked after him. But Karcsi couldn't take care of himself, let alone my child, so I made two promises to myself while I was in hospital.

Zoli was eleven and a half at the time and to me he was just a little child, but he needed to learn to look after himself if we were to find ourselves in such a situation again. It was not my intention to teach him to cook. but if he could use the gas cooker he could fry his own eggs or heat up his lunch. We didn't have microwaves to make our lives easier in those days.

I didn't even dare give him a knife, so I used to cut his bread and make sandwiches for breakfast, but I had to change that because no one would look after him if I was not there. What would happen to him if I died during an operation or had a heart attack from all the stress? When I'd decided to start a new life with Zoli in Hungary, I didn't think about the fact that we would be dependent on each other. If something happened to me, my son would be all alone without any help.

I needed someone I could rely on for everything, someone I could trust with my child if I needed to. That someone had to be Potyi, who had proven herself over the years.

The other promise I made in the hospital was that I would do everything I could to bring her and her little girl to Hungary. I needed my sister and Zoli needed his little sister.

It took me more than a year and a half to accomplish my plan, but I finally succeeded. In the meantime, however, many other things happened to me that I will write about because they were also important parts of my life.

After I came home from the hospital, I was off work for two or three weeks because of my hand. As I'd planned, I tried to teach Zoli to be independent while I watched my husband go completely mad. The old man also drank wine but a two-litre jug would last him two or three days, while Karcsi drank it all at once. He got drunk quickly, then slept for a few hours and drank more.

I used to say that Feri was not an alcoholic because he only drank when he was with other people, but the opposite was true of Karcsi. He liked drinking alone, which meant that he was an alcoholic. Because he was drunk more often than he was sober, he was sacked from his job and couldn't find another one for a long time. He was completely out of control that winter and became increasingly aggressive towards me.

We fought almost all the time, mostly over money or Zoli, and I got fed up with it all. Once, while I was ironing, he came to me drunk and asked me for money for cigarettes but I wouldn't give it to him. He started shouting at me and then raised his hand as if he were going to hit me. When I saw this, without thinking, I picked up the hot iron and held it in front of me.

'You want to hit me? Come on!' I shouted at him, then took a step forward and swung the iron towards his face.

Karcsi was so surprised that he started to back away and ran out of the room. I put the iron back in its place, sank into the armchair and began to sob. No one could ever hit me again and yet he had tried. Why was this happening to me? What had I done to deserve this? I'd been so afraid when I saw him raise his hand to me that I could have thrown the hot iron in his face. Would I have done that to protect myself?

A few days later, Karcsi tried to come at me again. He provoked me and yelled at me until I finally grabbed one of my boots with a thick, heavy heel and threatened him with it. 'If you don't stop, I'm going to smash your head in with this!' I shouted, losing my temper.

'All right, all right, just calm down,' he said more quietly and quickly left the kitchen.

I didn't recognise myself; it wasn't me who said those words. I didn't start crying as I had done the last time, but I was shaking like a leaf.

It was that winter, or perhaps early spring, when a similar incident occurred. Karcsi was drunk for the second time that day and wandering around the kitchen talking nonsense. Zoli was sitting quietly at the table and I was washing up after dinner.

Suddenly Karcsi took a small coffee cup from the kitchen drawer and threw it on the floor, where it immediately shattered. I thought he'd dropped it by accident so I said nothing. Then he took the next one and threw it on the floor, and then a third. I got very angry because they were the nicest cups in that shabby kitchen cupboard.

'Stop it!' I shouted at him. 'They were your mother's coffee cups.'

I didn't even finish the sentence when Karcsi grabbed the clock and slammed it to the ground. It was an old-fashioned metal alarm clock; it shattered with the violent impact and a piece of it flew towards Zoli's feet. I'm not sure if it hit him, but the sight of it made my head spin. He couldn't hurt my child!

With the pot in my hand, which still had the rinse water in it, I jumped up and started hitting Karcsi on the back with all my strength. He must have been hurt because he ran screaming out of the kitchen and returned a few seconds later with his father. Zoli, frightened, sat on a chair and I stood motionless in the middle of the kitchen which looked like a battlefield.

'Look what she did,' Karcsi complained to his father. 'She hit me on the back with the pot.'

'All right, calm down both of you. Stop it!' the old man shouted unnecessarily as we had already stopped.

'I didn't do that.' I pointed to the floor and resumed washing up.

I was stunned by what had happened. How could I lose my temper and hit my husband? By hurting my child he had brought out the beast in me but I had no regrets; I would have done it again any time.

That was how much I had changed. Ten years earlier I was the abused wife living in fear with her husband; now I had become the abuser who beats her husband without a second thought.

I am not proud of what I did, but I think it was the right thing to do. I didn't want to be a victim anymore; it was time to stand up and show him that I wasn't afraid of him. My only regret was that it all happened in front of Zoli and I didn't know how it would affect him in the future.

Can you guess how this incident affected Karcsi? He saw what I was capable of and, although we still fought a lot, he didn't dare lay a hand on me again. Later he kept telling me that this was not my house and if I didn't like something I could leave. These were partly the old man's words; he was sure that I was only using them, that I wanted them out of the house and wanted it for myself.

The wine finally ran out and Karcsi sobered up, found a job and went to work like a normal man. Our fights became less frequent, but still the phrase 'you can get out of here' kept coming out of his mouth. I once said to him, 'You'll keep saying that until we actually leave!' It was just an empty threat, though, because where else could we go?

I couldn't wait for the weather to get better so I could get out in the garden and work. Last year's planting had gone so well, I had enough tomatoes, peppers, cucumbers, green beans and many other things to last all summer. Not only did I not have to go to the shop, but I'd also made several jars of pickles and tomato juice for the winter.

Gardening was comforting – but only until I saw the old man behind me. At such times my stomach would clench and my nerves would be on edge because I knew what he was up to. He would follow me into the garden just to annoy me and criticise my work. I put up with his teasing for a while, but one day I snapped. When he started poking my pepper plants with his rake because he thought I had planted them too close together, I'd had enough.

'Enough, leave me alone! I did the same thing last year and they turned out fine. But if you know better, do it your way! I've had enough of this!' I shouted at the old man, then threw what I was holding to the ground and walked away.

Later that night I had an argument with Karcsi about something stupid, and the phrase 'you can get out of here' came up again. That's when I really got fed up, fed up with the whole thing. These two people were not worth ruining myself for. My heart was aching from the stress and my nerves were out of control. I needed some peace and I couldn't get it in this house, so I had to do something.

A few days earlier, I'd heard from a colleague that there was a cottage for rent on the main road so I went there the next day after work. It was quite expensive but as I had just received my salary, I put down the first month's rent. Then I went home, Zoli and I packed our things and put the bags on the bikes.

We were almost on our way when Karcsi arrived. He looked at us curiously, but I just told him, 'We're leaving.'

Without waiting for him to answer, we pushed the bikes onto the road and cycled to our new home. The old man was in the garden so he didn't realise he had succeeded in his plan to chase us out of their lives.

Ironically, a few days after I left Karcsi, we would have been married for a year. My first marriage lasted three years and my second didn't even last a year. What was wrong with me? How could I ruin my life like that? My parents and my grandparents lived together for decades; even though their lives were difficult, they stayed together. Why couldn't I do the same?

I could have been more patient with Karcsi and done everything the old man wanted, but then I would have sunk to their level and I couldn't live like that. I wanted to change the terrible conditions so that I wouldn't be ashamed in front of people. I wanted to make our lives better, but for them everything was fine the way it was. I was tired of the constant fighting and bickering; I needed peace.

To the old man I was an intruder who refused to live by his rules. He hated me and made no secret of it, so it was hard to be patient with him. But I couldn't understand why Karcsi didn't like my son. Zoli was a good child, his teachers never complained about his behaviour and he had no problems with his studies. He went to a badminton club and learned to play the trumpet, which he did quite well. He could have taken the trumpet home from school to practise, but Karcsi wouldn't let him because he was annoyed by the 'noise'.

The first time I heard Zoli play was at the Mother's Day celebration, when he played such a beautiful song that I cried with emotion. When he finished, several mothers and the class teacher were also wiping away their tears. They congratulated me and praised my son for his skill. I was so proud of him, but when I told Karcsi about it he laughed and then got angry. Was my husband jealous of my son? Was that why he was so mean to him? I couldn't do anything about it because Zoli would always come first for me.

The house I rented was only slightly smaller than Karcsi's but I liked the layout much more. To the right of the front door was the bathroom, to the left was a small kitchen, opposite was the dining room, which was also the living room, which led to the bedroom. The owner was an elderly lady who had been taken in by her daughter; they lived on the other side of the courtyard.

Fortunately the house was rented out furnished and I could use everything in it. Of course, this 'luxury' came at a price because after paying the rent I had little money left for food. There was no garden with fruit trees and vegetables, so I had to buy everything in the shop. Zoli turned twelve that summer and had already taken a student job picking cherries so that we could have a little more money.

A few weeks after we moved, I realised that I might have been hasty in my decision to leave Karcsi. It wasn't our financial situation that worried me because I could live on buttered bread all month if I had to. I had wanted quiet, stress-free days and hoped I would get them in the new place but I was wrong.

The old lady who was supposed to be living with her daughter in the big house only went there to eat and sleep and spent most of her time with us in the little house. She was already there when she saw me coming home from work; or more than one occasion she was sitting in the kitchen waiting for me because she could come in at any time with her own key.

At first I ignored her but it became increasingly annoying. She would sit with us for hours on and, although she was not mean or annoying like my father-in-law, I was increasingly irritated by her presence.

She talked about the same things almost all the time and I knew her stories by heart. When she wasn't talking about herself or her late husband, she was scolding the previous tenants.

Her daughter, who was a disabled pensioner and sat at home all day, also visited often but at least she didn't stay long.

A Romanian couple had lived in the house before me and the old woman said they stole from her. The only strange thing about the story was that I found most of the stolen items she listed hidden in the house. I don't think she had mental problems but something was wrong with her, that was for sure.

After a while I lost patience with her and couldn't wait for her daughter to call her for dinner or to go to sleep so I could spend some time with Zoli. I had no peace or privacy in that house either – and I even paid for it.

One evening when I was finally alone with Zoli someone rang the doorbell. I was surprised to see Karcsi at the gate, but although I hadn't told him where we were moving to, nothing in the village could remain a secret.

He wasn't drunk but he must have had two or three beers to give him the courage to come and see me. He was a little shy, but he wanted to know how I was and what the rented place was like. I couldn't tell him the truth so I said that everything was fine and that Zoli and I were doing well.

His visits became more frequent and I can honestly say that I didn't mind. It was such a strange relationship, because it was like he was flirting with me but we were actually married.

While I listened to my landlady's boring stories for the hundredth time, I sometimes thought about Karcsi. Now he wasn't the annoying figure I'd run away from but the one I looked forward to seeing in the evenings. He didn't stay more than a quarter of an hour and we only chatted at the gate because my landlady forbade me to let him in the house, but it was enough to brighten my day a little.

One Sunday evening he came to my house with half a tray of homemade pastries. He even apologised that his weren't as good as the ones I made, but I didn't mind: it was the gesture that really touched me. After Zoli and I left Karcsi's home I didn't bake anything because the money was for food, not dessert.

The next time he brought me a jar of jam from the pantry, then a tin of fruit and some pickles, even though I didn't ask for anything. He said I had worked hard growing them so I was entitled to some. It was during these visits that Karcsi showed me a side of him I hadn't seen before.

Once I met my former neighbour in the shop and we had a chat. She said that my flower garden was very nice and that Karcsi usually weeded and watered it in the evening. She also said that she'd seen the old man hoeing the front garden in the morning and that his arm must be hurting because it was tied in a sling with a scarf. When I heard that, I imagined the old man scratching my seedlings with one hand and I felt so sorry for him. For a moment I forgot about his meanness, his malicious remarks; all I saw was a gnarled old man with a bandage around his neck.

That moment passed quickly because I knew that my father-in-law hadn't changed a bit in the last few months. Even though Karcsi kept telling me how much he missed me and that I should go back to them, I didn't give in. One day he even said that the old man had sent him to call me home, but I didn't believe him.

'Maybe you've just realised that you're better off with me than without me?' I asked him, but he didn't answer.

Although we were getting on well now, I felt that if we got together again Karcsi would sooner or later show his ugly side, and I didn't want that. When I mentioned this to him, he swore he wouldn't and promised to behave himself.

'You say that when you're sober, but when you get drunk, you'll want to lay hands on me again,' I told him.

'I'll never do it again!' he swore. 'I won't get drunk again, but I can have a beer or two, can't I?'

'My problem is not with one, two or three bottles of beer! You get drunk when there's wine in the cellar and you don't sober up until it's gone. Can you change that for me?'

Karcsi didn't answer; the uncertainty was written all over his face.

'I didn't think so,' I said disappointedly, then turned and went into the house.

I wanted to give him another chance, but I was afraid it would end up like my first marriage; Robi had blown his second chance because he couldn't give up drinking for me. Why should this be any different? Karcsi didn't turn up for a couple of days; he was probably sulking about what I'd said.

We had been living in the rented house for almost three months when things started to disappear. One day I came home to find the kitchen set missing from the wall, not just the ladle or the meat fork but the whole six-piece set. I thought the old lady must have taken it to her daughter's house, even though they had a fully equipped kitchen. When she came round, I didn't ask her about the set because it was hers and she could do what she wanted with it.

The next afternoon the old lady was waiting for me in her usual place in the kitchen with a big grin on her face. I could believe that she was happy to see me, but I couldn't even pretend to be happy; all I wanted was a free afternoon or a weekend with no one at home but me and Zoli.

If you haven't been in this situation before, I hope you understand what I'm talking about and why my patience was wearing thin. She began to tell her story. I wanted to start cooking but I couldn't find the pot I needed anywhere. I remembered washing it the day before and putting it back in its place, but it was gone.

'Where is the pot in which I cook the soup?' I asked quietly, as if muttering to myself, but the woman heard me and was almost indignant at my question.

'Well, it must be there, because I haven't taken it anywhere!'

'Well, I didn't take it anywhere either!' I replied, not very kindly. It was an embarrassing situation and I ended up using another pot to cook in.

The next day my shower gel disappeared from my bathroom. When I entered the room, I immediately noticed that a family picture was missing from the wall, too. That's when I realised what was going on. The woman had accused her previous tenants of stealing things but I think she'd hidden them because I had found some of the 'stolen items' in the house. Now it was my turn to be the one 'stealing' from the poor old lady.

You can be sure that my already frayed nerves didn't need this circus. If word got around the village that I stole from her, I might as well run away or go straight home to my mother.

I didn't know what to do. When I saw her coming towards me with a big smile on her face, I thought I was going to explode with rage. 'Where did the picture go from the wall?' I asked her straight away, without even saying hello.

The old lady looked at me in astonishment, but when she saw my angry face she confessed that she had taken the picture to her room.

'And the set of spoons and the pot?' I asked her next.

'I didn't touch them,' she said meekly.

'Well, I didn't touch them either! I don't want anything from you!'

She could see she was getting on my nerves so she thought it was best to leave. It wasn't worth arguing with her because it was my first afternoon off in three months.

By the evening, I'd managed to calm down but I knew that this could not go on. When Karcsi showed up at the gate later and told me he would change and I should come home, I said yes without thinking. 'I'm coming. Pick us up this time tomorrow.'

I knew what was waiting for us if we went back there, but I also suspected what would happen if we stayed with the old woman. I had to choose between two evils, and at that moment Karcsi seemed the better option.

The next day, I told my landlady that I had made up with my husband and we were going back to him. We packed our things, Karcsi came to get us and we slept in our 'own' bed that night.

If you had to guess whether anything changed after I went back, what would you say? Probably no – and unfortunately you would be right. The first month went by and I probably scared the old man a bit because he tried to resist picking on me. Sometimes I even saw a forced smile on his face, but it was more pathetic than friendly.

Karcsi was tolerable with Zoli, similar to when I'd brought my son here two years ago. It seemed incredible that we had only lived there for two years (minus the three months) and so much had happened to us.

Unfortunately, there was more bad than good but there was nothing I could do about it. I considered myself an optimistic person and I wanted to believe that our future in this house would be better than our past, but I couldn't.

After a month passed, our lives became hell again. I think by then the two men felt safe and, knowing we had nowhere to go, they picked up where they'd left off. The old man was sucking my blood and driving me crazy and Karcsi was picking on Zoli, which I couldn't ignore.

A month after we moved back home, my dear husband got drunk and yelled in my face, 'Go back to where you were! Why did you come home?'

'But you invited me home, didn't you?'

'I certainly didn't!' he lied. 'You wanted to come back, but why?'

What could I say to him? Remind him of his promises, his vows to change and treat us well? It was useless to say or do anything because these two people were incapable of changing.

That autumn the grape harvest was rather poor but I still ate a lot of it to reduce the amount for making wine. One day the old man caught me munching on his grapes and scolded me, but I talked back. 'What's the wine for?' I asked him. 'The more there is, the more the circus!'

He mumbled something and left. I went from eating his grapes in secret to eating them in front of him; I was determined to ruin his nerves like he was ruining mine. But no matter how hard I tried, the grapes turned into a small barrel of wine that was waiting for my alcoholic husband in the cellar.

As I'd had to pay rent in the summer, I couldn't put any money aside so we couldn't order the firewood until the autumn, and even then only in small quantities. The old man didn't help financially; he only put in as much as he needed for wood, the rest he didn't care about. My father-in-law had a very nice pension (I happened to see his pension slip once) but he never gave me any money for utilities or food. If he needed bread or something else, he would send Zoli to the shop (that's what the child was good for) and count the change in front of him to check that he wasn't a penny short.

Karcsi found it difficult to bring home his salary because coffee, beer and cigarettes were more important to him than having enough wood to keep us warm in the winter. It was already very cold in November, so the little wood we had was quickly used up and what I had ordered from my next pay cheque had not yet arrived. By mid-December we were in big trouble but Karcsi didn't care because by then the wine was drinkable and it warmed him up.

Zoli and I collected all the wood and waste that could be burnt in the courtyard, but after a while we ran out of that too. I took two bags of dusty coats and old shoes from the attic and burned them all. Yes, I know I polluted the air because sometimes the smoke from the chimney was so bad that I was ashamed for the neighbours to see it. I apologise to the environmentalists, but I had no choice; I didn't want to freeze to death with my child in that cold house.

The old man complained that he had no wood and slept in a coat, but I think he stored it in his house, because there was always smoke coming out of the chimney at night. As I didn't go into his house, I couldn't be sure.

There was a huge log in the back garden, at least two metres long and about seventy centimetres in diameter, which must have arrived sometime in the summer. I asked Karcsi several times to saw it into pieces and split it but he wouldn't lift a finger. If you burned coal or ordinary wood, the tiled stove kept the heat in until morning, but the rags burned fast so the house cooled down very quickly.

One Saturday morning Karcsi went down to the cellar as usual. He no longer drank wine from a glass or a pitcher but straight from the barrel, using a rubber hose. An hour later he was drunk and lying on Zoli's bed in the kitchen next to the cold stove.

I had absolutely nothing to burn that day, so to warm us up while I ate breakfast with Zoli, I turned on one of the gas hobs. The gas cylinder was running out fast and was expensive, so I could only use it for cooking, but there was nothing else left.

When I saw Karcsi sleeping soundly and snoring heavily, I started to get nervous. He was not cold because he was drunk; if it was up to him, we'd freeze to death. He was the man of the house and he was supposed to keep his family warm. How could he do this to us? I had learned to split small pieces of wood with an axe but I couldn't manage the big log, it was a man's job.

I was so angry with Karcsi that I went over and shook his shoulder to wake him up and make him do something. 'Get up and chop that log, because we have nothing to make a fire with!' I shouted.

He shouted at me to leave him alone and turned over but I kept shaking his shoulders and shouting until he finally sat up on the bed. 'Send your child out, let him do it!' he growled, which made me even angrier.

'You want the child to do your work? Aren't you ashamed of yourself?'

'If you don't like it, you can get out of here!' He gave the usual line then got up and stomped over to the table.

I could tell by the way he was walking that he was still drunk; looking back, I know I should have kept my mouth shut but I didn't. We continued to shout at each other, then Karcsi picked up the knife on the table and held it over his head. His hand stopped halfway in the air and I froze.

We stared at each other for a while...

I'll stop here for a moment and let you imagine the situation in the kitchen.

In Karcsi's upraised hand there is a knife with a blade thirty centimetres long and a centimetre wide. I am standing opposite him, frozen, the tip of the knife half a metre from my heart. Zoli is standing at the other end of the table looking at us in horror.

We stayed like that for only a few seconds, staring at each other, but it felt like an eternity. Karcsi's confused, drunken eyes changed in an instant, as if he had suddenly sobered up and realised what he was doing. By then he was looking at me in fear, not because he was afraid of me but because he was afraid of himself, of what he was about to do.

Silently, he lowered the knife and with his other hand bent the end of the blade. Finally he threw the now-useless knife on the floor and stormed out of the kitchen.

I didn't move from my seat – I was still in shock – but when Zoli came to me, we sat on the edge of the bed. We were both shaking with fright but we didn't speak, we just looked at each other.

How could it happen to me again? Ten years ago Robi had almost taken my life and now it was only a matter of time before Karcsi stabbed me in the heart in front of my son. A year ago, when I'd hit him with the pot, I'd thought I was no longer afraid of him and that I could defend myself, but now I was so frozen that I couldn't move and he could have easily stabbed me. But if I'd tried to defend myself, I might have been lying in the middle of the kitchen. I guess I'd been lucky again – but why did these things keep happening to me?

It was my fault too, I shouldn't have provoked him, but my nerves were shot, I couldn't keep my mouth shut and it had almost cost me my life. When it had turned out that Karcsi had epilepsy, I had stood by him and this was what I got in return. What's next?

Karcsi and his father sawed the logs that day and by the afternoon the fire was crackling in the stove. A few days later the next load of wood arrived, so our problem was solved for the time being.

I knew Karcsi regretted what he'd done but I couldn't forgive him; I couldn't even look at him. I didn't speak to him for days even when he was picking on Zoli. I was tired of it all and I think I got depressed. Maybe that was why I didn't notice that Karcsi stopped drinking overnight.

It was weeks before I noticed that he didn't go down to the cellar or drink beer in the kitchen like he used to. Maybe pulling a knife on me had scared him so much that he gave up drinking. I wasn't too happy about that because he could change at any time, but he stayed sober and his epileptic seizures stopped. I knew that because his teeth grinding and twitching at night had stopped and he no longer had seizures during the day.

If you think my life got better with my non-alcoholic husband, you are wrong. Sure, it got a little easier because we argued less but it was still far from normal. He still wouldn't leave Zoli alone and that pissed me off.

'How many cups of tea have you had?' he asked my son once. 'You're like a sponge.'

'Why can't he drink as much as he wants? Did you buy the tea or the sugar in it?' I asked angrily.

'I didn't, but it's running out,' he said, laughing. Maybe he was joking but I was getting upset about everything.

One day I worked overtime in the sewing room and didn't get home until it was dark. Karcsi was in the kitchen having dinner and Zoli was sitting in the armchair in the dark room.

'Why are you sitting in the dark?' I asked him, surprised.

'Because Karcsi told me not to turn on the light, not to waste electricity,' he replied quietly. Wouldn't things like that make you angry?

There was a lot of this going on in the house and it usually ended in a fight. 'Why do you keep hurting this child?' I asked Karcsi once.

'Let him get used to harshness,' he laughed.

When I heard that, I realised something. I think Karcsi was teased and made fun of at school because of his stutter or his short stature so as an adult he compensated, but even if I was right he shouldn't have treated my son like that.

Nevertheless a good thing happened to Zoli that year, and I was very happy about it. Although he was still a beginner in the trumpet group, he was entered in a competition and we went together. Students from schools in the area were invited to the big music hall to show what they could do. The children played different instruments and were very good, so the jury had a hard time.

Zoli's name was called out during the results announcement as he had won first place in the novice group. As he walked up to the stage to receive his certificate, my chest literally swelled with pride. I had never been so proud of anything or anyone in my life as I was of him. It's true that Zoli didn't make a big career in music because life took him in a different direction, but that day was unforgettable for us.

Spring came and I managed to get Karcsi to build a small terrace in front of the kitchen. It cost him almost nothing because he built it himself with a welding implement borrowed from a friend and some scrap iron he'd found. He even made me a space for flower boxes on both sides of the patio. He put on a corrugated iron roof, also from the scrap, to protect the front door from the rain. He even made a gutter for the house by cutting two long plastic pipes lengthwise and laying them on the roof. It was not a pretty sight, but it served the purpose.

Eventually I had balcony boxes in which I had flowers, and thanks to my friends the windowsills were not left without plants either. From then on, when someone entered the courtyard, the first thing they saw was not the old, ugly building but my beautiful flower garden. In winter it was all shabby and ugly again, but there was nothing I could do about that.

Sadly, it was not enough to make the garden and the house look good on the outside when we were being 'eaten' by mould on the inside. I ventilated and washed our clothes all the time, but as soon as they were in the wardrobe they smelt musty. I heard in the shop that there was a product that, when mixed with wall paint, stopped the mould from spreading for a while.

When I told Karcsi to paint the house with it, he wouldn't hear of it. 'It's too much work and I don't have time. And what will the old man say?'

'I don't care what the old man says! It's not his health that's destroyed by this mould, it's ours. If you don't want to do it, I will! Just help me move the furniture away from the wall.'

He agreed. After I bought the paint and tools, we moved the furniture over the weekend and were shocked to see what was behind it. The walls were thick with mould, as were the backs of the beds and wardrobes.

It was a lot of work, but it had to be done. I had less time than Karcsi because of the sewing, housework and gardening, but I got on with it. I scraped the nasty mould off the walls, and even though I covered my nose and mouth with a scarf, I inhaled a lot of it. Karcsi saw how hard I was working so he started to help me and together we finished painting the room. I wanted to burn the cupboards but we didn't have money for new furniture, so I cleaned them and put everything back where it was. The tiled stove made the kitchen walls less mouldy so we got those done quicker.

I was glad we'd done it, but especially glad that Karcsi was there to help me. It also helped that Zoli was out of sight because he was doing student work again.

What do you think the old man thought? He was shouting about the terrace too, but the painting was killing him. He kept grumbling because he thought we should spend the money on firewood and not on painting. 'We didn't ask you for money for the wood before and we won't ask you in the future,' I told him.

Although I was busy, I had to look after the garden because I needed vegetables all year round. The old man kept coming up to me just to annoy me. One day, when I saw him coming towards me, I didn't even wait for him to open his mouth, I just shouted rudely, 'Go away.'

He was so surprised that he turned and walked away and then he didn't bother me for a while. I was brought up to respect the elderly but my father-in-law did not deserve my respect because he was the meanest man I had ever met.

Since he no longer came to bug me in the garden, he would come into the kitchen, sit down on a chair and start talking while I was cooking. My landlady used to irritate me when she sat in the kitchen for hours on end but now the old man was driving me up the wall, even though he only stayed a short time.

I think I really started to hate him when I found out he was no better than my ex-father-in-law. After his wife's suicide, he and Karcsi blamed each other for her death. It turned out that Karcsi had left the weedkiller out, but before his mother could drink it the old man had hit her on the head with a shovel because she was drunk again. She had been using a walking frame for years, so what the old man did to her was disgusting – and it wasn't the first time.

I played this card against him once when he was getting on my nerves. 'Why won't you leave me alone? Do you want me to kill myself too?' I asked him.

He pulled the most frightened face I'd ever seen and ran out of the kitchen, but he came back the next day because driving me mad was part of his daily routine.

When I started writing about Karcsi, I was planning to complain less about my father-in-law but I realize that I can't avoid complaining because he was the source of all my problems.

He took our antagonism to a masterly level, especially after Karcsi stopped drinking and behaved more normally around me. He was always scolding his son and saying bad things about him, which I often did not let him get away with; in the evenings he would call me names while eating what I'd cooked.

One morning I went to the back garden with a white bucket, but according to him I had a sheet with me to have fun with a guy at the back of the garden. Instead of defending me, Karcsi listened to his spiteful father and later told me everything even though I didn't want to listen to him.

I'll stop complaining for a while; I just wanted to give you an idea of what was going on around me and why my nerves were shot.

In the summer, Zoli and I went home to my family for a week and told Potyi the good news. It was time to bring her and Leda to Hungary but it took a long time to find a place for them to rent. Work was not a problem because my boss promised her a work permit if she came over, but they had no place to live. There were hardly any houses for rent in the village at that time, especially at affordable prices, but I eventually found one. It was a small summer house with a sofa, a cupboard, a table and a tiny stove in the corner. The kitchen and shower room together were no more than three square metres, but the house cost half as much as my previous rent so I took it straight away.

Potyi and Leda arrived in August and I could finally breathe a sigh of relief. My sister started working in the sewing shop, so Zoli took care of the little girl and in September he took Leda to kindergarten in the mornings.

When I brought Zoli back to Hungary, it soon became clear that I had separated him from his little sister. Now I had managed to put that right but it took me years to realise the pain I caused my father because Leda was the apple of his eye. At first Potyi and her daughter went home every month, but after she got her work permit she only visited the family once a year, like us.

After the little girl disappeared from his life overnight, my father became increasingly sad, maybe even depressed; years later he could hardly speak, as if he had lost the ability. He didn't die because of that at the age of seventy-six; his lungs collapsed from smoking. I still felt guilty; I had started the avalanche. However, Potyi and Leda had a better life and sacrifices had to be made.

This better life did not begin that year, not in winter. We were glad of the cheap rent because Potyi had some money left for food and firewood, but we hadn't counted on the cold. The walls of the house were thin, there was only one door, and the frost on the glass didn't disappear for two hours after the fire had been lit. Moreover, the small iron stove did not keep the heat in for long so that by morning the window and the door were again covered with ice. I felt sorry for Potyi, but at least they lived in peace.

When spring came, my sister helped me with the garden so they could have some of the harvest too.

Despite the old man's protests, I had planted a raspberry bush along the fence, which grew beautifully and was full of fruit. I was proud of my work because that was the only way we could eat such precious fruit in those days.

Zoli finished eighth grade and started working again during the summer holidays to earn some pocket money. The secondary school where he'd been accepted was in a nearby town but because he would have had to take the bus and train every day, I enrolled him in a dormitory. It seemed like a good solution for Karcsi and his father that my son would only come home at weekends, but I didn't expect it to be so hard on me.

The rumour about the dormitory was that the big boys bullied the little ones and picked on them like recruits in the army. Zoli was a small, quiet boy and I was very worried about him. The day when he moved in and I saw his roommates and the older boys wandering around the corridor, my heart sank even more.

I said goodbye to him with tears in my eyes and when I got home I was at the end of my tether; my nerves were shot. Slumped in an armchair, I began to sob as bitterly as if I had lost him forever. Years before, when my little boy had lived with my family, I hadn't worried so much about him because he was safe but now he could get hurt and I wouldn't be there for him.

The next day I couldn't get rid of these thoughts and they almost suffocated me. I managed to get to work but I ended up in the armchair again at home. I looked at the clock and saw that afternoon school was over and Zoli would be home from school soon. I heard the gate open and my son pushing his bike towards the woodshed; I knew it was him because I recognised the sound of the coloured berries rattling on the spokes of his bicycle. Then, in a flash, I realised that Zoli was in the dormitory and it had been an hallucination. I started sobbing again and didn't stop for a long time.

The next afternoon I didn't sit in the chair but lay down on the floor in the middle of the room and stayed there for a while. Karcsi called me several times for dinner but I didn't move. I was so weak and so sad that tears were falling from my eyes; it was as if I were mourning someone, but there was no one to mourn because Zoli was coming home for the weekend.

Karcsi got tired of it all, came over, grabbed my hands and tried to lift me up, all the while talking kindly to me. 'Get up, change your clothes and eat something.'

I had neither the strength nor the inclination, but I let him help me up. When I looked out of the window, I was shocked to see that it was completely dark. I felt as if I had just got home from work but hours had passed while I lay crying. What was happening to me – was I going mad?

I had fallen into such a deep depression that I was not only physically but mentally exhausted. I needed help. Looking back, my fear for Zoli was not the main cause of my condition, it was the stress I was under. It's true that Karcsi was less annoying since he'd stopped drinking but the old man did his best to drive me mad. It seems he had achieved his goal.

The next day the GP sent me to the psychiatric ward because it was obvious that something was wrong with me. I had recovered from a nervous breakdown before but now I was a nervous wreck again. While waiting for the bus I started to feel sick and panicked; I was sweating and my hands were shaking from the nervousness in my stomach. I was dizzy and gasping for breath, but the bus arrived before I could pass out and I quickly got on it.

If I could have sat down, maybe my nausea would have gone away but as usual there was hardly any room even to stand. The fact that people were panting all over me on the overcrowded bus made me feel even worse. Due to my weak nerves, I became panic-stricken that day and the antidepressant and mood-altering drugs did not help. Later I was given a stronger type of sedative, which I took for more than two years until my nerves recovered. The anxiety and panic in crowds went away much later after I had made some changes in my life.

For the next two years, apart from changing job, not much happened to me. In my new job I propagated and rooted plants under sterile conditions in laboratory, which I loved because it was interesting and varied.

Zoli got used to college and he never had a problem with the older boys, and I got used to seeing him only at weekends. The interesting thing was that my little boy started to grow so suddenly that at sixteen he was as tall as Karcsi; two years later he was 1m 90cms tall. Not only was he taller than my husband, he was also smarter.

As I was depressed and living on tranquilisers, Karcsi treated me better than before. We were fine during weekdays but as soon as Zoli came home from college, my husband went out of his mind. Just as his father couldn't leave me alone and stop picking on me, Karcsi couldn't leave my son alone. Weekends were spent fighting, crying and almost always with the same old words: 'This is my house and if you don't like it, you can leave!'

I always hoped that one day I would have a house where no one would tell me what to do and what not to do. To make it more than just a dream, I took out a five-year building society contract with a monthly deduction from my salary. This amount, with interest and the promised government subsidy, wouldn't buy a house but it would be enough for a mortgage. That was my goal, but Zoli found another way to make a better life for us.

He had just turned sixteen when one day he decided that he was going to work in England when he finished school. He said it so seriously and firmly that it stopped me in my tracks.

'To England?' I asked. 'So far away?'

As the saying goes, history repeats itself. A few years earlier I'd left my family in search of a better life and I rarely saw them. Soon Zoli would leave me, and he probably only visit me once or twice a year.

It was scary even thinking about it because England was a foreign country to us and so far away, but I didn't even try to talk him out of it. It was what my son wanted to do and I respected his decision. We still had a few years together and I hoped it would be easier to let him go when the time came.

What I didn't expect was to have to let Potyi and Leda go that summer. My sister had met a man who lived in a nearby village and was raising his daughter and granddaughter on his own. They dated for a while then suddenly decided to move in together. I was happy for them, but I was afraid that my sister would be disappointed. When I looked at myself and my relationships, I hadn't made many good choices in my life; however, Potyi was luckier than me because fate brought her together with a good man.

They got married in the autumn and a few days before the following Christmas they had a little girl called Rubin. Leda had a little sister and a daddy who loved her and raised her as his own.

Potyi's life was going well, but I couldn't say the same for mine. My new psychiatrist decided that the strong sedatives were no longer justified so she started to reduce my medication and eventually stopped it altogether. She said that at thirty-six I was too young to be on sedatives and that I should change my life to avoid going back for psychiatric treatment, but I couldn't see any way out.

Another two years passed and Zoli completed his A-levels, then studied a trade that would help him get on in England. He said he could always find work abroad as a cook or a waiter, so he chose those professions. My little boy, now grown up, was planning his future with a sense of purpose and I was very proud of him. He worked through the summer holidays, bought things I couldn't afford and got his driving licence at the age of eighteen, again with his own money.

While he was moving forward, Karcsi was 'stumbling' in one place. Over the years, he'd worked at every job in the village but never stayed long so I couldn't count on his salary because it was sometimes there and sometimes not. Then the idea came up for him to become a security guard, for which he had to do a course that cost quite a lot. Somehow we found the money (maybe we borrowed it from someone) and my husband got the certificate.

Soon after that he got a job of which he was very proud in Budapest at a railway station. The security company paid him a pretty good salary but before we could get back on our feet financially, Karcsi was an addict again – this time not to alcohol (fortunately he hadn't touched it for years) but to mobile phones!

At the time, all three of us had old mobile phones that we'd bought second-hand, but that was not good enough for Karcsi, who was working in the capital. He was always exchanging his phone or buying a new one and somehow he always ended up on the losing end of those 'good bargains' and regretted it financially. In one year he had at least fifteen phones pass through his hands, which drove me crazy. He was like a child who couldn't resist the next toy he saw in the shop window.

It was also around that time that cash payments stopped at my workplace so I had to open a bank account for my salary. The bank advised me to get another card and have a joint account with my husband and I took their advice.

Since many shops did not yet accept debit cards, I used to withdraw an amount from my account and use it for shopping. Sometimes I noticed something was wrong and there was less money in my account than I remembered. The following month it was a similar situation and when I went to withdraw the last part of my payment, my account was empty.

Outraged, I went to the bank and questioned the teller because I was sure they had done something with my money but when I got an answer I was mortified. The last bit of the money had been withdrawn from my account the night before from the ATM at the station in Budapest.

That was when I realised that it was my husband who was stealing from me, and not for the first time. The money was for food – how could he do that to me?

When he came home from work in the morning I questioned him, but he denied everything. Then he blamed Zoli, saying he'd stolen my card and taken the money.

'How can you say that?' I demanded. 'What was my son doing at your workplace last night?'

He had nothing to say: he was caught. I demanded the card back and he threw it on the table with the remaining money and stormed out of the kitchen.

I was so mad at him, I nearly exploded. He had accused Zoli of stealing to cover himself. Years ago, his father had called me a thief even though Karcsi was the one who was taking his pension, not me. How could someone steal from his own family?

As if that were not enough for one day, the old man came into the kitchen and made me very angry about something. Just because I stopped complaining about him a while ago doesn't mean our relationship had changed. My father-in-law had been destroying my nerves for nine years and as a result I had to take medication for my heart too.

I went to work in the afternoon in a very bad mood. I felt sick, my heart was pounding, and sometimes it felt like I was being stabbed with a knife. If this went on, one day I'd have a heart attack and I'd be dead.

I felt so bad that I started crying in the laboratory while I was cutting the plants. Luckily I was sitting alone and the mask I was wearing absorbed my tears so no one noticed, although that was the least of my worries at the time.

'How can I be so unfortunate? How long must I put up with this? Will I never have a peaceful life?' I was thinking these things when suddenly something inside me said, 'I've had enough! ENOUGH!!! Time to change my life!'

The inertia, the uncertainty, suddenly disappeared and I knew what I had to do.

The week before, I'd heard that my brother-in-law had got the job he'd applied for and it came with a staff apartment. They were due to move in a month and, to make sure their house wasn't empty, they were looking for a lodger or family member to keep things tidy. It had never occurred to me that I could be that family member but that afternoon it all came to me: yes, that was the solution. I could see a way out.

Over the weekend I spoke to my brother-in-law who was nice enough not to charge me rent if I kept the house and garden in order. Zoli was delighted with the news and couldn't wait to move out but Karcsi had an interesting reaction. I think he didn't believe we would leave, or was hoping I would change my mind. He was wrong: I had made up my mind and there was no going back.

A month later, when the removal van stopped in front of the house, my husband left home so he wouldn't see me leave. The old man had gone into the garden early in the morning so he didn't know what was happening. We had managed to keep the move a secret until then, and I was hoping we could get away without him noticing, but we couldn't. After putting the bikes on the truck, there were just a few pots of flowers left which I was about to take with me when the old man appeared in the courtyard.

'What's going on?' he asked, puzzled.

'Nothing! We're leaving.'

'But what's going to happen to me? And what about the house?'

'Take it to your grave!' I replied and left him.

It was not nice of me but it just came out and it felt so good. For nine years all I had heard was that I was a nobody who was trying to cheat them out of their house. I don't want your house, take it to your grave!

I quickly got into the van. We were almost on our way when the old man stopped us. He literally stood in front of the car and wouldn't let us go. The man who had made my life miserable and ruined my nerves for nine years now refused to let me go, but it was too late.

'Let's go,' I said to the driver and he backed up then swerved around my father-in-law who was waving his walking stick. Karcsi later told me that when he went home that day, the old man threw himself on the ground in the courtyard and cried like a child for me.

He died at the age of ninety-one, six months after we moved away. After the divorce, I kept in touch with Karcsi for a while but we eventually drifted apart. While he was living in a workers' hostel in Pest, he sold his house and gambled the money away overnight in a casino. I knew he was in bad company and I told him not to sell his house, but he wouldn't listen. He told me I was no longer his wife and to stay out of his life. His mates in Pest had a strong influence on him and he wanted to be one of them at all costs, so I had no choice but to let go of his hand.

About two years had passed when I heard from him again. He was unemployed and homeless so he went back to the village and stayed with old friends. Sometimes I saw him on the street but he was embarrassed and ashamed, and turned away quickly. He had a lot to be ashamed about because he had made a mess of his life by not appreciating what he had. Since then he has been living on odd jobs and moving around, staying with friends or family members. His father should have known that it wasn't me he had to fear but his own son.

That's the end of Karcsi's story, but before I continue with mine I'd like to tell you a little about Robi, Zoli's father. Since he was a part of my life, my first great love, I thought it might be interesting to tell you what happened to him.

After his mother died, my ex-husband went on a binge and spent everything he had on booze. Because he didn't get his mother's pension anymore, he couldn't pay the utilities and after a while he accumulated a lot of debt on the flat. At that time the housing mafia was flourishing in Ukraine, including Transcarpathia, and many people including Robi fell victim to it.

When he was offered the chance to have them pay off all his debts and get a less valuable flat in exchange for his flat, he gladly agreed. He signed all the papers they put in front of him and moved into the new flat, unaware that it was a scam.

A few months later, Robi was found dead in his apartment. He was only forty-eight years old, and because his death was suspicious the police sealed off the apartment and opened an investigation. In the end, it was not clear whether he had been murdered or overtaken by alcohol; neither did I find out who arranged the funeral or where he was buried.

Zoli went home after he received news of an inheritance from relatives and, with the help of my brother, tried to find out what had happened but wherever they went, whoever they asked, they ran into walls.

What they did find out was that the flat had never been in Robi's name; he was one of four people who had been registered there with a temporary address in the last year. It was obvious that he was defrauded and Zoli's inheritance was lost.

After the way he had treated me during our marriage, you might think Robi deserved his fate but I was no longer angry with him. Time had healed my wounds and I had forgiven him. Whatever kind of person my ex-husband was, he didn't deserve to end his life like that.

Chapter 7

Because I have more to tell you, I will now continue with my life story. I was thirty-eight and my son was nineteen when we moved away to start a new life in my brother-in-law's house. Luckily I didn't have to change jobs because I travelled from one village to the other by bicycle. In good weather it took me forty minutes, but in winter it took me an hour because of the icy roads. Despite dressing warmly and wearing three pairs of gloves, I nearly froze to death on the bike in temperatures of minus ten to fifteen degrees, but I survived because it was nothing compared to what I'd endured from Karcsi and his father.

I didn't regret leaving them for a moment; I finally had peace of mind and that was worth everything. Thanks to them, Zoli and I could stay in Hungary but I think I had paid them back in full and I have no regrets. It was time for me to start my own life.

My son was in his last year at school and then he had to find a job and save money to go to England, so we had two or three more years together before my big boy started a new life.

The winter passed. In the spring three of my colleagues and I were sent to Germany to learn how to work with a new type of machinery; once we got the hang of it, we would train people back home. I was quite apprehensive as I had never been abroad before; I was mainly worried about the language but I had a Russian colleague there who helped me a lot with translation.

I was really sorry that my father hadn't taught me German when I was a child, but maybe because I had German blood I found it relatively easy to learn the language. By the end of four months, I knew a lot of words and could communicate quite well with my colleagues and bosses. That was when I realised that no matter what country I was in, if I could speak the language I could somehow get by.

This opportunity not only brought me financial and experiential benefits but completely changed my life. It opened up the world to me and I was no longer afraid of the unknown. I wondered what it would be like to go to England with Zoli. If we were both earning, we would be able to save enough money to buy a house much sooner. After months in Germany, the idea of England as my next destination was not so scary.

My son took the news well and was relieved that he didn't have to leave me alone, so we started planning our future together in this unknown country.

After finishing school, Zoli took a job as a customer service representative in a bank in Budapest. His starting salary was not high but he managed to save some money every month. We calculated that we would need to save for about two years to pay for the plane tickets, rent, deposit and living expenses for the first few weeks. In order to get a job there, I also needed to speak some English.

In the autumn I enrolled on a language course with classes twice a week after work,. They say that English is much easier to learn than German, but I disagree; it was difficult for me because German was still fresh in my mind and I kept mixing up words. Maybe I should have waited a while, but I didn't have time.

The course was also quite tiring as the school was in a town that could only be reached by bus and train. After cycling home from work, I either cooked something quick or studied a bit then walked to the bus stop. I got home late in the evening and had to get up early in the morning to go to work.

This went on for a while before something changed. I had a colleague called Anita who came to work from a village further away and she had a car. As she drove down our street on her way to work, she offered me a lift to and from our workplace. You can imagine how happy I was as winter was approaching and I already knew what to expect on freezing days.

Anita picked me up every morning and dropped me home in the afternoon, for which I was very grateful. At first we drove in her old car but in mid-December she replaced it with a new one that was bigger and much faster.

She had only had it for three days when the accident happened. I went out at the usual time in the morning and waited for her. It was early and very cold, but despite the sub-zero temperatures the roads were dry and passable. Anita arrived on time, I quickly hopped in and we were off to work. The road between the two villages was unlit and the sun was just starting to rise over the horizon, so it was still quite dark. We were chatting and laughing about something when suddenly we spotted a broken tree branch in front of the car's headlights.

Anita pulled the wheel to get around it and we shifted into the other lane. The car skidded, the front hit the side of the road and it spun round a few times in the air before finally landing upside down in the field.

I didn't see much. I remember the tree branch, a sinking feeling in my stomach from the sudden change of lane, then the sky, the ground, the sky, the ground ... and darkness.

When I regained consciousness, I didn't know where I was. I couldn't see anything and I didn't understand why I was in such a strange position, like I was hanging upside down. Then it dawned on me: we'd had an accident.

'Anita, Anita, are you okay?' I asked but there was no answer. 'She's not dead, is she?'

I shuddered in terror. I tried to undo my seatbelt but my hands were shaking so badly that I couldn't. I was groping around in the dark but eventually I found the buckle and unfastened it.

'Call for help,' Anita said, and I was relieved to hear her voice. I reached for the door to open it but felt only the cold ground beneath my hands. Where had the door gone? I was completely confused. Not only was the car upside down but it was tilted on its side on my side, and buried into the ground. It was impossible to get out.

It was getting lighter and my eyes were getting used to the dimness, so I looked around the inside of the car. The windscreen glass was smashed so I decided to try and climb through it.

A car passed by; the driver saw us and came quickly to help. First he freed Anita from her seatbelt and pulled her out of the wreck, then he pulled me out. While he called for an ambulance and the police, I climbed back into the car to get our bags with our phones and documents.

I don't know if it was because of the accident or because it was so cold, but I was shaking so badly I could hardly stand. The stranger saw how bad I was and invited us to get into his car until the ambulance arrived.

Strangely, Anita handled the situation perfectly well, or perhaps she didn't really realise what had happened. As soon as we got into the car, she started making phone calls while I stared numbly ahead.

My shaking began to subside and suddenly something interesting happened: I felt the presence of my Nana beside me. Yes, Nana, my second mother! I didn't see her and I didn't hallucinate, I just felt her there and it filled my heart with warmth.

Nana had died more than twenty years ago but although I was very hurt by her loss, time healed my wounds and I rarely thought of her. I knew at that moment that it was not the seatbelt or the airbag that saved my life, it was her. She was my guardian angel and she didn't let me die in a car accident that morning.

I felt safe and calm but the sirens of approaching police cars jolted me out of that state. I no longer felt the presence of my Nana and that frightened me. I started shaking again.

The police closed off both sides of the road and started the investigation. We were not questioned, they just talked to the man who came to help us and then one of them went to the overturned car to look at it. I followed him with my eyes, but I would rather not have done so because the sight was horrible.

Anita's beautiful new car was a total wreck. Its wheels were pointing skywards and you could now see the debris lying around the wreck. When I saw it, I literally freaked out. There was no way to get out of an accident like that alive, so I was sure that I wasn't going to survive it either. Maybe I was bleeding internally or my heart would stop in the ambulance on the way to hospital. But where was the ambulance?

I looked down at my trembling hands and was shocked to see that my knuckles were bleeding, probably from the shards of glass in the windscreen. When I touched the top of my head, which had been hurting for some time, my hair was covered in blood.

I was in a complete panic because I was sure I was going to die. My heart was pounding, my chest hurt and it was getting harder to breathe. Then I thought, I have to tell someone; no one knows what's happened to me. I couldn't call Zoli because I knew how frightened he would be and I didn't want that. Potyi would tell him the good or bad news later so at least he wouldn't worry about me until then.

I called my sister and tried to talk to her, but I could hardly speak. My voice was shaking, my throat was choked with tears, and I could hardly breathe. 'We had an accident, we are waiting for the ambulance. Don't tell Zoli yet. I'll call you from the hospital,' I groaned and hung up quickly.

'This could be the last time I talk to her,' I thought, and it made me feel even worse. I was scared to death and I could barely control myself. By the time the ambulance arrived I was almost out of my mind.

'She's in shock,' the paramedic said to his partner after looking at me.

They put me in the ambulance and put something on my index finger that was connected to a machine and measured my pulse. I think they also gave me a breathing mask because by the time we got to the hospital my breathing had recovered and my heart was beating normally.

On the way, the paramedic kept telling me not to worry, that everything would be fine. Thanks to his reassuring voice, I calmed down and my fear of death passed.

At the hospital it turned out that I had no serious injuries; I had got away with a few scratches. The skin on my head was torn but the wound was not deep and did not need stitches, nor did the cuts on my knuckles. As for the chest pain, I was told that it was caused by the airbag and that it was normal. After my wounds were treated I was discharged home on my own responsibility, but Anita had a sore neck and was kept in hospital for a few days for observation. Before I left, the police arrived and questioned me about the accident.

They said we were very lucky because if the car had skidded twenty centimetres further we would have hit one of the trees; instead we flew into the field between the two trees. I might have agreed with them if I hadn't felt Nana's presence after the accident. I'm sure it wasn't luck but my guardian angel watching over me. I couldn't die then and there; life had something else in store for me.

Since Anita's car was a write-off, I had to start cycling to work again. The weather was not kind to me that winter so I had a hard time. In January the temperature was always below zero and it snowed a few times, which made life even more difficult.

I thought about giving up; much as I loved my job, it was too much for me. Not only was I freezing in the cold, but once I fell on the icy road between the two villages and could hardly get back on my bike. I was lucky because I only hurt myself slightly, unlike my colleague who fell the same morning and broke his ankle. He had to have surgery to put his leg back together with screws and didn't come back to work for months. That could have happened to me at any time so I seriously considered resigning, but my problem was solved in time.

There was a bus that went through several villages and picked up workers to take them to a factory. As it was not run by our company I was not allowed to take it, but a colleague of mine knew the driver and arranged the ride for me. After that, although not legally, I took the workers' bus to work for 100 forints a day. This went on for a month until the driver told me he was going on holiday but his colleague knew about me and would pick me up at the bus stop in the morning. The man was from the village, his name was Otto and it turned out that I knew of him. Our sons were classmates and his ex-wife worked with me, so I had heard a lot about him.

What I'm about to write may seem unbelievable or rather ridiculous, but I don't mind because I want to tell you about it. When I got on the bus in the morning and gave Otto the money, our hands touched and something happened. It was as if I'd been hit by a little bolt of lightning, though looking back I'd say I was hit by Cupid's arrow because something happened to me, that's for sure! I blushed and was so embarrassed that I didn't dare look at the driver after I sat down.

As soon as we entered the village, I got up and went to the door to get off quickly when it opened. Otto started talking to me and the bus moved so slowly that I thought we would never get there. We finally arrived and when the door opened I literally ran away.

'My God, what is happening to me?' My heart was pounding and my face was burning like I had a fever. Needless to say, I thought about Otto all day. I was just as distraught on the way home, and that didn't change the next day. The English course didn't make much sense either, because my mind was elsewhere.

I was almost forty-one at the time but I felt like a fourteen-year-old girl who had fallen for a boy. It must have been something like love at first sight – in our case, love at first touch. From the moment our hands touched, I felt an inexplicable attraction to Otto that was both exciting and terrifying. He awakened feelings in me of which I had never dreamed. All my previous relationships had failed and I'd given up on love. To avoid another disappointment, I had to do something as quickly as possible.

Before I got off the bus the next afternoon, I told the driver that I would not be at the bus stop in the morning because I would be cycling to work from tomorrow onwards.

'Why?' asked Otto anxiously and loudly enough that I think everyone on the bus heard. 'Because of the money?' he asked but more quietly.

I didn't expect this question and I didn't know what to say. 'Yes, it's the money,' I said. 'Also the good weather is coming and I like cycling.'

'The weather isn't that good yet. At least ride the bus while I'm the driver. And from tomorrow you won't have to pay for the trip.'

'Okay,' I said quickly and got off the bus.

'Why did I say yes when I should have said no?' I asked myself. I was so shocked by his reaction that I had answered without thinking, even though I had planned otherwise. But why was he so upset that he could no longer take me? It certainly wasn't the money because from the next day I could travel for free.

Otto was a middle-aged, very handsome man, and his slightly stubbled face and grey hair made him even more attractive. His ex-wife told me that when he was young he was the coolest guy in the village and all the girls were in love with him. Guys like that didn't even notice me back then, I was invisible to them, so why should it be any different now?

A few days later Otto asked me if we could go out in the evening. I immediately said no. 'I'm busy. I attend an English course and I'll be home late.'

'Then at least give me your phone number so I can call you later.'

'No,' I said firmly, then I got off the bus quickly. I wanted to say yes because I'd just been asked out on a date by the man I was secretly in love with, but I couldn't.

That evening after the course, as I got off the train and was about to go to the bus stop I was shocked to see Otto coming towards me. 'What are you doing here?' I asked him.

'Waiting for you. I thought you might be hungry so we could go somewhere for dinner.'

'How did you know which train I was coming on and when?' I asked, still puzzled.

'I have connections,' he said with a laugh, then pointed towards his car. 'Shall we go?'

I could say that I was hungry and that's why I went with him, but that's not true. I liked this man and it was hard to say no to him but I also needed to talk to him. I had plans for my future and he wasn't part of them. He needed to know that I was leaving the country soon and wouldn't be coming back for a while. This dinner wasn't about getting to know each other, it was about saying goodbye – but it turned out differently.

Otto took me to a cosy restaurant that couldn't have been more romantic. The candlelit dinner, soft music and the sparkling eyes of the man sitting opposite me completely blew me away. I hadn't felt that good in a long time and I wouldn't have minded if the evening had never ended.

Otto was no ordinary man, and I was very impressed by him. He wasn't trying to impress me by gushing about himself for hours on end like my previous boyfriends, he was genuinely interested in me. Whatever I talked about, he listened with curiosity, not cutting me off to make himself the subject again. He was attentive and polite, which impressed me; he made me feel not like a grey mouse but someone who mattered.

It turned out that we had a lot in common, but it was fishing what we both truly loved. I told him about my childhood and how many small fish I used to catch in the water of the Latorca, and about Robi and his friends with whom we often went fishing in the surrounding rivers and lakes. It was good to share these experiences with someone who had the same passion and knew what I was talking about. When I told him that my biggest catch was a one-kilo carp, he laughed.

'We throw those back into the lake because they are considered undersized. Next time I'll take you with me and you can catch bigger fish than that.'

And that was the end of it because there wouldn't be a next time. I had to tell him the truth, even if it ruined the wonderful evening. 'As much as I'd like to, there won't be a next time. I'm taking an English course because my son and I are going to England soon, and we're going to stay there for a couple of years.'

Otto didn't say a word but his face said it all. He looked at me with such sad eyes that I almost cried. 'How can I cause such sadness to someone who hardly knows me?' I wondered.

'Then at least let's hang out until then,' he said finally.

How could I say no? He was different from the men I had been with before and his eyes told me that I interested him, so I said yes. I longed for his love and I wanted to be happy, even if it couldn't last long.

Otto kept his word and took me fishing, which was an exhilarating experience. I caught a four-kilo carp all by myself, and I was over the moon. If you are a fisherman or know someone who is, you will know how I felt that day. My only regret is that we didn't have smartphones and I couldn't take a picture with the giant fish in my hands.

The following weekend we went on a trip to an area that looked eerily similar to Transcarpathia. When we arrived, my eyes welled up with emotion. On our first date in the restaurant, I'd mentioned that I often felt homesick and missed the mountainous countryside where I was born. He took me to a place like that; wasn't that romantic?

Our 'hanging out' together went so well that two months later I moved in with Otto and cancelled my plans to go to England. I chose happiness instead of money and a better life, and Zoli went to London on his own.

Otto became part of my life, and I couldn't imagine my future without him. The love I'd felt for Robi and Peti was nothing compared to the love I felt for Otto. They say that opposites attract, but I think true love is only possible between two people who are alike; we were soul mates, and once we found each other our happiness knew no bounds.

If you think this story has a happy ending, you are wrong. We had a lot in common but our relationship was not smooth, though even if we sometimes argued or fought, we always made up afterwards and got over it. We loved each other and could talk about our problems, which helped us through our difficulties.

Otto and I didn't get married and we didn't take the 'for better, for worse, in sickness and in health' vows, but it was obvious I would have done anything for my partner because he was the most important person to me after my son.

It took me eight-and-a-half years to realise that the unspoken vow was only obvious to me. I had a health problem, which I won't go into detail about, and I needed a major operation. The doctor said it would take a few weeks for me to recover, so I decided to prepare for that period.

For years I had baked our bread because Otto didn't like the kind you buy in the shops; he didn't like anything with preservatives or colourings. We grew what we could in order to eat healthy, chemical-free food. We kept pigs and there were years when we had seventy chickens running around the poultry yard that I had raised from chicks. My vegetable garden was large enough to feed three families, but according to Otto more was better than less. I filled the pantry shelves with jams and pickles, and the cellar was full of potatoes and several crates of apples and walnuts after the autumn harvest.

We lived well, we had everything we needed but it was a lot of work. At first Otto did his bit and helped as much as he could, but then he stopped doing what he thought was 'women's work'. As the years went by the 'women's work' increased and I couldn't cope. It was too much for me but I didn't complain; I did it willingly. I was sorry about the trips and fishing trips becoming less frequent though; in the end we didn't go anywhere because we didn't have the time.

So eight-and-a-half years went by and then I had to go under the knife. To make sure that Otto had nothing to worry about, in the two months before the operation I prepared food for several weeks ahead and baked bread, which I froze. I also put several portions of his favourite cake in the freezer so that there would be no shortage of it while I was recovering.

A few days after the operation I was discharged from hospital. I had to rest and take it easy; I couldn't do much else, as I was very weak and dizzy, so in the beginning I spent a lot of time in bed. Even so, I wouldn't let myself go: I walked several times a day to the poultry yard, then to my vegetable garden and back.

Ten days after the operation I dared to walk to the back garden to the fruit trees, which was quite a distance from the house. After lunch, I told Otto I was going to rest for a while because I was quite tired, and he replied, 'You'd better pull yourself together, because I've had enough of washing up!'

You can't imagine how I felt at that moment.

'Can't you do that much for me?' I asked, and the tears started to flow.

I was so disappointed, I can't even tell you. I would have done anything for the man I loved and I'd done my best. I'd worked eighteen and often twenty hours a day to make sure he had everything he needed. When I was well, I did all the housework and he couldn't do the washing up for me?

I was very disappointed in him, and from that day on things had changed between us. I'd be lying if I said that was the moment the love faded or the pink mist cleared from my eyes, because it wasn't. The exhilarating feeling we'd had at first – what we called love – turned into liking each other after a while, and that was fine. That love gave me the strength to work day and night to please my partner who was important to me. But on that day I realised that I was really just a servant serving my master, and that realisation left its mark on our relationship.

For the next few months I did everything in the same way, but out of necessity, not willingly. My enthusiasm was gone and nothing gave me any pleasure. The knowledge that I was being taken advantage of made me bitter and unhappy, but there was nothing I could do about it.

In the autumn came the kitchen renovation that had been a topic of discussion and debate for some time. I wanted some changes to make my work easier, but Otto insisted on his ideas.

I argued that I spent half of my life in the kitchen and needed these changes, but he was adamant. 'This is my kitchen and everything will be the way I want it!' he almost shouted.

'If that's the way you want it then I'm leaving you!' I shouted back, ending the argument.

Probably thinking I was bluffing, Otto said nothing. For the first time, I had stood on my feet to put pressure on him to see if I could get something out of him.

The renovation began and I waited until the last minute for him to change his mind and do what I had asked but that didn't happen. Otto stuck to his principles; because that kitchen was really his, everything was done the way he wanted it.

Chapter 8

Two months later I was in London, celebrating my fiftieth birthday with my son and his fiancée, Zsuzsa. I was devastated and heartbroken by our break-up but I managed to recover and start a new life in the UK.

I'm sorry that life with Otto ended like that, but it wasn't all my fault. We both made mistakes because our relationship faded and the flame that burned in our hearts died. I didn't notice when we grew apart and I became neutral to Otto. In hindsight, I would say that I spent too much time in the kitchen and garden doing housework, while Otto spent his time at his friend's house next door or sitting in front of the computer listening to smart people talking.

Fishing, which was our passion, slowly disappeared from our lives; we no longer had any mutual interests and in the end we had very little in common. If we had realised this in time, we might have been able to change things and we'd still be together, but it seemed that our love story could not have a happy ending.

I'm fifty-seven now and I can't believe I've been living in London for more than seven years. Thanks to Zoli and Zsuzsa and the new environment, I left the past behind and moved forward. They planned to move back home for good once their house was built and the baby was born, but I wanted to stay; it was time to pursue my own dreams.

I had learned to manage my money well, to budget what little I had, and I saw an opportunity to save money here. My goal was the same as it had been nine years ago, before Otto.

I'd heard too many times from Karcsi, my second ex, that 'this is my house, and you can get out of here', and I didn't want to hear it from anyone else ever again. I longed for an apartment or a small house of my own where I could renovate the kitchen or arrange it the way I wanted. Those bad memories inspired me to work hard and eventually make my dreams come true.

The English course I had started in Hungary ten years earlier was of little use to me because I had forgotten everything I'd learned, so I started from scratch. At the age of fifty, I went back to school to learn the language as well as I could. After a month and a half of unemployment, I got a job as a cleaner in a factory. The work was hard and the evening classes were tiring, but I needed them because at least they took my mind off Otto and our break-up.

I studied hard for two-and-a-half years, which paid off. By then I spoke English well enough and it gave me confidence, so it was time to move on. I left the factory and got a job in retail that I still do today, and I love it. If you remember, once upon a time I had wanted to work in a shop like my aunt who was my role model. It's been forty years since then and life has taken me in different directions, but now I'm in a good place and enjoying my job.

But that's not the only thing I've achieved because last summer I finally bought my first property, so I can tick that off my bucket list, too. I've got a small two-bedroom house with my own courtyard and garden, which is just right for me. The best thing about it is that it's just a few streets away from my family. Zoli and Zsuzsa stayed in London for three more years, but as soon as their house was finished they moved back home, and soon after a baby boy was born.

David is now four-and-a-half years old and is an adorable little rascal who has inherited his big, beautiful eyes from his mother and his mouth from his father and me. My little grandson has brought me joy and happiness and I'm sure Zsuzsa's parents feel the same. He has become everything to us and that's the way it should be.

This is where my life story ends, because I have told you everything that has happened to me so far. It's been a long and bumpy journey, but if I could go back in time I wouldn't change much. All the bad things I've been through have only strengthened me and pushed me towards a better life.

Nana was right when she told me as a child that 'Once will be better'. I think that time has finally come, and I am now comfortable with myself. I am happy with my life because I have fulfilled all my dreams: I'm living well and I have my own little home where I can soon settle in happily, but none of this would be complete without a loving family waiting for me at home.

Where we are born is not our choice, but as soon as we have the opportunity we can change it and aim for a better life. We cannot avoid our destiny, but we can shape our lives and it is up to us how we live them. The first love is not always the last, and the second may not last forever, but you will never know if you are stuck in one place.

If you're an abused woman (or man) and your life is eerily similar to mine then take action! I moved on too, not once or twice, and how glad I am that I did. If you don't have the strength or you can't do it alone, get help! You deserve happiness too, but don't expect it to fall into your lap. Do something about it because life can only get better.

If you are in a relationship that is not bad but not the right one, change it! Don't let the fire in your heart go out and be neutral towards each other! Organise programmes, have new experiences to tell your grandchildren about one day. There is no perfect relationship, just as we are not perfect, but we can still strive for better, for something more beautiful.

But if you choose to live your life alone, there's nothing wrong with that. Find the right path, *your* path, and live your life to the best you can. At fifty-seven, I am a happy single woman who has achieved everything I wanted in life. I wish you the same. Find your way to happiness and never stray from it!

www.ingramcontent.com/pod-product-compliance
Lightning Source LLC
Chambersburg PA
CBHW070659120526
44590CB00013BA/1022